D1606042

Television Series
of the 1980s

Television Series of the 1980s

Essential Facts and Quirky Details

VINCENT TERRACE

ROWMAN & LITTLEFIELD
Lanham • Boulder • New York • London

Published by Rowman & Littlefield
A wholly owned subsidary of The Rowman & Littlefield Publishing Group, Inc.
4501 Forbes Boulevard, Suite 200, Lanham, Maryland 20706
www.rowman.com

Unit A, Whitacre Mews, 26-34 Stannary Street, London SE11 4AB

British Library Cataloguing in Publication Information Available

Library of Congress Cataloging-in-Publication Data

Names: Terrace, Vincent, 1948– author.
Title: Television series of the 1980s : essential facts and quirky details /
    Vincent Terrace.
Description: Lanham : Rowman & Littlefield, 2017. | Includes index.
Identifiers: LCCN 2017011642 (print) | LCCN 2017027587 (ebook) | ISBN
    9781442278318 (electronic) | ISBN 9781442278301 (hardback : alk. paper)
Subjects: LCSH: Television programs—United States—Plots, themes, etc.
Classification: LCC PN1992.3.U5 (ebook) | LCC PN1992.3.U5 T47 2017 (print) |
    DDC 791.45/750973—dc23
LC record available at https://lccn.loc.gov/2017011642

Printed in the United States of America

Contents

Introduction   vii

The A-Team   1
Airwolf   6
Alf   8
Amen   11
Baywatch   14
Cagney & Lacey   23
Charles in Charge   25
Cheers   29
China Beach   36
Coach   40
The Cosby Show   43
Dear John   47
Designing Women   49
Empty Nest   55
The Fall Guy   62
Family Matters   64
Family Ties   68
Full House   74
Gimme a Break   80
The Golden Girls   82
The Greatest American Hero   89
Growing Pains   92
Hill Street Blues   97
Hunter   103

It's a Living	107
Kate & Allie	111
Knight Rider	113
Life Goes On	117
MacGyver	122
Magnum, P.I.	125
Mama's Family	130
Married . . . With Children	135
Matlock	141
Matt Houston	144
Miami Vice	145
Moonlighting	147
Mr. Belvedere	150
Murder, She Wrote	153
Murphy Brown	156
Newhart	163
Night Court	169
Perfect Strangers	174
Quantum Leap	177
Remington Steele	180
Roseanne	183
Saved by the Bell	189
Scarecrow and Mrs. King	194
The Simpsons	197
St. Elsewhere	203
Star Trek: The Next Generation	210
T.J. Hooker	214
Too Close for Comfort	216
21 Jump Street	219
Webster	223
Who's the Boss?	225
The Wonder Years	229
Index	235
About the Author	245

Introduction

This is the fourth in a series of books that relate the quirky (trivia) facts associated with select television series that premiered between January 1, 1980, and December 31, 1989. Series prior to this era can be found in *Television Series of the 1950s, Television Series of the 1960s,* and *Television Series of the 1970s.*

This is *not* a book of essays or opinions, and information is based on viewing the episodes of the series listed; it is a presentation of facts only, such as that Alex P. Keaton (*Family Ties*) cried for the first time when he learned his father worked for a nonprofit organization (PBS); Larry, Darryl, and Darryl (*Newhart*) operated a business called "Elegant Mouse, Rat and Weasel Skins for the Discriminating Buyers Who Are Tired of Wearing Feathers" and B.A. Baracus (*The A-Team*) had the Social Security number 554-04-3106. It will also reveal why MacGyver was reluctant to use a gun; who acquired a job as a waitress because she knew you bring the plate to the table, not the table to the plate; and why Ben Matlock always wore white suits.

If these few facts capture your attention, then you will be amazed by the many thousands of facts that are contained within these pages and that can be found only here.

Programs that premiered in the 1970s but continued first-run production into the 1980s are not included here. Information on these programs can be found in the volume *Television Series of the 1970s*:

Archie Bunker's Place
B.J. and the Bear
Buck Rogers in the 25th Century
Diff'rent Strokes
The Dukes of Hazzard
Eight Is Enough
The Facts of Life
Fantasy Island
Happy Days

The Incredible Hulk
Laverne & Shirley
Little House on the Prairie
Lou Grant
The Love Boat
Taxi
Three's Company
Vega$
The Waltons
WKRP in Cincinnati

The A-Team
(NBC, 1983–1987)

Cast: George Peppard (John "Hannibal" Smith), Dirk Benedict (Templeton Peck), Mr. T (B.A. Baracus), Dwight Schultz (H. M. Murdock), Melinda Culea (Amy Allen), Marla Heasley (Tawnia Baker).

Basis: Four military fugitives, called the A-Team, use their combat expertise to assist people threatened by unscrupulous characters.

OVERALL SERIES INFORMATION

John Smith, Templeton Peck, and B.A. Baracus, American soldiers stationed in Vietnam during the war, are ordered by army colonel Samuel Morrison to rob the Bank of Hanoi of 100 million yen as a means of ending the war. It is Sunday, January 27, 1971. The team is successful but arrested when Morrison, secretly a North Vietnamese supporter, frames them for the theft and disappears with the money. The team is sent to the Fort Bragg military prison in North Carolina but escape before they can be tried. Smith, Baracus, and Peck retreat to the Los Angeles underground, where they become soldiers of fortune (the A-Team) but also fugitives wanted by the army (the A-Team case is Military File 1-HG-4227; $10,000, then $20,000, has been offered for their capture). Hannibal, B.A., and Peck were with the 5th Special Forces. Hannibal named his team after the Operation Detachment Alpha Units, called "A-Teams."

Military brass suspect that H. M. Murdock is the fourth member of the A-Team but can't prove it (Murdock, a helicopter pilot, was on another mission at the time and secretly joined the team after his discharge). General Hunt Stockwell (Robert Vaughn) captures the team in 1986 (following failed attempts by Colonel Roderick Decker [Lance LeGault], the man who originally caught the team; Colonel Lynch [William Lucking], the man in charge of Fort Bragg; and General Harlan "Bull" Fullbright [Jack Ging], Lynch's replacement). The team is tried at Fort Owen in California and convicted of desertion but freed to

1

Seated: George Peppard; standing: Dirk Benedict, Dwight Schultz, and Mr. T.
NBC/Photofest. ©NBC

Hunt to perform special missions. Langley, Virginia, becomes a permanent base for the A-Team, and they operate under the code name Empress 6 (Hunt's code is Empress 1). The team's mobile phone number is 555-6162, and NRB 729 is Hunt's limo license plate number. Eddie Velez joins the A-Team as Frankie Santana, a Hollywood stunt man, and Judith Ledford becomes Carla, Hunt's aide.

JOHN "HANNIBAL" SMITH

FBI File Number: 61-5683-1.
Social Security Number: 844-31-3142.
Position: Colonel and Commander of the 5th Special Forces Group (in the pilot he is a lieutenant colonel).

Awards: Silver Star, Medal of Honor, Army Distinguished Services Medal, Legion of Merit, Purple Heart.

Occupation: Soldier of fortune and head of the A-Team. Hannibal also works as an actor, portraying the Aqua Maniac, the Slim Monster, or Killer Gator in horror films (mentioned titles are *Aqua Mania, Aqua Mania II, The Snake from the Center of the Earth,* and *The Monster from Camp Runamuck*). At such movie sites, Murdock runs Face's food catering truck. The team is also part owner of the Golden Pagoda Restaurant and receives 10 percent of the value of anything they recover for a client.

Aliases: Mr. Lee, the elderly owner of Mr. Lee's Chinese Laundry Shop on 6th Street in Los Angeles (clients must meet with Mr. Lee for Hannibal to determine that it is not a military trap); Hugh Howland, real estate mogul; U.S. Air Force Colonel Brown; Jack Daniels (a wino); TV personality Gene Shalik; music promoter Johnny B; Irish restaurateur Shawn O'Shea III; and Danny Diamond, "personal manager to the stars."

Favorite Gun: An M-60 he calls "Baby."

Favorite Expressions: "I love it when a plan comes together" and "You've just hired the A-Team." He also gets "on the jazz," a feeling of excitement during each case.

Vice: Smoking cigars.

Rules: "The team doesn't date female clients because it distorts the team's thinking and is dangerous"; "Not to be out of contact with each other for more than 30 minutes."

B.A. BARACUS

FBI File Number: 615683-3.

Social Security Number: 554-04-3106.

Rank: Sergeant (ordinance, weapons, and munitions officer).

Real Name: Bosco Albert Baracus (also said to be Elliott Baracus). He was called "Scooter" by his mother and earned the nickname B.A. (Bad Attitude) for his temper.

Place of Birth: Chicago's South Side on November 3, 1955 (where he lived at 700 Foster Avenue). He now lives at the Regina Hotel in Los Angeles.

Character: A special fondness for children (runs a day care center and volunteers at the L.A. Youth Center). He played football in college and is distinguished by a Mohawk haircut and lavish gold jewelry (especially his chain-link necklace). He is the team's mechanic and drives a black-with-red-trim 1983 GMC Series G van.

License Plate: 2L8 3000 (then 5TT 6162, S96 7238, 2A 22029, and 2E14859).

Injury: Sustained an enemy gunshot wound to the shoulder ("Waiting for Insane Wayne") and a leg wound ("Black Day at Bad Rock").

Catchphrases: "I pity the fool," "Don't mess with me sucker." With reference to Murdock: "Shut-up fool" and "You fool."

Favorite Drink: Milk.

Greatest Fear: Flying. Hannibal has to devise ways (usually by drugging his milk) to get B.A. from one place to another by plane. Hannibal has a two-by-four block of wood he calls "B.A.'s beddie-by stick" (to knock him out).

Blood Type: A-B negative (same as Murdock).

Nickname: Called "The Big Guy" by Murdock.

Aliases: Boxer Volcano Johnson (Hannibal played his manager Jimmy Pearl) and musician Ignatius Blacktop.

Relatives: Mother, unnamed (Della Reese).

TEMPLETON PECK

FBI File Number: 61-5683-2.

Social Security Number: 522-70-5044.

Rank: Lieutenant (a wanted poster mistakenly lists Peck as a captain in the episode "Blood, Sweat and Cheers").

Real Name: Richard Bancroft.

Place of Birth: Los Angeles.

Parents: A. J. and Samantha Bancroft. Their son, Richard, was orphaned at the age of five when they deserted him. Templeton mentions he wandered into and was raised at the Guardian Angels Orphanage in Los Angeles. It is not explained how Templeton acquired his name (he toyed with Alvin Brenner, Al Brennan, Al Peck, Holmes Morrison, and Morrison Holmes before choosing Templeton Peck). He later learned that his father remarried and he has a stepsister (Ellen, played by Claire Kirkconnell).

Education: St. Mary's High School (football team member and named "All City Quarterback"); member of the Sigma Chi fraternity in his unnamed college.

Nickname: Called both "Face" and "Faceman" (due to his good looks and charm).

Ability: Master con artist (the TV series *Dragnet* was his inspiration). As Hannibal says, "Face will give you the shirt off his back then go out and scam one for himself."

Favorite Scam: Miracle Films ("If it's a good picture, it's a Miracle"); he has a script, "The Beast of the Yellow Night," ready for "production."

Home: A beach house (that he scammed) at 1347 Old Balboa Road.

Car: A white 1984 Corvette (plate IHG 581).

Aliases: Father Shawn O'Herlihy, Father Foley, and Michael DeLane, *Fine Arts* magazine critic.

Fear: The word "commitment" (he is not prepared for marriage).

Note: In the opening theme, when Dirk Benedict is credited, a Cylon robot is seen (reflecting Dirk's time on the series *Battlestar Galactica*). Tim Dunigan played Face in the pilot (replaced when it was felt that he was too young to have served in Vietnam).

H.M. MURDOCK

Full Name: Never revealed. Murdock claims his initials stand for "Howling Mad" (he is called "Jim" in one episode and refers to himself as "Matt Murdock" in another).

Rank: Captain. Prior to Vietnam, H.M. was a pilot for the Thunderbirds precision flight team. He performed heroic missions during the war, was wounded twice, served two tours of duty, and was awarded the Silver Star and three unit citations. He worked for the CIA in 1967 and 1972 and claims that his experiences have damaged his psyche. He pretends to be insane to secretly help Hannibal and lives at the Veterans Administration Psychiatric Hospital, Building 16, Section 18, Area 8, in Los Angeles. He has been diagnosed with paranoid delusions, and "ammonia" is the key word that triggers his aggression. B.A. believes that "he ain't pretending he's crazy," and Hannibal must devise ingenious ways to sneak Murdock out of the hospital for an assignment.

Blood Type: AB-negative (same as B.A.).

Pets: Billy (invisible dog) and Wally Gator (a baby alligator).

Houseplant: The Little Guy.

Heroes: The Range Rider (from the 1950s TV series) and Captain Belly Buster (the mascot for the Burger Heaven food chain).

Favorite TV Show: The Rifleman. As a kid, he watched *The Uncle Buckleup Show* (in 1984, Hannibal played Ruff the Bear on the show; aired on KCEA-TV, Channel 3).

Secret Weapon: Mike, a skunk he uses as a diversion.

Aliases: Professor Nutty Buddy; Rex the Wonder Dog; Captain Ahab; The Range Rider; Captain Cab, Knight of the Road; Logan Ross, Russian spy; Clothing Inspector No. 6.

Trademarks: His leather jacket ("Da Nang 1970" is on the back); his T-shirts (with sayings such as "Sensuous and Strong," "Wong for the Road: Chinese Delivery," "Stamp Out Cellulite," "This Space Is Unoccupied," and "Minds Are for People Who Think").

Favorite Singing Group: The Lennon Sisters.

Quirks: Doesn't listen to the radio "because all the music I need is in my head"; often thinks he is invisible; can read and speak Chinese (but doesn't know how he does it).

B.A.'s Affectionate Term for Murdock: "Fool."

OTHER CHARACTERS

Amy Amanda Allen, called Triple A, is a reporter for the *Los Angeles Courier-Express* (as seen on the paper's building; the *Tribune* is seen when an actual paper is needed). She became a part of the team when she hired them to find a missing reporter and became involved in the case. Her car license plates read IFH 450, IFHJ 480, and ILBJ 1247. Amy, only in first-season episodes, can be seen in opening theme visuals in the following two seasons when the inside of B.A.'s van is shown.

Tawnia Baker, Amy's friend and a reporter, replaces her when Amy is transferred overseas to Jakarta. Like Amy, Tawnia has virtually no trivia information. Her car license plate reads 854 022 (later 1JFY 515), and she lives at the Mirabella Apartment Complex. In the episode "The Battle of Bel Air," when Tawnia is using a computer, her screen name is "Tanya Baker." She left the team to marry and join archaeologist Brian Leftcourt (Barry Van Dyke) on an expedition.

Airwolf
(CBS, 1984–1986; USA, 1987–1988)

Cast: Jan-Michael Vincent (Stringfellow Hawke), Ernest Borgnine (Dominic Santini), Jean Bruce Scott (Caitlin O'Shaughnessy), Alex Cord (Michael Archangel).

Basis: A Vietnam vet (Stringfellow Hawke) uses an experimental attack helicopter (Airwolf) to perform missions for the U.S. government.

STRINGFELLOW HAWKE

Stringfellow, the son of Alan and Mary Hawke (deceased), is a man with few friends. He has a brother, Saint John (pronounced Sin-Jin), and lives in seclusion in California with his dog, Tet (named after the Tet Offensive). His one enjoyment appears to be playing the cello. Aviation, especially helicopters, became an obsession with him, and during the Vietnam War, he served as a chopper pilot (later captain of the 328 AHC Unit). It was at this time that Saint John, a member of the unit, was captured by the enemy, and his fate is now unknown.

Stringfellow left the army in 1973 to become an agent for The Firm, a government organization that performs secretive missions to protect the country. He is bitter that the U.S. government has done little to find Saint John.

It is 10 years later. Stringfellow has resigned from The Firm, and Dr. Charles Moffet (David Hemmings), a Firm engineer, had developed Airwolf, an attack helicopter that he plans to sell to a foreign power (Libya), for $5 million. Michael Archangel, head of The Firm, recruits Stringfellow to retrieve it. Stringfellow, with the help of his friend Dominic Santini, rescues Airwolf but chooses to keep it to force the government to find Saint John; in the meantime, he will use Airwolf to help Michael when necessary. To protect Airwolf, Stringfellow has hidden it deep in a hollow mesa in the desert (discovered by Dominic) that he calls "The Valley of the Gods" (but is referred to as "The Lair"). Christopher Connelly plays Saint John in flashbacks.

DOMINIC SANTINI

Dominic "Dom" Santini is the owner of Santini Air, a helicopter charter service based at the Van Nuys Airport (also given as the Municipal Airport) in California. He was a close friend of the Hawke family, and when Stringfellow's parents drowned in a boating accident, Dominic raised Stringfellow (then age 12) and Saint John (it has to be assumed that there were no other relatives; Dom and Hawke's father were friends and served in the Korean War together).

Dominic was born on the island of San Remo and calls Airwolf "The Lady." He is a skilled helicopter pilot and has equipped his red, white, and blue Jet Ranger copters with cameras for movie and television stunt work. He is divorced from Lila Morgan (Diane McBain); their daughter, Sally Ann, died from a drug overdose. When inside shots of Airwolf are shown, Stringfellow usually pilots while Dom sits in the back. Dom often wears a blue Santini Air jacket with a red cap; his jeep license plate is 1-BOX-070, IDT 0406 is his station wagon plate, and 2G 15626 is the plate of the Santini Air gas truck.

Relatives: Niece, Holly Matthews (Barbara Howard).

OTHER CHARACTERS

Caitlin O'Shaughnessy, a pilot for Santini Air, was born in Texas and served as a deputy helicopter pilot with the Texas Highway Patrol, Aerial Division. At Texas A&M University, Caitlin was a member of the Kappa Chi sorority and lives at 703 La Sorda Place in Van Nuys. She is being trained by Hawke as a backup pilot for Airwolf.

Michael Coldsmith Briggs III, code name Michael Archangel, is head of The Firm; he wears a patch over his left eye and walks with a cane (injuries sustained when Moffet blew up the Airwolf test site). Angel One is his code to Airwolf; FIRM-1 is his limo license plate. He is assisted by several beautiful women throughout the series: Gabrielle (Belinda Bauer, then Deborah Pratt), Rhonda (Leigh Walsh), and Lydia (Sandra Kronemeyer). Michael dresses in white; his agents are called the Zebra Squad, and his superior is apparently a man named Zeus (never made clear).

AIRWOLF

Helicopter Type: Black-with-white-underbelly Bell 222.
Government File: A56-7W.
Cruising Speed: 300 knots.

Maximum Speed: 662-plus miles per hour when the main rudder is disengaged; in some episodes the top speed is mentioned at Mach 2.

Height Limit: 82,000 feet.

Air Code: Ranger 26.

Armaments: Four 30-mm chain guns (in the wings); two 40-mm wing cannons.

Air-to-Air Radar Missiles: Redeye (short range); Sidewinder and Sparrow (radar homing); Phoenix (programmable, radar homing).

Air-to-Surface Missiles: Hellfire (short range); Copperhead (long range); Maverick (infrared radio imaging); Strike (electromagnetic homing).

Warheads: Bull Pup (radio controlled); Harpoon (radio controlled, anti-sky).

Abilities: Radio scanners to identify and analyze objects; turbo engines for fast flight; movie and infrared cameras; electrical defense (produces a severe shock to unauthorized personnel attempting to board it).

REBOOT (USA VERSION)

Michael Archangel has been transferred to the Middle East, and Jason Locke (Anthony Sherwood) has become head of The Company (not The Firm). Jo Ann "Jo" Santini (Michele Scarabelli), Dominic's niece, now works with him at Santini Air.

After acquiring positive proof that Saint John is alive, Stringfellow attempts a rescue mission but is seriously injured in a helicopter explosion that kills Dominic. Jo, determined to continue with the mission, is stopped by Jason Locke and U.S. Air Force pilot Mike Rivers (Geraint Wyn Davies), who have tracked Airwolf through infrared high-resolution photography. Jason, learning what has happened, allows Jo to proceed with a mission that successfully frees Saint John (Barry Van Dyke) from his Vietnamese captors. Fearing that Airwolf could fall into enemy hands if returned to the government, Jason keeps it and forms a new Airwolf team: himself, Jo, and Saint John.

Jo is called "Little Lady"; the team's code to the Airwolf hideout (now called "The Company Store") is "Wolf"; their code to Santini Air (now run by Jo) is "Cubs" (e.g., "Wolf to Cubs"). During assignments, Saint John often uses "Plan B" (make it up as you go along). Donnelly Rhodes appeared as Jo's father, Tony Santini. Further information on Stringfellow is not mentioned.

ALF

(NBC, 1986–1990)

Cast: Max Wright (Willie Tanner), Anne Schedeen (Kate Tanner), Andrea Elson (Lynn Tanner), Benji Gregory (Brian Tanner), Paul Fusco (voice of ALF).

Basis: An Alien Life Form (ALF) finds refuge with (and creates havoc for) an Earth family (the Tanners) after his spaceship malfunctions and he crashes into their garage.

ALF

Real Name: Gordon Shumway.

Character: Short and furry (burnt-sienna color) with off-black eyes, a large snout, four teeth, and an enormous appetite (he has eight stomachs).

Home Planet: Melmac. "Are you going to finish that sandwich?" is its motto; it has a purple moon, and people consider a mouse and a Tupperware lid as good-luck charms. The monetary system is based on foam (gold is worthless), and the word "stupid" translates as slang for a rich person. Melmacians live to the age of 650.

Parents: Bob, Biff, and Flo.

Birthday: ALF is 229 years old (in Earth year 1986) and is first mentioned being born on the 28th of Nathanganger, then on August 12 and October 2, 1757 (his was a two-part birth). Melmac exploded on the day ALF turned 228 (due to a nuclear disaster; ALF jokes this happened when "everybody plugged in their hair dryers at the same time"). He escaped right before the disaster, and it was the Tanners who named him ALF.

Body Temperature: 425 degrees.

Blood: Green.

Fear: Snails and being discovered.

Favorite Food: "Everything with everything on it."

Favorite Melmac Breakfast: Cats Benedict (he enjoys felines, especially Siamese cats).

Favorite Earth Breakfast: Spaghetti, Jell-O, and eggs.

Favorite Take-Out Food: Pizza (which he orders via the Tanner house account at the Pizza Barge).

Education: Melmac High School (a student for 122 years); Melmac State College (where he earned degrees in software and pedestrian crossing).

Home: When ALF first moved in with the Tanners, he lived in the laundry basket next to the washing machine (he hides under the kitchen table when the doorbell rings); he later resides in the attic. When he uses the telephone, he calls himself "Alf Tanner."

Melmac Occupation: Host of the TV series *Mr. Science*; bearded lady in the circus; car salesman; male model (at the age of 150); and captain of the Codsters, a Bouillabaisse-ball team (like Earth baseball but with fish parts as the ball; fish gills are sold at concession stands; their "baisseball" trading cards feature such players as Mickey Mackerel and come in packages with tabby and Persian cat–flavored bubble gum).

Military Service: The Orbit Guards (to "Guard the Orbits—whether they want it or not").

Quirks: Believes Earth TV reflects real life. If ALF diets, an enzyme imbalance occurs, and he becomes Wolf, "a primitive Melmacian hunting machine." Melmacians gain weight from the inside and explode if they are not careful.

Favorite Earth TV Shows: Gilligan's Island and the mythical *Polka Time* and *Midwest General* (a soap opera).

Favorite Comic Book: Shana, Mistress of the Universe.

Earth Fascination: Ventriloquism (a craft he tried to master with a dummy named Paul).

Medical Issue: When Alf hits his head, he develops amnesia and believes he is Wayne Schlagel, an insurance salesman.

Pet: When ALF asked Willie for a pet, he bought him an ant farm.

WILLIE AND KATE TANNER

William (middle name Francis), called Willie, and Katherine (called Kate) are the parents of Lynn, Brian, and, in later episodes, an infant named Eric. They met at Amherst College in Massachusetts (Willie as a science major, Kate as an art history major). They married on July 11, 1967, and honeymooned in Niagara Falls, New York, at the Duke of Mist Hotel. Willie also serves as captain of the Neighborhood Watch.

Address: 167 Hemdale Street in Los Angeles (the locale is also given as San Francisco).

Telephone Number: 555-8531 (later 555-7787 and 555-4044).

Occupation: Kate is a housewife; Willie works for the Los Angeles Department of Social Services. He mentions that at the age of 17, he was called "Boxcar Willie," as he hopped freight trains traveling around the country.

Willie's Hobby: His shortwave radio (call letters KC276XAA) and talking to people around the world. It was actually Willie's radio that caused ALF to crash when its frequency interfered with ALF's and caused him to lose control. Willie considers ALF his personal nightmare.

Family Car: A 1982 Ford (license plate not seen).

Family Pet Cat: Lucky, then, after Lucky's passing, a cat named Lucky II (called "Flipper" by ALF).

Relatives: Kate's mother, Dorothy Halligan (Anne Meara); Willie's brother, Neal Tanner (Jim J. Bullock); Willie's uncle, Albert (Elisha Cook Jr.).

LYNN AND BRIAN TANNER

Lynn attends South Bay High School and wanted to attend her parents' alma mater but was unable due to the extra expenses required to care for ALF ($10,000 a year); she instead chose State College. Lynn possessed an inferiority complex (felt she was not as pretty as other girls in class) until ALF stepped in and entered her in the Miss Southland Beauty Pageant (her talent was clog dancing) and boosted her confidence (even though she lost). On Melmac, the judges wear swimsuits in beauty pageants, and the contestants rate the judges. Lynn wears a locket that has a picture of actress Mary Tyler Moore on one side and Elvis Presley (from the film *Change of Habit*) on the other side. Brian attends Franklin Elementary School and played a vegetable in his school play.

FINAL EPISODE ("CONSIDER ME GONE")

While using Willie's shortwave radio, ALF receives a Malmacian signal from two friends who tell him of a new home planet. ALF, wanting to join them, leaves the Tanners, unaware that his presence is known by the Alien Task Force. However, before ALF can leave, he is captured; the 1996 TV movie *Project ALF* concludes the story. ALF has been imprisoned. Gilbert Milfoil (Martin Sheen) is determined to eliminate ALF, while scientists Rick Mullican (William O'Leary) and Melissa Hill (Jensen Daggett) believe ALF should live. Their efforts to free ALF comprise the story, with the Tanner family not seen or mentioned.

Amen

(NBC, 1986–1991)

Cast: Sherman Hemsley (Ernest Frye), Clifton Davis (Reuben Gregory), Anna Maria Horsford (Thelma Frye).

Basis: Ernest Frye, a pastor stuck in the past, and Reuben Gregory, a modern-day thinking pastor, clash over what is best for their church.

ERNEST J. FRYE

Position: Pastor of the First Community Church of Philadelphia. Ernest's father founded the church in 1936, and it currently hosts one weekly mass; its competition, the First Methodist Church, offers four services per week.

Marital Status: Widower (his late wife was named Larraine).

Meeting: Larraine Tillman, a nurse at County General Hospital, first met Ernest, a law student working for Al's Delivery Service, when he brought flowers to a patient. It was love at first sight, and they married shortly after. Larraine passed away five years after giving birth to their daughter, Thelma.

Occupation: Lawyer (his shingle reads "Attorney-at-Law, Ernest Frye—Where Winning Is Everything"). It is mentioned that Ernest graduated last in his class at law school. He later becomes a judge and begins a church day care center ("Deacon Land").

Home Address: 5719 Liberty Avenue 19198.

Phone Number: 555-3707.

Law Office: Room 203 on 56th Street (also given as 159 Olive Street).

Parking Space Sign: "Don't Even Think of Parking Here."

Fear: Snakes.

Pet Dog: Peanut.

Blood Type: A-positive.

Favorite Magazine: Popular Gospel.

Favorite Food: Meatball topped pizza.

1982 Sedan License Plate: KNC 481.

Hope: To win the lottery and help the church (he buys one ticket a week).

State Senate Race: Ran for Pennsylvania state senator under the slogan "Vote for Ernest Frye and Get a Piece of the Pie"; he lost against an imprisoned incumbent, 19,372 to 43.

Opening Theme: As two young girls jump rope, Ernest joins in and jumps 11 times.

Relatives: Estranged father-in-law, Ben Tillman (Moses Gunn); he deserted the family when Ernest and Larraine married.

Flashbacks: Larraine, Ernest's wife (Anna Maria Horsford).

REUBEN GREGORY

Mother: Josephine Gregory (Jane White).

Position: Assistant pastor at the First Community Church of Philadelphia. He also teaches theology at Baxter Women's College.

Place of Birth: Cleveland, Ohio.

Education: Morehouse College (a BA in theology), Yale Divinity School (degree in religious education), Union Theological Seminary (doctorate in Christian studies). He also has an undergraduate degree in economics.

Duties: Conducting the Sunday morning service; overseeing the church's teen hotline (295-TEEN) and discussing church matters with parishioners via his "Pastor's Pow Wow." Reuben began preaching in Cleveland in 1976 and was host of the *Sunrise Semester* TV show.

Address: An apartment (931) at an unnamed location.

Arrest Record: Jailed for picketing against racism at the South African embassy.

Relatives: Aunt, Martha (Vivian Bonnell).

THELMA FRYE

Relationship: Ernest's daughter; later Reuben's wife (1990).

Age: 31 (when the series begins).

Address: 5791 Livingston Street.

Trait: Nags and whines until she gets what she wants.

Fear: Flying.

Education: West Holmes High School. (Where she was called "The Un-date-able." In the pilot episode Ernest mentions that Thelma was jilted 20 times in 10 years; in the third episode he says 16 times in 10 years.) She has flat feet but won the 100-yard dash for her track team.

Favorite Subjects: Science, English, and home economics.

Military Service: U.S. Army (serial number 111382595).

TV Commercial: Spokesgirl for Bake Rite Flour.

TV Show: Thelma's Kitchen (which ended before the first episode aired, as her assistants, Reuben and Ernest, managed to destroy the set while she was preparing a meal).

Occupation: Real estate agent for the firm of Underwood-Baines.

Nickname: Thelma calls Reuben "Sweet Potato."

Child: The final episode finds Thelma and Reuben becoming the parents of an unnamed boy. They previously attempted to adopt Jeanette (Gloria Briscoe) through the Women's Christian Alliance, but after three weeks, her aunt and uncle came for her.

Relatives: Aunt, Leola (Rosetta LeNoir).

Flashbacks: Thelma, age five (Alexaundria Simmons).

OTHER CHARACTERS

Rolly Forbes (Jester Hairston) is the elderly church board member who continually insults Ernest; he is Thelma's godfather and married Thelma's aunt, Leola Henderson Forbes (Rosetta LeNoire, then Montrose Hagnis). Rolly mentioned that he served in World War II and, after his discharge in 1944, joined the church.

Amelia Heterbrink (Roz Ryan) and Cassietta Heterbrink (Barbara Montgomery) are the spinster sisters who are members of the church board and the choir; 555-1765 is their phone number.

Baywatch

(NBC, 1989–1990; Syndicated, 1991–2001)

Cast: David Hasselhoff (Mitch Buchannon); Yasmine Bleeth (Caroline Holden); Pamela Anderson (C. J. Parker); Kelly Packard (April Giminski); Donna D'Errico (Donna Marco); Brooke Burns (Jesse Owens); Shawn Weatherly (Jill Riley); Carmen Electra (Lani McKenzie); Heather Campbell, then Gena Lee Nolin, then Jennifer Campbell (Neely Capshaw); Erika Eleniak (Shauni McClain); Alexandra Paul (Stephanie Holden); Nicole Eggert (Summer Quinn); Ashley Gorrell (Josephine "Joey" Jennings); Brandon Call, then Jeremy Jackson (Hobie Buchannon).

Basis: A showcase for the glamorous female lifeguards attached to the Baywatch Division of the Los Angeles County Lifeguards at Malibu Beach (also said to be Sunset Beach) as they risk their lives to protect beachgoers.

OVERALL SERIES INFORMATION
The radio call letters for Baywatch headquarters are KMF 295; Sam's Surf and Dive is the beach store. Bucky's Ocean Grill (also seen as Bruce's Beach Burgers and the Beach Hut) is the eatery (a regular hamburger is $3.00; $3.75 for a cheeseburger). Early episodes place the lifeguards with the Beach and Harbors Unit of the Los Angeles County Lifeguards. Santa Monica Bay is also mentioned as the beach they are patrolling.

MITCHELL "MITCH" BUCHANNON
Place of Birth: Phoenix, Arizona (dialogue claims in 1952 and 1954).
Parents: Al and Irene Buchannon. Irene (Anne Jeffreys) is suffering from Alzheimer's disease; Al is deceased.
Brother: Buzz Buchannon.
Ex-Wife: Gayle (Wendie Malick). Gayle, a consultant for Captain Chuck's Chicken and Fixin' franchise in Columbus, Ohio, ended their marriage in

1992 due to Mitch's total dedication to his work (at this time, Gayle burned Mitch's surfer dude cap; Mitch crushed Gayle's favorite ceramic duck).

Son: Hobie (named after a famous surfboard company). He lives with Mitch and later becomes a lifeguard and had a dog named Rocky in NBC episodes.

Address: 1311 Talanca in Venice, California.

Education: West Palisades High School (in Los Angeles), where he and Gayle met.

Occupation: Senior lifeguard. As a rookie, Mitch was assigned to Outpost Tower 33, later Tower 2, Tower 27, and Tower 12. He was promoted to captain (1997) and assigned to an office at Baywatch headquarters. Mitch, who enjoys Hawaii as his place for excitement and relaxation, later establishes the International Lifeguard Training Center, a camp based on the north shore of Oahu, Hawaii (seen under the final-season title of *Baywatch: Hawaii*).

Favorite Sports: Surfing, kickboxing, and racing boats and dune buggies.

Favorite Group: The Heat Rays (a mythical version of the Beach Boys).

Military Career: Served as a navy SEAL (skilled in hand-to-hand combat).

Talent: Sings and plays the guitar. Mitch had dreamed of becoming a singer, and this is reflected in the episode "Wet and Wild," where Mitch envisions what his life may have been (seen through footage of David Hasselhoff's concerts).

Background: As a child, Mitch loved detective movies (especially *The Maltese Falcon*) and yearned to become a private detective. He was groomed to follow in his father's footsteps and become an architect. He joined his father's firm after college but felt miserable and quit after two months. At some point, Mitch became a lifeguard, and in 1983, he spent one year in Australia as part of a lifeguard exchange program.

Adopted Child: Joey Jennings. In 1995 Kyla, Joey's con-artist mother, is killed in a car accident. Mitch takes on the responsibility of caring for her (Hobie's nine-year-old friend) when he learns she will be sent to an orphanage.

Patrol Car Code: KF 295, then 208 Lincoln.

Patrol Car License Plate: 18903 (then 3E9 1063, 6G05770, and 4J061 197).

Personal Car License Plate: 200T 456.

CAROLINE HOLDEN

Place of Birth: New York City on June 14, 1968.

Sister: Stephanie Holden (see below).

Measurements: 36-26-34. She is a brunette, wears a size 7 shoe, and stands 5 feet, 5 inches tall.

Occupation: Lifeguard (works out of Tower 1 at Baywatch).

Favorite TV Show: Charlie's Angels.

Character: Although she expressed interest in becoming a lifeguard in high school, Caroline yearned to become an actress. Before achieving either, she married and later divorced environmentalist Frank Baxter for infidelity. It was at this time that she began her lifeguard career at Baywatch (moving in with Stephanie and C.J.). She also pursued acting and left Baywatch for a role on the TV soap opera *Shannon's Hope*. While Caroline did wear tight, cleavage-revealing red swimsuits like most of her counterparts, she often relaxed in a bikini in her off-work hours.

STEPHANIE HOLDEN

Place of Birth: New York City on July 29, 1963.

Measurements: 36-23-33. She has brunette hair, wears a size 4 dress and a size 8 shoe, and stands 5 feet, 10 inches tall.

Car License Plate: 2HEX 864.

Occupation: Lifeguard (originally commanded Outpost Tower 18 before becoming a lieutenant). She was later the administrative assistant, and, although wearing her red Baywatch swimsuit and assisting in rescues, she was often relegated to office duty at Baywatch headquarters (and attired in a black skirt, white top, and high heels).

Favorite Movie Actresses: Katharine Hepburn and Sophia Loren.

Character: Caroline's older sister. (Their father lost his life in a helicopter crash during the Vietnam War. She and Caroline were then abandoned by their mother and raised by their grandmother.) She is dedicated to work and rooms with C.J. and Caroline. She keeps in shape by jogging and exercising and has a fear of helicopters. Stephanie appeared on the NBC version as Mitch's girlfriend, a lifeguard at the time. (Mitch walked into the men's locker room and saw Stephanie, who had mistaken it for the women's locker room, changing into her swimsuit. The two became friends and dated. When the relationship became serious, Stephanie broke it off by leaving Mitch, as she was married but only separated from her husband.) Stephanie originally left Baywatch (1994) to set sail on an around-the-world cruise but returned five months later when she missed being a lifeguard. She was well versed in all operations at Baywatch—from rescuing people at sea to commanding a boat to training teenage girls as part of the Junior Lifeguards. In 1997, while on a boat called *Chance of a Lifetime*, a sudden storm engulfs the craft. Lightning strikes the mast and kills Stephanie when it falls on her.

C.J. PARKER

Full Name: Casey Jean Parker, although she prefers C.J.

Place of Birth: Las Vegas, Nevada, on July 1, 1967.

Mother: Shelley Sands (Connie Stevens), a Las Vegas exotic dancer. She was originally said to be a bookkeeper for Tony Blantoin (David Groh), a Las

Vegas businessman. C.J.'s unseen father was addicted to gambling, and, being around the casinos, C.J. became hooked on gambling at one point.

Measurements: 39-24-34. She has blonde hair and blue eyes and stands 5 feet, 7 inches tall. Because she shows considerable cleavage, it is said, "Wherever C.J. goes, men are not far behind."

Occupation: Lifeguard (works out of Tower 25, then Tower 16). She pilots the boat *Lifeguard 1* ("Rescue One" is her radio code) and was an ocean lifeguard, volleyball coach at Malibu High School, and then a white-water river rafting guide before joining Baywatch.

Sports Car License Plate: 3DT 368 (then 3JM5 193).

Abilities: Trained in lifeguard rescue skills, scuba diving, kayaking, hang gliding, rock climbing, kickboxing, and jet skiing. She can also play the saxophone.

Character: Believes in karma, fortune-tellers, mermaids, and even elves. She left Baywatch for a marriage to a rock star that failed and reestablished herself as the owner of C.J.'s Bar and Grill at the Turtle Bay Resort and Marina in Hawaii.

APRIL GIMINSKI

Place of Birth: Wisconsin on January 29, 1975.

Measurements: 34-24-34. She is blonde, has green eyes, wears a size 8 shoe, and stands 5 feet, 4 inches tall.

Occupation: Lifeguard (previously a lifeguard at Lake Watanabe in Wisconsin).

Character: Gives of herself to help others and is thought of as the wholesome, old-fashioned girl next door. She never pretends to be something she is not and follows the rules, never rushing into the water without thinking first.

DONNA MARCO

Place of Birth: Alabama on March 30, 1968.

Measurements: 34-22-34. She has blonde hair and blue eyes and stands 5 feet, 5 inches tall.

Occupation: Businesswoman (under the name D.J. Marco "because it makes business easier"). Donna first appeared on the spin-off *Baywatch Nights*, wherein she owned a beach nightclub called Nights; she became a lifeguard when the series ended.

Character: Appears too perfect for the job (a gorgeous girl who should be admired). She is athletic (skilled in rock climbing), finished second in her class at lifeguard school, and proved to be a responsible lifeguard when it came to rescues; her private life was different: She earned money prior to Baywatch (and her nightclub) by entering beauty pageants. In one later shoot, she posed in *Playboy* magazine wearing her Baywatch swimwear. She was reprimanded, as lifeguards are role models, not magazine eye candy.

JESSICA "JESSE" OWENS
Place of Birth: Texas on March 16, 1978.
Measurements: 36-25-36. She wears a size 10 shoe and a size 8 dress and stands
5 feet, 8 inches tall.
Occupation: Lifeguard (Jesse mentions that 80 percent of what lifeguards do is
look after children who become lost at the beach).
Character: As a teenager, Jesse was arrested and convicted of riding in a stolen
car with her then boyfriend. Because she was underage (16), she was not
criminally prosecuted. Jesse, a poor student in school and often troublesome
to her parents, left home at age 19 and drifted around the country until
she found a job at Baywatch in its maintenance department. With a steady
income, Jesse was now anxious to pursue her dream of becoming a movie
and TV stuntwoman. One evening, while alone on the beach, Jesse saves
a drowning person but quietly disappears after doing so. Several similar
rescues occur, and the press dubs Jesse "The Mystery Girl." When Mitch
discovers her secret, he convinces her to become a lifeguard.

JILL RILEY
Place of Birth: Wisconsin on July 24, 1959.
Measurements: 35-25-35. She has blonde hair and blue eyes and stands 5 feet,
8 inches tall.
Occupation: Lifeguard (works out of Tower 27 with Mitch).
Character: The daughter of a middle-class family and somewhat of a tomboy,
as she enjoyed sports. At the age of 15, she fell in love with fishing. Every
weekend, Jill would fish from a rowboat on Lake Motawanakeg and read
while waiting for a bite. Halfway through the book *Wuthering Heights*, she
got a nibble, then a bite, and reeled in a large striped bass that she prepared
for dinner that night. Jill always gives of herself to help others. She is never
careless and always figures out the best procedure in a rescue. When Jill
tried to save children during a shark sighting, she was attacked by a shark,
lost a great deal of blood, and suffered massive internal injuries (requiring
more than 200 stitches). She appeared to be improving at Webster Memorial Hospital, but complications set in, and Jill died from a blood embo-
lism. She never had the opportunity to finish reading *Wuthering Heights*.
Pamela Bowen played Jill in the 1989 TV movie pilot *Baywatch: Panic at
Malibu Pier.*

LAILANI "LANI" MCKENZIE
Place of Birth: Hawaii on April 20, 1972.
Measurements: 36-23-35. She wears a size 4 dress and a size 8 shoe and stands 5
feet, 3 inches tall.

Occupation: Lifeguard.

Character: Proud of her Hawaiian heritage; she has the fiery temper of her father, a naval officer of Scottish descent, but the mellow attitude of her Hawaiian mother. Lani had aspirations to become a dancer and performed as Kyla at the Club Rio. She left Baywatch for a dancing career in Manhattan and later entertained at C.J.'s bar in Hawaii.

NEELY CAPSHAW

Place of Birth: Minnesota on November 25, 1971.

Measurements: 35-24-34. She has blonde hair and brown eyes, wears a size 10 shoe, and stands 5 feet, 9 inches tall (all for Gena Lee Nolin as Neely).

Occupation: Lifeguard (she worked previously at Huntington Beach before her transfer to Baywatch in 1995). Neely also modeled lingerie and appeared in the *Inside Sports* magazine swimsuit edition.

Character: Neely is cold and calculating (schemes to get what she wants) and believes that being a good swimmer is the most important requirement for a lifeguard ("If you're not a good swimmer to reach the victim then nothing else matters"). Neely defies rules and regulations (like flirting with beachgoers and drinking on the job) but always manages to come out on top (believing her gorgeous looks can get her out of trouble). The "stiff punishments" she received amounted to switchboard duty. While she has to be the star attraction wherever she goes, in a crisis she will risk her life to save a drowning person. She left Baywatch to become a businesswoman. Neely (Heather Campbell) was first seen in a one-time role in the fifth-season episode "Wet and Wild" as a rookie lifeguard fired for drinking on the job and filing a false sexual harassment charge against lifeguard Matt Brody when he refused her advances (he was dating C.J. at the time). In the sixth-season premiere, "Trapped Beneath the Sea, Part 1," Neely (Gena Lee Nolin) returns to Baywatch when Stephanie Holden is ordered to rehire her in exchange for her dropping a lawsuit against the county for false dismissal. Neely becomes romantically involved with Mitch, and they marry in the seventh-season three-episode arc, "Bon Voyage" and "White Thunder at Glacier Bay, Parts 1 and 2." Jennifer Campbell then became Neely (Gena left to star in her own series, *Sheena*), but the character appeared only in a recurring story wherein it is learned that Neely tricked Mitch into marrying her to acquire some stability in her life. In Neely's final episode ("Wave Rage"), she is again fired for her devious actions.

SHAUNI MCCLAIN

Place of Birth: California on September 29, 1969.

Measurements: 38-24-36. She is 5 feet, 6 inches tall and wears a size 8 shoe.

Education: South Central High School in Los Angeles (later said to be Valley High School; her wealthy parents gave her $50 for each "A" on her report card).

Address: 3360 North Canyon Drive.

Occupation: Lifeguard (assigned to Tower 17; also the pilot of *Rescue Boat 1*).

Character: Suffered from a fear of people drowning and would often hesitate when administering CPR. She and lifeguard Eddie Kramer became a couple and left Baywatch in 1992 to raise a family in Australia. Shauni uses Bohemian Love Sun Block Lotion.

ROBERTA "SUMMER" QUINN

Mother: Jacqueline "Jackie" Quinn (Susan Anton).

Place of Birth: Pittsburgh on January 13, 1972.

Bra Size: 34C. She wears a size 10 dress and a size 6 shoe and stands 5 feet, 3 inches tall.

Education: Malibu Beach High School; Penn College.

Occupation: Lifeguard (assigned to Tower 26).

Character: The youngest of the lifeguards (17 years old), who prefers to be called by her nickname "Summer." Jackie, her single mother (her husband deserted her), and Summer live in a trailer park. Jackie runs the beach diner, Jackie's Summer Place, and Summer attends school while training at Baywatch. Summer's greatest fear during training was diving off the 100-foot pier. She left Baywatch to attend college in Pennsylvania.

OTHER LIFEGUARDS

Eddie Kramer (Billy Warlock) was born in Philadelphia in 1961. He joined the Los Angeles County lifeguards as a teenager and was assigned to Baywatch under Mitch's command. Eddie, orphaned as a child, went through 17 different foster homes and learned life's lessons from the streets, which gave him a tough exterior. He had a sister named Lonnie (drowned in a swimming pool at age seven), and during the great Los Angeles earthquake, he delivered twins when he came across a woman in labor. He and Shauni became close and moved to Australia to raise a family.

Ben Edwards (Richard Jaeckel), born on Long Island (New York) in 1926, is a seasoned lifeguard and one of the original founders (known as the Red Knights) of Baywatch in the 1950s. He retired in 1994 but served as a mentor to Mitch, whom he first met in rookie school. Ben became disabled (now walks with a cane) when he crushed his hip after jumping from a great height to save a drowning fisherman. He received a promotion to lieutenant, then captain, before retiring.

Cody Madison (David Chokachi) was born in Indiana on January 16, 1968. He is a former Olympic swimmer and was first romantically involved with C.J., then Lani. Cody's parents were first said to be living in Indiana, then to have drowned in floods that ravaged the state when he was younger. A medical exam revealed in 1996 that he had an irregular heartbeat and could no longer work at Baywatch.

Captain Dan Thorpe (Monte Markham) is the head of Baywatch (stationed in Tower 21 when he was a rookie). His ex-wife was named Doris; when she left him, he bought himself a red Miata sports car. He was replaced by Stephanie Holden in the episode "Tequila Bay."

Craig Pomeroy (Parker Stevenson) was married to Gina (Gina Hecht, then Holly Gagnier) and left Baywatch to pursue a career as a lawyer. *Sea Hunt* was his favorite TV show.

Matt Brody (David Charvet) was a lifeguard trainee and introduced in the episode "River of No Return" as Eddie Kramer's replacement and Summer's romantic interest (Matt won the "Rookie of the Year" award, and 853 DTS is his license plate number). Dirk Benedict and Josette Prevost played his parents, Aaron and Vivian Brody.

Logan Fowler (Jaason Simmons), born in Tasmania, Australia, on July 20, 1970, became a part of Baywatch through an exchange program. He was a top lifeguard in Australia but could not replicate that success at Baywatch. He had a failed romance with Caroline Holden (who was not ready for marriage) and married the wealthy Kathleen Huntington to get his green card and remain in California.

SPIN-OFF

Baywatch Nights (1995–1997). Mitch (David Hasselhoff), unhappy being a lifeguard, joins with his friend Garner Ellerbee (David Alan Williams), the beach patrol officer, and Ryan McBride (Angie Harmon), a young investigator newly arrived in Santa Monica from New York, to form the Buchannon-Ellerbee-McBride Detective Agency at 200 Beach Boulevard above a nightclub called Nights. Singer Lou Raymond (Lou Rawls) first owns the club; he is replaced by D.J. Marco (Donna D'Errico).

TV MOVIE UPDATE

Baywatch: Hawaiian Wedding (Fox 2003) reunites original cast members of both *Baywatch* and *Baywatch: Hawaii* to end the series. Mitch (David Hasselhoff) has retired and is now engaged to Allison Ford (Alexandra Paul). Allison works as a travel agent and is a dead ringer for Stephanie, but that likeness is not mentioned. Mitch's son, Hobie (Jeremy Jackson), is a lifeguard at Baywatch; C.J.

(Pamela Anderson) is now the owner of C.J.'s Bar and Grill at the Beach Turtle Bay Resort. Caroline (Yasmine Bleeth) is now an actress (which was her dream from *Baywatch*). Neely (Gena Lee Nolin) is now a businesswoman. Summer (Nicole Eggert) returned to Baywatch as a lifeguard after graduating from college. The story focuses on Mitch and Allison's wedding.

Cagney & Lacey
(CBS, 1982–1986)

Cast: Meg Foster, then Sharon Gless (Chris Cagney); Tyne Daly (Mary Beth Lacey).

Basis: New York City Police Department detectives Chris Cagney and Mary Beth Lacey investigate crimes based on their differing opinions rather than departmental procedure.

CHRISTINE "CHRIS" CAGNEY

Place of Birth: Westchester, New York.

Age: 38 (in third-season episodes, making her birth year 1944).

Father: Charlie Cagney (Dick O'Neill). Her mother died when Chris was 19.

Address: 11 West 49th Street in Manhattan.

Occupation: Detective with the 14th Precinct, Homicide Division. She (and Mary Beth) previously worked with the 23rd Precinct's John Squad (posing as prostitutes to nab men who pay for sex). Chris liked the assignments; Mary Beth complained it is tough on her feet ("Cops' feet aren't made for hookers' shoes").

Precinct Association: Member of the Community Board (oversees minor cases).

Education: Holy Cross Grammar School; Mount St. Michael High School.

Dodge Car License Plate: 562 BLA (later 437 BLA, then 801 FEM).

Badge Number: 730 (then 790).

Car Code: 312 (then 27 and 394).

Marital Status: Single ("Because I understand about commitment and responsibilities"; something she is unable to handle ever since a psychic told her "I was going to marry, live on a farm and have four children").

Addiction: Alcohol. Chris, like her father, has a serious drinking problem but is attempting to control it through AA meetings.

Favorite Bar: Flannery's Bar (then O'Malley's Bar).

Trait: Hates to lose at anything; punches or kicks something when she is angry.

Case Approach: Gather the obvious evidence and proceed from there.

Relatives: Brother, Brian Cagney (David Ackroyd); niece, Bridget Cagney (Amanda Wyss).

MARY BETH LACEY

Place of Birth: Queens, New York.

Father: Martin Biskey (Richard Bradford).

Husband: Harvey Lacey (John Karlen), a freelance construction worker.

Children: Harvey Jr. (Tony LaTorre), Michael (Troy Slaten), and Alice (Donna and Paige Bardolph).

Maiden Name: Mary Beth Biskey.

Address: In the first season, Mary Beth lives in Manhattan (Apartment 4E in a building with the street number 333). Harvey is the building's superintendent. For the remainder of the series, they live at 7132 West 46th Street in Jackson Heights, Queens, New York (although said to be living there for 15 years). Harvey now works in construction. As a kid, Harvey raised pigeons. He has an inner-ear affliction that causes him to lose balance at great heights. He calls Mary Beth "Babe," and *Lucks 'n' Bucks* is his favorite TV game show; Harvey dislikes it when Mary Beth and Chris discuss police matters at dinner. Tuesday is Harvey's bowling night, and he and Mary Beth order pizza from Luigi's.

Phone Number: 555-1519.

Philosophy: Mary Beth and Harvey agree on cars: "Drive 'em till they die."

Occupation: Detective with the 14th Precinct, Homicide Division; previously a member of the 23rd Precinct's John Squad (posing as hookers) with Chris.

Education: St. Catherine's Grammar School; St. Helena's High School. In the fifth grade, Mary Beth was called "Mary Beth Number 2" to distinguish her from fellow student Mary Beth Lazonne (called "Mary Beth Number 1").

Car Code: 312 (then 27 and 394).

Badge Number: 763 (also seen as 340).

Former Habit: Smoking.

Dislike: Missing-persons cases (as she becomes too emotionally involved).

Case Approach: A stickler for details (treats each piece of evidence like a puzzle that can lead to a successful conclusion).

Favorite Bar: Flannery's Bar, then O'Malley's Bar.

Note: Loretta Swit played Chris Cagney in the pilot film, Robert Hunter was Harvey Lacey, Jamie Dick was Harvey Lacey Jr., and Evan Routband was Michael Lacey.

TV MOVIE UPDATES
In *Cagney & Lacy: The Return* (1994), Mary Beth is now a lieutenant, and Chris is married to James Burton (James Naughton). The cast is also reunited for *Cagney & Lacy: Together Again* (1995), *Cagney & Lacey: The View Through the Glass Ceiling* (1995), and *Cagney & Lacey: True Convictions* (1996).

Charles in Charge
(CBS, 1984–1985; Syndicated, 1987–1990)

1984–1985 Cast: Scott Baio (Charles), Willie Aames (Buddy Lembeck), Julie Cobb (Jill Pembroke), James Widdoes (Stan Pembroke), April Lerman (Lila Pembroke), Jonathan Ward (Douglas Pembroke), Michael Pearlman (Jason Pembroke).

1987–1990 Cast: Scott Baio (Charles), Willie Aames (Buddy Lembeck), Sandra Kerns (Ellen Powell), Nicole Eggert (Jamie Powell), Josie Davis (Sarah Powell), Alexander Polinsky (Adam Powell), James Callahan (Walter Powell).

Basis: A college student's (Charles's) experiences as a live-in helper for a busy working couple: Jill and Stan Pembroke with three children, Lila, Douglas, and Jason (1984–1985), and Ellen and Robert Powell and their children, Sarah, Jamie, and Adam (1987–1990). The address 10 Barrington Court in New Brunswick, New Jersey, is used for both versions of the series.

CHARLES
Place of Birth: Scranton, Pennsylvania.
Mother: Lillian (Ellen Travolta), a widow who first operates Sid's Pizza Parlor, then the Yesterday Café.
Career Ambition: To become a teacher.
Education: Scranton Elementary School (where he won the seventh-grade spelling bee with the word *quixotic* and had a ventriloquist act with a dummy named Muggsy); Scranton High School (where he formed a band called the Charles Tones); Copeland College (in New Jersey, majoring in education).
Nickname as a Child: "Doodlebug" (as called by his mother).
Show Gimmick: Neither Charles nor his mother has a last name.
Favorite Movie Star: Darby Peterson (mythical).
Favorite Seafood Eatery: The Grotto.
Favorite Hamburger Eatery: The Lamplight.
Medical Issue: Unnamed, but any bump on the head will cause Charles to become Chazz Lamborghini, a tough-looking biker (a second head bump reverses the condition).

Chazz's Girlfriend: Tiffany (Denise Miller), who is just there when Chazz appears.

Charles's Girlfriend: Gwendolyn Pierce (Jennifer Runyon), a gorgeous blonde who also attends Copeland College.

First Teaching Experience: Student teacher at Central High School.

Final Episode: Charles leaves the Powell family to pursue his teaching degree at Princeton University.

Relatives: Uncle, Joe (John Astin), "The Pickle King of Brooklyn"; cousin, Anthony (Justin Whalen); aunt, Sally (Ellen Travolta).

BUDDENCE "BUDDY" LEMBECK

Relationship: Charles's best friend.

Place of Birth: California (he mentions being a Leo).

Education: Copeland College (a political science major and a member of the Scuba Club). An aptitude test revealed that he is a jack-of-no-trades and best suited for jury duty. In high school, he was voted "Class Flake." Mr. Hobbs (a goat) is the college mascot, and Buddy's theory regarding college is "only take courses with less than five books to read" (any more will cause him to cheat).

As a Kid: Had a dog named Kitty and a hand puppet named Handie.

Residence: The college dorm (where he has been banned from bringing livestock into the room and performing chemistry experiments).

Pets: Arlo (an ant who lives in a plastic ant farm), Lloyd (lizard).

Character: A bit dim-witted and claims he receives mind transmissions from the planet Zargon. His denseness could be attributed to his smashing 57 cans of beer against his forehead ("I could have done more if the cans were empty"). He believes that singer Barbara Mandrell loves him (her autographed photo to him reads "Love, Barbara"), and he is most proud of his autographed Mickey Mantle baseball (which Buddy signed for Mickey when Mickey was unavailable). And, of all the troublesome situations in the world, the question that bothers Buddy most is "Why won't the park ranger let Yogi Bear have a picnic basket?" (from the *Yogi Bear* cartoon series).

Radio Host: The *Buddy Lembeck Show* on the Copeland radio station, WFNZ.

Fear: Clowns.

Money-Making Idea: Clone Charles and market Charles Live-In Housekeepers as a company called "Charles Are Us."

Girlfriend: The often talked about but rarely seen Nurse Bennett (Kelly Ann Carr).

Relatives: Father, Clarence Lembeck (Lewis Arquette); Grandmother, Gloria (Ruta Lee); sister, Bunny Lembeck (Mindy Cohn); cousin, Dudley Krantz (Willie Aames).

JILL AND STAN PEMBROKE

Jillian, called Jill, is a theater critic for the *New Jersey Register*. Her father, Harry Gardner (Dick O'Neill), called her "Jillybean," and in high school she was called "Pixie." Stanley Albert, called Stan, is one of 49 vice presidents in an unnamed company. Like Jill, virtually nothing else is revealed (other than their favorite eatery being Willie Wong's Chinese Palace). Rue McClanahan appeared as Stan's mother, Irene (who, with Charles's help, attempted to start a pizza business called Mama Garabaldi's Pizza).

LILA, JASON, AND DOUGLAS PEMBROKE

Lila Beth, the eldest child, attends Lincoln Elementary School, then Northside High School. She is described as being "sweet, lovely and dots her *i*'s with little hearts." She reads *Co-Ed* magazine and calls Buddy "Goon Machine." Lila is a member of the Circle of Friendship Club and longs to wear makeup and high heels. She played softball on Stan's company's team but was so bad that she was assigned deep-roving right field.

Jason and Douglas, like Lila, have virtually no background information. They attend Lincoln Elementary School and have a pet feline named Putty Cat. Jason is mischievous and an average student at school, while Douglas strives for "A" grades but was heartbroken when he received an "F" for a book report on *TV Guide* (his teacher didn't consider it classic literature). He, Jason, and Lila have Kellogg's Bran Flakes for breakfast. Julie Mercer (played by Liz Keifer) was the original live-in helper.

ELLEN AND ROBERT POWELL

Ellen is a real estate broker, and Robert (James O'Sullivan), her husband, is a navy commander on assignment in the South Seas. He is infrequently seen (only when on leave), and his father, Walter Powell, a retired navy officer, also resides in the home to help Charles care for his grandchildren. Ellen was born in New Jersey and attended Central High School (apparently where she and Robert met). After graduating, Ellen chose to study journalism at Copeland College while Robert chose to follow in his father's footsteps and become a navy man. Nothing else is stated. While Charles tries to use psychology to deal with the children's problems, Walter, a member of the John Paul Jones Society, believes that stories about his naval experiences are better teaching tools.

Ellen's Relatives: Cousins, Joan Robinson (Kay Lenz), Amanda Colfax (Nicole Eggert), Melanie Colfax (Olivia Burnette); uncles, Steve Colfax (David Braf), Michael Colfax (Michael Manasseri).

Walter's Relatives: Father, Ben "Buzz" Powell (Dabbs Greer). Ben mentioned that his wife's name is Florence.

JAMIE PEMBROKE

Relationship: Ellen and Robert's eldest child.

Education: Central High School (where she is a cheerleader); the Better Image Modeling School.

Nickname: Called "Little Scooter" by her father.

Career Ambition: Fashion model.

Shoe Size: 5; she has blonde hair.

TV Commercial: Banana Cream Shampoo.

Job: Waitress at Sid's Pizza Parlor.

Cult: Joined (but quit) the Followers of Light.

Beauty Pageants: Won titles in "The Miss Brunswick Beauty Pageant" and "The Yesterday Café Beauty Pageant."

Character: Very pretty but too eager to grow up. Her quest for more freedom often placed Charles in a difficult position, as it is his responsibility to make sure she is making the right decisions without making it look like he is controlling her life.

SARAH PEMBROKE

Relationship: Jamie's younger sister.

Education: Central High School (a member of the Shakespeare Club).

Career Ambition: Writer or novelist.

Job: Freelance reporter for the *New Brunswick Herald* (writes stories geared to teenagers). She also starred with Jamie in the Banana Cream Shampoo TV commercial.

First Published Story: "What It Is Like to Be a Teenager" (for *Teen* magazine).

Character: The most sensitive of the children. She has more common sense than Jamie and maintains a straight "A" average. Unlike Jamie, Sarah will not venture beyond the limits that Charles and Walter have placed on her.

Pet Turtle: Ross.

Favorite Doll: Rebecca.

Favorite Poets: Elizabeth Barrett Browning and Emily Dickinson.

Ambition: Ending world hunger and war.

Beauty Pageant: First runner-up in "The Yesterday Café Beauty Pageant."

ADAM PEMBROKE

Adam, the youngest child, attends an unnamed grammar school, then Central High School (an average student). He is a bit mischievous and enjoys hanging out with his grandfather, Walter (it appears he wants to become a navy man and enjoys hearing about Walter's experiences traveling the world when he was in service).

Cheers

(NBC, 1982–1993)

Cast: Ted Danson (Sam Malone), Shelley Long (Diane Chambers), Kirstie Alley (Rebecca Howe), Rhea Perlman (Carla Tortelli), Nicholas Colasanto (Ernie Pantusso), George Wendt (Norm Peterson), John Ratzenberger (Cliff Claven), Woody Harrelson (Woody Boyd), Kelsey Grammer (Frasier Crane), Bebe Neuwirth (Dr. Lilith Sternin).

Basis: Cheers, a Boston bar, provides the setting for a look at the life of its owner (Sam), his staff (Diane, Carla, Rebecca, Coach, and Woody), and his principal patrons, Cliff, Frasier, and Norm.

OVERALL SERIES INFORMATION

Cheers, located at 112½ Beacon Street, was established in 1889 as a bordello called Mom's (it became Cheers in 1895; Sam purchased it from Gus O'Malley in 1976). The wooden Indian, Tecumseh, stands by the front door; Melville's Fine Seafood Restaurant (owned by John Allen Hill) operates above Cheers (the stairway that connects the two is called "Sam's Stairway"). Gary's Old Towne Tavern is Sam's competition. Exterior images of Cheers were filmed at the Boston bar The Bull and Finch Pub. When the first episode begins, Sam is seen walking out of the bar's pool room; the final episode shows him entering the pool room.

SAMUEL "SAM" MALONE

Place of Birth: Boston.

Brother: Derek Malone (George Bell), an international lawyer.

Education: Boston Prep School.

Marital Status: Divorced (from Deborah).

Occupation: Sam was a ballplayer with the Boston Red Sox (relief pitcher; wore jersey 16). He was nicknamed "Mayday," and a bottle cap he found on the field became his good-luck charm. He turned to alcohol when his career began to falter and was released; shortly afterward, he purchased Cheers as a place "where everybody knows your name." He also dreams of opening a waterfront bar called "Sam's Place."

Character: Gruff in his tone but actually kindhearted. Sam recalled that he first noticed the difference between men and women when he was in sixth grade. He has a little black book of girls he dated, feels that he has "the look" that attracts women, and is famous for his infatuation with Diane, his prim-and-proper barmaid.

Car: Sam mentions driving a Corvette.

Front row: Ted Danson and Shelley Long; back row: John Ratzenberger, Nicholas Colasanto, Rhea Perlman, and George Wendt. *NBC/Photofest. ©NBC*

Biggest Regret: Selling Cheers to the Lillian Corporation when he felt he needed a change of life. He bought a ketch and set out on a trip around the world. Shortly after, the ketch sank, and he became stranded on an atoll he called "No Brains Atoll" (for selling the bar, which he now missed). He regained ownership of Cheers when the corporation became involved in a scandal and sold it back to him for 85 cents.

Biggest Fear: Losing his hair (so much so that he has his hair insured).

TV Work: Commercials for Fields Beer; substitute sportscaster at Wrigley Field.

Business Venture: Pooled resources with patrons Norm and Cliff to open the ill-fated Tan 'n' Wash (a tanning salon and coin-operated laundry).

DIANE CHAMBERS

Place of Birth: Boston.

Parents: Spencer (deceased) and Helen Chambers (Glynis Johns). Diane was born prematurely at eight months. Spencer called her "Muffin."

Pets: Elizabeth Barrett Browning (a cat, after her favorite poet); Freddy Frogbottom (toad).

Plush Toys: Mr. Jammers (giraffe); Mr. Buzzer (bee); Brian the Lion; Gary Gorilla.

Occupation: Barmaid. Diane, a college student, first met Sam when she entered the bar after breaking up with her boyfriend, Professor Summer Sloan (Michael McGuire). Sam, feeling sorry for her, hired her as a waitress despite her lack of experience. Diane is also an art student and held jobs at the Third Eye Bookstore, as a checker at Hurley's Supermarket, and as a substitute teacher at Boston University.

Education: Boston University (majored in psychology and a member of the Phi Epsilon Delta sorority house; to fulfill her physical education requirements, she took a bowling course). In high school, she was voted "Most Likely to Marry into Old Money."

Interests: Rare first-edition books and ballet.

Relationships: Diane dated her psychologist and bar patron Frasier Crane. They had planned on a honeymoon in Italy, but Diane broke the engagement when she felt that a marriage would not work; Frasier called the experience "The evil days when darkness fell over the earth." Diane then embarked on a sexual spree in Europe. When she found sex overpowering her, she checked into the Abbey of St. Anshelins in Boston, where the Sisters of the Divine Serenity cured her. A rocky romance with Sam followed. He believed that Diane was "allergic to commitment," while Diane felt that Sam had great difficulty saying the word "love." They had planned a Disney World honeymoon, but Diane called off the wedding in 1987 to pursue a writing career.

Book: The Heart Held Hostage (made into a TV movie that won a cable TV Ace Award as "Best Telefilm"). The book was published by Houghton Mifflin Publishers. Diane previously used the pen name Jessica Simpson Bourgales to help Sam write a book (that never materialized) about his days as a ballplayer and wrote a play, *The Losers*, based on her experiences at Cheers (Sam was named Stan; Carla, Darla; Norm, Ned; Cliff, Clark; and Frasier, Franklin).

Character: Diane is a dreamer, "and I have a habit of making those dreams come true." She entered the 45th Annual Miss Boston Barmaid Contest (1983) and won based on her beauty, perkiness, and congeniality. Diane is allergic to dogs and, to overcome a bout of depression, she checked herself into the Goldenbrook Psychiatric Hospital. She develops a facial tick when she gets nervous (she controls it by meditating) and is always very courteous to bar patrons (she addresses Norm as "Norman" and Cliff as "Clifford").

CARLA

Place of Birth: Boston.

Full Name: Carla Maria Victoria Angelina Theresa Apolonia Lozupone Tortelli Ludlow LeBec.

Religion: Roman Catholic (although Rhea Perlman is Jewish).

Maiden Name: Carla Lozupone.

Mother: Mama Lozupone (Sada Thompson).

Siblings: Sisters, Annette Lozupone (Rhea Perlman), Angela Lozupone (Carol Ann Susi), and Zia Lozupone (Oceana Marr); brother, Sal Lozupone (Randy Pelish).

Ex-Husbands: Nick Tortelli (Dan Hedaya), Dr. Bennett Ludlow (John Karen), Eddie LeBec (Jay Thomas). Jean Kasem played Nick's second wife, Loretta.

Children by Nick: Anthony (Timothy Williams), Sarafina (Leah Remini), Lucinda (Sabrina Wiener), Gino (Josh Lozoff), and Annie (Risa Littman, then Mandy Ingber). *Son by Bennett:* Ludlow (Jarrett Lennon). *Twins by Eddie:* Elvis (Danny Kramer) and Jesse (Thomas Tulah). Eddie was a hockey player for the Boston Bruins (wore jersey 38). Eddie's full name was given as Edward Raymond LeBec, although Carla insists his real first name is Guy (pronounced "Gee"). Carla used the "Le Mans" method of childbirth ("I screamed like a Ferrari"). She refused to follow a family tradition of giving her firstborn son (Anthony) her father's name and her mother's maiden name (which would have made him Benito Mussolini).

Occupation: Waitress at Cheers; previously worked at the Broken Spoke Bar.

Character: Nasty and wisecracking. As a child, she was so mischievous that her parents sent her to St. Clete's School for Wayward Girls. She was named after her grandmother's stubborn mule and was called "Muffin" by her brothers (who stuffed her ears with yeast and tried to bake her face). She danced on the TV show *The Boston Boppers* when she was 16, and in 1991, she entered the Miss Boston Barmaid Contest (she became "nice" for the duration and won the Miss Congeniality title).

Nicknames for Diane: "Fish Face," Pencil Neck," and "Squawkbox."

Quirk: Her humor is always at the expense of someone else ("It makes me laugh").

Phone Number: 555-7834.

Relatives: Cousins, Frankie (Anthony Addabbo) and Santo Carbone (Ernie Sabella).

ERNEST "ERNIE" PANTUSSO

Place of Birth: Boston.

Late Wife: Angela.

Daughter: Lisa Pantusso (Allyce Beasley).

Occupation: Bartender. He was a former pitching coach (nicknamed "Coach") for the Boston Red Sox at the same time that Sam was a relief pitcher. Sam hired Ernie when he became somewhat senile and was let go by the ball club. Ernie holds the record for being hit by more pitched balls than any other coach in minor league history.

Favorite Movie: Thunder Road starring Robert Mitchum.

Character: Ernie is also nicknamed Red (not because he has red hair but because "I once read a book"). He considers the blackouts he has to be a nice break in the day and has chosen 1:37 a.m. as his favorite time of day ("I don't know why, I just like it"). He has a habit of banging his head on the bar's serving area next to the beer dispensers and is the coach of a Little League baseball team called the Titans. Ernie is kind and gentle and always gives of himself to help someone in need. In a fond tribute to Nicholas Colasanto after his passing in 1985, the picture he kept of Indian Chief Geronimo in his dressing room was placed on the *Cheers* set (upper left stage wall) to remind the cast and crew that Ernie was a part of their lives. In some episodes, Sam can be seen wearing the baseball jacket that Coach wore.

Relatives: Niece, Joyce Pantusso (Cady McClain).

CLIFFORD "CLIFF" CLAVEN

Place of Birth: Boston.

Parents: Esther (Frances Sternhagen) and Cliff Claven Sr. (Dick O'Neill). Cliff owns a condo, and it appears that his mother also lives there.

Occupation: U.S. Post Office letter carrier. He first worked the Meadow View Acres route near the airport, then the South Central Branch route before becoming district supervisor of Subdivision A, Grid L. The Flannigan's dog (on his route) and the day the now nonexistent Sears catalog came out (putting an extra strain on him) were his biggest fears. He also won the Postman of the Year Award (Greater Boston).

Quirk: Has an opinion on any subject and claims to know everything about anything. He is an expert on tapeworms and an amateur inventor and gets drunk on nonalcoholic beer.

Favorite Snack: Hostess Twinkies.

Favorite TV Channel: The Weather Channel (for the Weather Bunnies: "You sort of develop a fatherly feeling after a while").

Association: The Knights of Semitar Lodge.

Belief: He is "the wing nut that holds Western civilization together." His car trunk contains an inflatable raft and cans of tuna fish (preparation for flooding when the polar ice caps melt due to global warming).

HILARY "NORM" PETERSON

Place of Birth: Boston.

Wife: Vera (who is never seen, only heard; voiced by Bernadette Birkett). Her maiden name is Vera Kreitzer. Norm does love her and puts up with her nagging. Norm, however, is loyal to the bar first: "Vera is somewhere down the line. I joke about her but she's all I got. I don't know what I'd do without her." It is unclear exactly how long they have been married. Norm first says 17 years, then 15 years, then 10 years.

Occupation: First worked as an accountant for H.W. and Associates. He then became a "corporate killer" (fires people) for Talbot International Accounting. He held one additional job as an accountant (Masters, Holly and Dickson) before starting his own home decorating business (first called AAAA Painting, then K&P Painting).

Military Service: Norm first mentions being in the U.S. Army (stationed at Fort Dix, New Jersey), then serving with the U.S. Coast Guard.

Favorite Activity: Eating and drinking beer.

Favorite Eatery: The Hungry Heifer Restaurant.

Favorite Snack Cake: Ho Hos.

High School Nickname: "Moonglow."

Childhood: A member of the Boy Scouts (quit when he didn't want to go hiking).

Bar Tabs: One at Cheers and one at Gary's Old Towne Tavern. Although Norm claims that he was always overweight, Sam mentions that when he first opened a tab for Norm, he was called "the skinny guy at the end of the bar."

Tattoo: Strange as it may seem, Norm has one on his butt that reads "I Love [seen as a heart] the U.S. Postal Service" (this reflects Cliff's job; Cliff, on the other hand, has one that reads "Vera" after Norm's wife).

REBECCA HOWE

Father: Franklin E. Howe (Robert Prosky), a navy captain.

Sister: Susan Howe (Marcia Cross).

Place of Birth: San Diego. She is 39 but claims to be 35.

Education: The University of Connecticut (earned a degree in business and was nicknamed "Backseat Becky").

Character: A talented cellist who found it difficult to live up to her parents' high expectations while growing up. Although slim now, she was overweight since she was 12 (weighed 300 pounds as a senior in high school). She hides her insecurities beneath her polished exterior and is always fashionably dressed. She is neurotic, whines, is easily exasperated, and is considered a frigid, no-nonsense "ice queen." Her smoking habit caused damage to Cheers when she tossed a lit cigarette into a Boston Red Sox trash can and the building caught fire (the bar regulars then frequented the bar Mr. Pubbs). She becomes overly romantic when she hears the song "You've Lost That Loving Feeling."

Occupation: The manager of Cheers when Sam sold it to the Lillian Corporation in 1987. She was fired shortly after when she was falsely accused of letting her boyfriend (Roger Colcord) use her secret computer code ("Sweet Baby") to access corporate information. In need of money, she worked as the Miracle Buff Girl (a wax preservative) at the Auto Show. When Sam reacquired Cheers from the corporation, he took pity on Rebecca and hired her as his bar manager (at $6 an hour).

Investment: $25,000 in Cheers to add a pool room and a new bathroom.

Favorite TV Show: Spenser: For Hire (its star, Robert Urich, is her favorite actor).

WOODY BOYD

Full Name: Huckleberry Tiberius Boyd, nicknamed "Woody."

Place of Birth: Hanover, Indiana.

Occupation: Assistant bartender. Woody wrote to all the big-city bars but received a response only from Ernie. They became pen pals. When Woody came to Boston and learned that Ernie had died, Sam hired him, feeling that is what Ernie would have wanted.

Education: Hanover High School.

Invention: A game called "Hide Bob's Pants."

Pet Dog: Truman.

First Childhood Disease: Chickenpox.

Favorite Sports: Fishing and duck hunting (he uses an empty Good & Plenty candy box as a duck call).

Character: A friendly person with a backwoods aura that makes him very likable. With aspirations to become an actor, he acquired only a commercial for a vegetable drink called "Veggie Boy" (broccoli, cauliflower, and kale juice). Woody mentioned having a girlfriend named Beth Curtis in Hannibal, but he married Kelly Susan Gaines (Jackie Swanson), the very rich and very spoiled daughter of Elliott (Richard Doyle) and Roxanne Gaines (Melendy Britt). Kelly has a collection of more than 1,000 Barbie dolls; Woody wrote her a song called "The Kelly Song." In the final episode, Woody becomes Third District councilman with the Boston City Council.

Relatives: Susan's Grandmother Gaines (Celeste Holm).

FRASIER CRANE

Place of Birth: Seattle, Washington.

Mother: Dr. Hester Crane (Nancy Marchand). His father, first mentioned as being a scientist, then a cop, is not seen.

Occupation: Psychiatrist.

Education: Harvard University; Oxford University.

Marital Status: Divorced (from Nanette Gooseman, a performer known as Nancy Gee).

Second Wife: In 1988, Frasier marries Dr. Lilith Sternin, a somber-looking woman who, according to Frasier, "rules the roost in her bra and panties." She is a psychiatrist on call at Boston Memorial Hospital and wrote the book *Good Girls/Bad Boys*; Whiskers and Whitey are her two favorite lab rats. When Lilith enters the bar, Norm exclaims, "Frost warning." She and Frasier eventually separated (but later reconciled) after Lilith had an affair with a coworker in an Eco Pod.

Son: Frederick Crane (Christopher Graves and Kevin Graves). He was born in November 1989 in the back of a taxicab; another episode, however, shows him celebrating a birthday in January.

Hobby: Collecting rare first-edition books. He also mentions having a spider collection.

Dog: Pavlov.

Favorite Author: Charles Dickens.

Character (Frasier): A psychiatrist who finds Cheers his own therapy from the pressures of work. He considers himself "the solver of all problems personal" and conducts traveling self-help $350 seminars called "The Crane Train to Mental Well-Being."

SPIN-OFFS

Frasier (NBC, 1993–2004). Frasier moves to Seattle to become the host of *The Frasier Crane Show*, an advice program on radio station KACL.

The Tortellis (NBC, 1987). Nick Tortelli (Dan Hedaya), Carla's ex-husband, is now married to Loretta (Jean Kasem). He owns Nick's Talent Emporium at 171 Hope Drive. Loretta, his main client, is a singer with the Grinning Americans (later called the Lemon Sisters). Later, they move to Las Vegas, where Loretta becomes a showgirl and Nick establishes Tortellis TV Hospital (at 6531 Veronna Street).

China Beach

(ABC, 1988–1991)

Cast: Dana Delany (Colleen McMurphy), Marg Helgenberger (K.C.), Nan Woods (Cherry White), Chloe Webb (Laurette Barber), Megan Gallagher

(Wayloo Marie Holmes), Jeff Kober (Dodger), Concetta Tomei (Lila Garreau), Brian Wimmer (Boonie).

Basis: A harsh look at the Vietnam War as seen through the eyes of the medical personnel (of the 510th Evac Hospital, 63rd Division) stationed at China Beach, the U.S. Armed Forces rest-and-relaxation facility in Da Nang, Republic of Vietnam. The hospital has 180 hospital beds and 33 surgical units but is unable to handle critical neurological surgery.

COLLEEN MCMURPHY

Parents: Margaret Mary (Penny Fuller) and Brian McMurphy (Donald Moffat).

Brother: Brenden McMurphy (John Laughlin).

Position: Triage nurse (represents the 50,000 women who actually served in Vietnam).

Serial Number: N91574.

Nickname: Called "FNG" (Fairly New Guy) when she first arrived.

Place of Birth: Lawrence, Kansas, in 1948.

Education: Lawrence High School (1962–1966). At the age of 18, after being inspired by John F. Kennedy to believe that she can make a difference, she chose to become a nurse. She joined the army, trained in Houston, Texas, and volunteered for duty in Vietnam (where she served from 1967 to 1969).

Religion: Irish Catholic.

Bra Size: 34C.

Belief: "I made a difference. I couldn't save them all [wounded soldiers], but I saved some. I mattered. We all did."

Greatest Wish: "A day without choppers" (as the helicopters brought the wounded). It never came true.

Civilian Life: In 1970, Colleen returned to Houston and worked as a nurse at the local hospital. Two years later, she became "a wild-at-heart free spirit" who took to the open road on her motorcycle. As the memories of Vietnam began to eat away at her, she purchased a car (license plate CN3 679) and drifted around the country until she settled in Portland, Oregon, in 1975. She acquired a job as a hospital administrator and married architect Joe Arenberry (Adam Arkin) in 1985. In 1988, the last we know of her character, she is the mother of a three-year-old girl named Maggie.

Relatives: Uncle, Conal (Harold Russell).

KAREN "K.C." COLOSKY

Place of Birth: Kansas City, Missouri, in 1949. She uses the initials K.C. to represent her hometown. Her middle name is Charlene.

Occupation: Prostitute (the only civilian on the base; charges $100 an hour for her services).

Blood Type: O.

Dana Delany, Nan Woods, and Chloe Webb. *ABC/Photofest.* ©ABC

Measurements: 34-25-36. She is blonde and 5 feet, 6 inches tall and wears a size 6 dress and a size 6½ shoe.

Best Friend: Colleen McMurphy. (They met in 1967 in the women's shower; K.C. noticed Colleen staring at her navel and remarked, "Never seen an outie before?" They joked and became close friends.)

Safety: As a child, K.C. loved the rain, as it made her feel safe (she would snuggle under the bed covers and gain a sense of security). On China Beach, the rains provide K.C. with the only sense of safety she can feel amidst the devastation that surrounds her.

Ability: Having people believe pathetic stories about herself.

Life Changer: K.C. became pregnant by General A. M. "Mac" Miller (Wings Hauser) in 1967. Later that year, while with Colleen in Saigon, K.C. gives birth (with Colleen's help) to a daughter she names Karen. Unable to care for Karen, K.C. hires Trieu Au (Kieu Chinh), a Vietnamese woman, to take the child "until I get my life together."

K.C.'s Fate: K.C. left China Beach in 1969 without Karen (now age two; played by twins Kelsey and Kirsten Dohring). She moved to Bangkok, where she first ran an export/import business, then in 1975 opened a nightclub called K.C.'s. It is at this time, with the fall of Saigon occurring, that K.C. realizes she must get Karen to safety. K.C. manages to get Karen (Shay Aster), now eight, onto a helicopter. With only seconds remaining, K.C. tells Karen to look up Boonie Lanier (a soldier from China Beach who loved her), "who'll take care of you." In Santa Cruz, California, in 1976, K.C. sees that Karen is safe, attending school, and with Boonie and his family. K.C., spying from a distance, leaves without approaching Karen. Finn Carter is Boonie's wife, Linda, and Adam (Sean Ryan), Gillian (Shannon Farrara), and Angela (Conni Marie Brazelton) are Boonie's children. A Christmas card sent to Colleen from K.C. reveals that in 1977, K.C. operated a diner called The Answer. By 1988, K.C. is a high-powered businesswoman, and she sees Karen for the first time in 12 years. Karen Lanier (Christine Elise), as she is now called, is attending college. It is the last we know of K.C. Boonewell G. "Bonnie" Lanier was with the First Marine Division, Icor, on China Beach. Karen considers him her father and uses his last name. Boonie always called K.C. "K.C. from K.C."

OTHER CHARACTERS

Laurette Barber is a singer and dancer with the USO (United Serviceman's Organization). She was an orphan and raised at the Perpetual of Hope Orphanage. While she entertained the service personnel, she also volunteered to help the wounded. When the USO tour moved to another base, Laurette was written out (it is assumed that she found a career in show business after the war).

Cherry White is an American Red Cross nurse who volunteered for duty in Vietnam. She was dedicated to helping the victims of a war that she felt was unjust. Cherry's greatest hope was finding her brother, Rick (Frederic Lehne), an army private who was reported as missing in action. One of the program's most emotional moments occurs when Cherry is killed by an enemy bomb during the Tet Offensive.

Wayloo Marie Holmes is the U.S. Air Force television reporter who covered the misery of China Beach, hoping it would lead to something better. It did, as she acquired a job as a reporter for ABC-TV in New York. In 1988, she became the host of the TV series *This Morning*. Kevin McCarthy appears as Wayloo's father, Congressman Holmes.

Major Lila Garreau is the hospital commander whose life is the army (having grown up in a military family). She was called "Scooter" and found herself pushing herself and her nurses beyond the call of duty. She married Sergeant Bartholomew Pepper (Troy Evans) and left the military to operate a gas station with him in Alabama.

Evan "Dodger" Winslow is the seldom-talking, tough (on the outside) but gentle (on the inside) combat soldier. Dodger felt that he was meant to die in Vietnam and remained behind when the China Beach personnel left in 1975. He befriended a Vietnamese girl named Cam Noi (Page Leong) and is last seen walking through a stream to escape the fall of Saigon. Next, he is in Red Lodge, Montana, and the father of a son named Archie (Tyrone Tan). He owns Archie's Bar and is hoping to build a church for Vietnam veterans out of an old school bus. Jean (Penelope Windust) and Archie Winslow (Tom Bower, then Richard Jaeckel) are his parents; Annie Winslow (Arlene Taylor) is his sister.

Coach
(ABC, 1989–1996)

Cast: Craig T. Nelson (Hayden Fox), Shelley Fabares (Christine Armstrong), Jerry Van Dyke (Luther Van Dam), Bill Fagerbakke (Michael Dybinski), Clare Carey (Kelly Fox).

Basis: A comical behind-the-scenes look at the life of a college football coach (Hayden Fox) as he struggles to shape a losing team into a winning team.

HAYDEN WILBUR FOX

Place of Birth: Spokane, Washington.

Education: Spokane High School; Georgetown University (another episode mentions Minnesota State University, where he played running back on the football team).

Occupation: Coach of the Screaming Eagles, the Minnesota State University football team. Hayden has been coaching the team for 21 years, and their biggest win was beating the Texas Wranglers (23 to 16) in the Pineapple Bowl in Hawaii.

TV Show: Host of *The Hayden Fox Show*, a weekly sports and interview program on KCCY-TV, Channel 6.

Magazine Covers: Sports Illustrated and *Collegiate Sports Digest.*

Award: The Curley O'Brien Award for excellence in coaching.

Marital Status: Divorced from Beth (Lenore Kasdorf) when the series begins; later married to Christine Armstrong (see below).

Daughter: Kelly Fox (by Beth); see below.

Address: Unspecified. He has a cabin the woods, as he likes to live away from people. The cabin is recognizable by a wooden Indian on the porch, a tree house, a basketball hoop, and a rubber tire on a rope (for football training). At the front door is a pledge paddle from the Beta Theta Pi fraternity.

Famous For: His "five-alarm chili" (served at his weekly poker game, which has a $2 limit).

Favorite Hangout: The Touchdown Club.

Transportation: A truck that he has cleaned at Helen's Car Wash.

Prize Possession: A pair of shoes once worn by football great Johnny Unitas.

Life Changer: In 1995, Hayden leaves Minnesota for a job in Orlando, Florida, as the coach of the Orlando Breakers, an NFL expansion team.

CHRISTINE ARMSTRONG

Parents: Mildred (Nanette Fabray) and Dr. James Armstrong (James Karen).

Place of Birth: Kentucky.

Education: St. Mary's High School; the University of Kentucky (acquired a degree in communications).

Husband: Hayden Fox (they met in 1986 at the United Charity Bowl). Hayden spotted her, thought she was the most beautiful girl he had ever seen, and forced himself on her. They married on November 25, 1992, and later had a child they named Timothy David (whose initials, T.D., stood for "Touch Down").

Occupation: Television personality. She first worked as a sportscaster on KCCY-TV, Channel 6, in Minneapolis, then as the host of *Christine's Sports Round Up.* She next hosted a failed pilot (*Magazine America*), then became the star of *Wake Up, Minneapolis,* an early morning information and news series. When she and Hayden move to Florida, Christine becomes the host of *Coach's Corner,* a postgame football series on Channel 5.

Character: Logical and sensible and tries not to let the littlest things upset her; but when they do "I have to be by myself" to work things out.

LUTHER VAN DAMME

Father: Not named (Paul Dooley).

Position: Hayden's assistant coach (he has been an assistant coach at various universities for 38 years, 21 years with Hayden). He is interested more in what happens behind the scenes than in the actual game itself. He was also the coach at Aberdeen College but was fired after one week for breaking NCAA rules. He fears having to coach alone.

Place of Birth: Danville, Illinois.

Education: Danville High School.

Salary: $32,000 a year.

Pets: Quincy (a dog) and Sunshine (a parrot). Luther received the parrot from his father 42 years ago; he feeds the parrot Acme Bird Seed.

Favorite Breakfast Cereal: Sweeties, the Full Sugar Cereal.

Dislikes: School recesses because he gets what he calls "the summer blues" (eats, gains weight, and spends the fall semester working it off).

Life Changer: Joins Hayden in Florida as the assistant coach of the Orlando Breakers.

Florida Address: Lives in a condo at Leisure Town (in Minneapolis, it was a small, unidentified apartment).

OTHER CHARACTERS

Michael Dybinski has been a student at Minnesota State for eight years (majoring in forestry) and Hayden's star player; he later becomes the staff adviser for incoming freshmen and the special teams coach (coordinating game strategy). Michael, who wears a size 14EEE shoe, has the nickname "Dauber" (given to him by Hayden, as his moves on the football field remind him of the dauber wasp). On Monday nights, Dauber joins Hayden and Luther for drinks at the Touchdown Club; his home doorbell chimes to the first notes of the show's theme, "The Coach Theme," by John Morris.

Judy Watkins (Pam Stone) is Dauber's girlfriend (whom he calls "Sweet Stuff"; she calls him "Honey"). She coaches the women's basketball team and is Hayden's nemesis (they simply do not get along when together). Marlene (Nancy Marchand) and Judge R.J. Watkins (John McMartin) are her parents (who live in her hometown of Atlanta; Pepper is Marlene's pampered poodle).

Kelly Fox is Hayden's daughter and a student at Minnesota State. She married fellow student Stuart Rosebrock (Kris Kamm) in her sophomore year (their marriage broke up when Stuart, a hopeful actor, left her to become the host of a kid's TV series called *The Buzzy the Beaver Show*; they divorced a year later). Kelly worked as a bartender at the Touchdown Club, and when she became a senior (1992), she chose to follow her dream of becoming an actress (posters from the films *Come Back Little Sheba*, *Othello*, and *Wonderful Town* can be seen on her dorm room wall). It is revealed that she later abandons acting for an office job in New York City.

The Cosby Show
(NBC, 1984–1992)

Cast: Bill Cosby (Cliff Huxtable), Phylicia Rashad (Clair Huxtable), Lisa Bonet (Denise Huxtable), Sabrina LeBeauf (Sondra Huxtable), Malcolm-Jamal Warner (Theo Huxtable), Tempestt Bledsoe (Vanessa Huxtable), Keshia Knight Pulliam (Rudy Huxtable), Geoffrey Owens (Elvin Thibideaux).

Basis: Incidents in the lives of an African American family (the Huxtables) living in Brooklyn, New York: parents Cliff and Clair and their children Sondra, Denise, Theo, Vanessa, and Rudy.

HEATHCLIFF "CLIFF" HUXTABLE

Parents: Russell (Earle Hyman) and Anna Huxtable (Clarice Taylor).

Brother: James Theodore (died of rheumatic fever at age seven; Cliff was eight at the time).

Address: 10 Stigwood Avenue.

Occupation: Obstetrician/gynecologist (works out of his home and at both Corinthian Hospital and Children's Hospital). Even though Cliff's first name is Heathcliff, the nameplate on the side of his house reads "Clifford Huxtable, M.D." (his name from the pilot episode); 331 is his office extension number.

Favorite Music: Jazz (he calls himself "Mr. Jazz").

Favorite Western Movie: Six Guns for Glory (starring Colt Kirby).

Childhood: Accidentally sat on his pet bird, Charlie, and killed it; a two-wheeler bike he called "Bob"; dreamed of becoming a drummer.

Favorite Hangout: Jake's Appliance Store.

Fault: No sales resistance; will buy items on impulse even though he doesn't need them; tends to gain weight (Clair refuses to let him eat junk food and restricts him to carrot juice, celery, and sprouts).

Education: Hillman College in Georgia (where he met Clair Hanks, the woman whom he would later marry; she called him "Baby Cakes," he called her "Lum Lum"). They married on February 14, 1964, and honeymooned at the Caralu Hotel in the Caribbean.

Favorite Newspaper: City Sun.

Trademark: Sweaters (varying from great to just plain awful).

Relatives: Great aunt, Grammie (Minnie Gentry).

CLAIR HUXTABLE

Parents: Al (Joe Williams) and Carrie Hanks (Ethel Ayler).
Sister: Sara (Yvette Erwin).
Maiden Name: Clair Hanks.
Education: Hillman College (when she and Cliff graduated, they celebrated with dinner at Michael and Ennio's Restaurant).
Dress Size: 8.
Occupation: Lawyer with the firm of Greentree, Bradley and Dexter.
TV Work: Panelist on the Channel 37 history discussion series *Retrospective*.
Favorite Restaurant: El Grande del Restaurante.
Character: Stricter with the kids than Cliff (who is more laid back when it comes to disciplining them). When Clair lectures the kids about something they did wrong, Cliff always agrees with what she says—"And that goes for me too."
Relatives: Cousin, Pam Turner (Erika Alexander).

SONDRA HUXTABLE

Relationship: The oldest child.
Education: Princeton University (it cost her parents $79,648.72 for her education). It is here that she met Elvin, a premed student, whom she later married (they became the parents of twins Nelson and Winnie; Sondra was in labor for eight days).
Nickname: Called "Muffin" by Elvin.
Occupation: Sondra studied to become a lawyer but put that aside to join Elvin in a business called the Wilderness Store. (Elvin felt he could not become a doctor due to a psychological problem: he could not charge people for medical help. With Cliff's help, he returned to medical school in 1990.) Elvin also held a job as Inspector 36 at Benrix Industries (checking pill bottle safety seals). He was discharged when an efficiency expert found they did not need 36 inspectors. At this point, Sondra enrolled in graduate school and a year later passed the bar exam. In 1992, after living with her parents, Sondra and Elvin moved to New Jersey to begin a new life. They also lived in an apartment (5B) where the "K" from the neon Valley Milk sign rested against the window.
Elvin's Relatives: Father, Lester (Deon Richmond); mother, Francine (Marcella Lowery).

DENISE HUXTABLE

Relationship: The second-born child.
Education: Central High School; Hillman College (dropped out after a year and a half when she received five "D's," one "C," and seven incompletes).

Occupation: Clerk at the Wilderness Store, then assistant to the executive assistant at Blue Wave Records (earning $25 a week); photographer's assistant.

Trait: Not the most responsible child. She wore fashions that often upset her parents (being a bit too suggestive) and annoyed Cliff by dating boys he didn't like.

Husband: Martin Kendall (Joseph C. Phillips), a divorced navy lieutenant (a graduate of Annapolis) with a young daughter, Olivia (Raven-Symone). Denise met Martin, stationed in Africa, on a photography shoot.

Dream: To teach disabled children (which she pursued by enrolling in education classes at the Medgar Evers College of the City University of New York).

Olivia Facts: Paula (Victoria Rowell) is her mother; her favorite song is "Pop Goes the Weasel"; Sparky, Dwayne the dog, and Howard the parrot are her invisible pets. The tulip is her favorite flower.

Note: In the final episode, Denise announces that she is pregnant.

THEODORE "THEO" ALOYSIUS HUXTABLE

Relationship: The third-born child (born in Brooklyn at Children's Hospital in 1968).

Education: Central High School (known as "Monster Man Huxtable" as a member of the wrestling team); New York University (majoring in psychology).

College Address: Apartment 10B of an unidentified Greenwich Village building.

Occupation: Student; counselor at the Seton Hall Communications Center (of the Rosa Parks Group).

Character: A bit naive and easily taken advantage of (especially by pretty girls). He was also called "Teddy," and dyslexia caused him to have atrocious grades in high school. In the final episode, Theo graduates from New York University with a science degree; it cost Cliff and Clair nearly $100,000 for his education.

VANESSA HUXTABLE

Relationship: The fourth-born child.

Character: A teenager anxious to grow up (Clair fears she is going to miss the best years of her life if she doesn't slow down).

Education: Central High School; Lincoln University in Philadelphia (where she became engaged to Dabnis Brickley [William Thomas Jr.], the maintenance man and 12 years her senior [Vanessa being 18 at the time]; they later broke off their engagement).

Rock Band: The Lipsticks (Clair ended Vanessa's career when she felt that the band outfits, a miniskirt and a stuffed bra worn over a leotard, were too suggestive).

Makeup: Purchases cosmetics at Nathan's Department Store.

Curfew: 10 p.m. (although good at keeping it, Clair believes that Vanessa often lies about where she goes "so she can neck in the woods").

Favorite Movies: 1930s and 1940s comedies.

RUDITH "RUDY" LILLIAN HUXTABLE

Relationship: The youngest child.

Teddy Bear: Bobo.

Goldfish: Lamont.

Favorite Ice Cream Flavor: Vanilla.

Favorite Sport: Football (she wears jersey 32 as a member of the Pee-Wee League football team; Cliff calls her "The Gray Ghost" for her speed).

Trait: Likes to throw video parties for her friends. Cliff looks on Rudy as his little girl and fears her growing up; as Rudy says, "It's a new age, Dad, get with it."

Bedtime: 9:30 p.m. (because when Cliff was nine years old, his bedtime was 9:30 p.m.).

SPIN-OFF

A Different World (NBC, 1987–1993). Set at Hillman College in Georgia, where Denise has enrolled (to continue a family tradition) but with an undecided major (she later drops out with a 1.7 grade-point average). She shares room 204 in the Gilbert Hall dorm with Jalessa Vinson (Dawnn Lewis) and Maggie Laughton (Marissa Tomei). Denise is a member of the track team (called "The Little Engine"); Maggie is an army brat and majoring in journalism. Jalessa, age 26, works in the cafeteria and later begins her own campus employment company, Jalessa Vinson May Temps. Colonel Bradford Taylor (Glynn Turman) is the calculus teacher (called "Dr. War"); Whitley Gilbert (Jasmine Guy) is an art major (resides in room 20S of Gilbert Hall) who becomes an art buyer for E.H. Wright Investments; and Dwayne Wayne (Kadeem Hardison), a math major (residing in Matthews Hall), becomes a math teacher.

Dear John
(NBC, 1988–1992)

Cast: Judd Hirsch (John Lacey), Jane Carr (Louise Mercer), Susan Walters (Mary Beth Sutton), Isabella Hoffman (Kate McCarron), Jere Burns (Kirk Morris), Harry Groener (Ralph Drang).

Basis: The activities of a group of people who attend the 1-2-1 Club, a support group for lonely, divorced and separated people in Manhattan. Meetings are held Friday nights at the Rego Park Community Center; Clancy's Bar is the hangout; the club is also called the One-On-One Club, and Smoke Enders hold their meetings on the same floor.

JOHN LACEY

John was born in Binghamton, New York, and now lives in Apartment 42 on Woodhaven Boulevard in Queens, New York. He was called "Moochie" as a kid, served in the Peace Corps, and teaches English at the Drake Prep School in Manhattan (he has office 215). His childhood dream was to play the clarinet (he took lessons at the Charles Moreloft Music School). Pineapple strudel is his favorite dessert, and he cares for Snuffy, Fluffy, and Snowball, the cats of his never-seen 92-year-old neighbor. John has an antique watch that was handed down to him from his father and was married to Wendy (Carlene Watkins, then Deborah Harmon), who, after 10 years of marriage, left him a Dear John letter: "Dear John, I know that this will come as a great shock to you and I pray that in time you will come to understand why I had to leave. The love I once had for you died many years ago although I have tried desperately to pretend otherwise. Wendy" (the theme, "Dear John," sung by Wendy Talbot, plays over this). Wendy ran off with John's best friend and took their son with them; John lost virtually everything in the divorce settlement.

Relatives: Parents, Phil (Stephen Elliott) and Charlotte Lacey (Nina Foch); John's son by Wendy, Matthew Lacey (Ben Savage, then Billy Cohan); aunt, Emma (Elizabeth Franz).

Flashbacks: John, age 13 (Peter Smith).

KATHERINE "KATE" McCARRON

Kate, maiden name Foster, is the daughter of Harry and Elizabeth Foster. She was born in Manhattan and is a graduate of Columbia University (has a degree in business administration). As a kid, she had a dog named Skipper and loved to help her mother around the house, especially when it came to preparing meals. Her love of cooking enabled her to open her own restaurant (Kate's Place). Kate is beautiful, always fashionably dressed, and looking for a man who will see her for her intellectual side, not for her looks; she is divorced from Blake McCarron (Corbin Bernsen).

Relatives: Sister, Lisa (Wendy Schaal); nephew, Danny (Judd Trichter); aunt, Trudy (Helen Page Camp).

MARY BETH SUTTON

Mary Beth was born in New York City and is the daughter of Everett Sutton (Wayne Tippert), the owner of the Sunshine Baby Food Company. As a child, Everett called Mary Beth "Sunshine Girl" and "Little Honey Bunny" and uses her picture on the jars of baby food. Mary Beth attended private schools and was a homecoming queen and a beauty pageant winner. She lives in an apartment (3A) of an unnamed building and is a columnist for the airline magazine *Above the Clouds*; she wrote previously for the TV soap opera *The Divided Heart*. Mary Beth is very attractive but feels that no one appreciates her. She always expects something bad to happen but is not sure how to act when something good happens. She believes that her view from her office window of Bloomingdale's department store is what makes New York the greatest city in the world.

LOUISE MERCER

Louise was born in Cheshire, England, and now lives in Apartment 5G of an unnamed building. She runs the support group and attempts to implement her strict aristocratic upbringing on members. Louise was married but became deeply depressed after her divorce and spent time at Meadowbrook, a mental institution. She is the mother of the often-talked-about but never-seen Nigel, and her claim to fame is being best friends with the Queen of England. She was first runner-up in a beauty pageant but crowned "Miss Cheshire" when the winner's bathing suit strap broke, exposing her breasts and disqualifying herself by running off the stage. Louise tries to take an interest in people's problems but often becomes depressed when she realizes her problems are even worse.

Relatives: Sister, Sarah (Jenny Agutter); mother, Aubrey Mercer (Lila Kaye); father, Nigel Mercer (Clive Revill).

KIRK MORRIS

Kirk, born in Scranton, Pennsylvania (in September), grew up on the streets (where he learned to become a con artist; he now survives on schemes). His occupation is a mystery; a peek into his wallet revealed him to be assistant loan officer at the Security Merchants Bank ("specializing in loans to single women"), Hollywood talent scout, and special White House adviser. His scams include "Mr. Kirk's Bikini Waxing," "Cuisine by Kirk," and "Stand-By Airline Tickets" (to Hawaii via Texas Universal Airlines). Carol (Kate McNeil), his ex-wife, left him for another woman. He lives at 36 Amsterdam Avenue (Apartment 306) and claims to be a published author (by his letters to *Playboy* magazine). Girls are uppermost on Kirk's mind, and John claims that when Kirk sees a girl, he thinks, "Does her bra unhook from the front or back?" He joined the 1-2-1 Club to meet women.
Relatives: Mother, "Mumsy" Morris (Pat Crawford Brown then Alice Hirson).

RALPH DRANG

Ralph is a constant worrier and works as a toll taker in Manhattan's Lincoln Tunnel. He has the ability to tell how much money people toss into the booth collection bin just by the sound the coins make. He lives in Apartment 3C (building not identified) and has *Star Trek* wallpaper on his bedroom walls. Molly (Megan Mullally), a toll collector who works three booths from him, is his love interest. He says he never knows if Molly is blowing him kisses or choking from car exhaust. His dream is to have two children with her: Penny and Buck. Ralph eats alphabet cereal in alphabetical order and is later promoted to equipment supervisor. He was replaced in 1991 by Annie Morono (Marietta DePrina), a hopeful actress looking for Mr. Right. She stuffs her bra to enhance her figure for auditions and is always in good spirits: "I'm a wonderful girl in a wonderful time with a wonderful life."

Designing Women
(CBS, 1986–1993)

Cast: Dixie Carter (Julia Sugarbaker), Delta Burke (Suzanne Sugarbaker), Annie Potts (Mary Jo Shively), Jean Smart (Charlene Frazier), Meshach Taylor (Anthony Bouvier), Julia Duffy (Allison Sugarbaker), Jan Hooks (Carlene Dobber), Judith Ivey (B.J. Poteet), Sheryl Lee Ralph (Etienne Toussaint).

Basis: Sisters Julia and Suzanne Sugarbaker struggle to work together to make their business, the Sugarbakers Design Firm (later called Sugarbaker and Associates—Interior Design), a success.

OVERALL SERIES INFORMATION

The company is located at 1521 Sycamore Street in Atlanta, Georgia. Its telephone number is first 404-555-8600, then 404-555-6878. Julia and Suzanne buy their goods from Fabric World. They are assisted by Mary Jo, Charlene, Anthony, Allison, Carlene, and B.J. Poteet.

JULIA SUGARBAKER

Mother: Perky Sugarbaker (Louise Latham).

Son: Payne Sugarbaker (George Newburn); he is married to Sylvia (Jocelyn Seagrave).

Brother: Clayton Sugarbaker (Lewis Grizzard).

Legal Guardian Of: Randa Oliver (Lexi Randall), a pretty, lively teenage girl (wore jersey number 3 and pitched for the Sugarbaker Giants Little League team).

Place of Birth: Georgia.

Home: A room above the business. Julia began the company (something she always wanted to do) after the death of her husband, Hayden McIlroy. She is currently dating Reese Watson (Hal Holbrook).

Annie Potts, Jean Smart, Dixie Carter, and Delta Burke. *CBS/Photofest. ©CBS*

Education: Chapel High School; Southern State University. She also studied art in Paris (the Gallery Pouzett displayed her series of fruit bowl paintings).

Quirk: "To get a vacation from being myself." At one point, she became Giselle and sang at the Blue Note Night Club.

Bra Size: 34. She is 5 feet, 5 inches tall and wears a size 7 shoe.

Trait: Ultrafeminine, laid back, very distinguished, fashionably but conservatively dressed.

Relatives: Nieces, Camilla (Ginna Carter) and Jennifer (Mary Dixie Carter).

SUZANNE SUGARBAKER

Place of Birth: Georgia.

Position: Sales representative (first said to be 14, then 12, years younger than Julia). Suzanne worked as a correspondent for the local TV station's "Action News Team" and accidentally burned down Design House '86 when she tried her hand at decorating.

Education: Chapel High School; Southern State University.

Home: A mansion (address not given).

Dislike: Art shows ("I'm sick of seeing small-busted women with big butts").

Character: While Julia is said to be brainy, Suzanne is said to be "the sister who got the big boobs"; she flaunts her sexuality by showing cleavage. Her first attempt at cooking was preparing a Thanksgiving dinner.

Bra Size: 36C. She is 5 feet, 9 inches tall and wears a size 6½ shoe.

Quirk: Exercises to the song "St. Louis Blues."

Pageant Title: Miss Georgia World of 1976 (her talent was twirling the baton; she was the only woman in pageant history to sweep every contest category except congeniality—something women in her family lack). Julia says "that when she walked down the runway in her swimsuit, five contestants quit on the spot." She also says that when Suzanne twirled her baton, "12,000 people jumped to their feet for 16½ minutes of uninterrupted thundering ovation." In another episode, the pageant is called the 1975 Miss Georgia U.S.A. Pageant.

Favorite TV Program: Sensational Breakthroughs (infomercial for new products).

Pet Pig: Noel.

Ex-Husbands: Dash Goff (Gerald McRainey), author of the book *Being Belled.* She was also married to J. Benton Stonecipher (her third husband) and Jack Dent, her second husband, a Major League baseball player.

Embarrassing Moment: During a fashion show, Suzanne appeared onstage in a skirt tucked into the waistband of her pantyhose.

Maid: Consuelo (never seen but said to be "the maid to end all maids"). By dialogue, Consuelo appears to be ultratemperamental (throws hatchets at the Good Humor man), throws fits, and is eccentric (howls at the moon and makes necklaces out of chicken bones). Her family is in the meatpacking business, and through it, Suzanne acquired her pet pig. She is, a Julia says, "totally psychotic."

CHARLENE OLIVIA FRAZIER

Parents: Bud (James Ray) and Ione Frazier (Ronnie Claire Edwards).

Brother: Odell Frazier (George Wurster).

Sisters: Carlene, Darleen, Harleen, and Marlene.

Position: Julia's assistant. She previously worked as a salesgirl at Kemper Cosmetics.

Place of Birth: Little Rock, Arkansas (but grew up in Poplar Bluff, a small town where the only eatery was Bob's Quick Bite).

Education: Poplar Bluff High School (member of the cheerleading squad, the Mules); Three Rivers Secretarial School (in Missouri); Claritin University (in Atlanta; studied psychology).

Home: The Grand Ghostly Mansion of Atlanta (supposedly haunted).

Heroine: Julia Sugarbaker.

Favorite Song: "I'll Be Seeing You."

Shoe Size: 8.

Religion: Baptist.

Pride and Joy: Her autographed picture of Elvis Presley.

Hobby: Collecting thimbles.

Book: Charlene and Mary Jo wrote the children's book *Billy Bunny.*

Husband: Bill Stillfield (Douglas Barr), a U.S. Air Force colonel (they married in 1989 at the rooftop garden at the Dunwoodie Hotel; "Ave Maria" was their wedding song).

Daughter: Olivia (born in 1990). Prior to Olivia's birth, Charlene had a dream in which her "guardian movie star," Dolly Parton, helped her through the birth.

Relatives: Mother-in-law, Eileen Stillfield (Beany Venuta).

MARY JO SHIPLEY

Father: Dr. Davis Jackson (Geoffrey Lewis).

Brother: Skip Jackson (Blake Clark).

Maiden Name: Mary Jo Jackson.

Position: The firm's decorator and buyer.

Education: Franklin Elementary and High Schools.

Religion: Baptist.

Fixation: Breasts (she wishes she was as voluptuous as Suzanne and feels that a big bust means "power and respect"—not only from men but also from women). She contemplated implants to become a 36C but declined.

Best Time of Her Life: "Raising my two children."

Pet Dog: Brownie.

Title: Voted "Parent Volunteer of the Year" by the PTA in 1991. Her daughter, Olivia (Priscilla Weems), was a contestant in the Miss Pre-Teen Atlanta Beauty Pageant.

Ex-Husband: Ted Shively (Scott Bakula), a gynecologist (he later married Tammy [Eileen Seeley]). Ted claims that Mary Jo has the best behind he has ever seen (even after spending time in Japan, where, he says, "women have great rear ends").

OTHER CHARACTERS

Allison Sugarbaker is Julia and Suzanne's cousin. When a poor economy forces Suzanne to leave the country (1991) for a business opportunity in Japan, Allison buys her home and share of the company. She worked previously "as a seeing-eye person" to a Mrs. Digby, who was allergic to dogs, in New York. She was fired for dying her blonde hair brown. She now works as Julia's office manager and is a member of the self-help group Common Sense and suffers from OPD (obnoxious personality disorder).

Carlene Dobber joined the firm as the receptionist when Charlene (her cousin) moved to England to join Bill (now stationed overseas). She worked previously for Ray Flat's Flatbed Furniture Store. She was born in Poplar Bluff, takes evening classes at college, and is leader of Girl Scout Troop 6523. As a child, she watched *Chip and Dale* cartoons ("because they had manners"). Ray McKinnon played Carlene's ex-husband, Dwayne Dobber.

Bonnie Jean Poteet becomes Julia's new partner (1992) when Allison leaves the firm to begin a Victoria's Secret lingerie catalog franchise. She was born in Texas (later moved to Atlanta) and prefers to be called B.J. She is a recovering alcoholic and first worked as a go-go girl (swung her tassels to the song "Proud Mary"), then as "the fastest court reporter in Houston." She married a litigant (James Poteet) whom she fell in love with during a trial she was covering. Their marriage was short lived: while dancing in a Conga line, James, the wealthy owner of a contracting firm, died of a heart attack, and B.J. inherited his money. B.J., who enjoys buying things for people, joined the firm after contacting Julia to redecorate her home.

Anthony Bouvier, the company's delivery man, became a partner in 1990 after he acquired his contracting license (number L-3303). He is an ex-con (arrested for participating in a liquor store robbery) and served time in Cell Block D of Atlanta State Prison. He is now attending law school, does volunteer work at the Home for Wayward Boys, and is the director of the Atlanta Community Theater (where Julia starred in a production of *Mame*).

Relatives: Anthony's father, Charles Bouvier (Bill Cobbs); Grandma Bouvier (Frances E. Williams); aunt, Louise (Marilyn Coleman).

Etienne Toussaint, a Las Vegas Follies Bergère showgirl (at the Tropicana Resort and Casino), became Anthony's wife after he broke up with the dim-witted Vanessa Chamberlain (Olivia Brown, then Jackee Harry). They were married at the Isle of Capri Wedding Chapel in Las Vegas by a judge who moonlights as an Elvis Presley impersonator. Etienne likes to be called "E.T." and considers herself "The Ebony Princess" (she calls Anthony "Tony, because he's my tiger"). When E.T. first joined the Follies Bergère, she forgot the words to the songs and sang, "Blah, blah, blah, blah." E.T.'s mother was one of 14 children, and E.T. is one of nine; she wants four children with Anthony ("After four, you can't get your figure back").

Alice Ghostley appeared as Bernice Clifton, a somewhat senile friend of Julia's who now lives in Atlanta at the Hillcrest Leisure Condominium. She also hosts *Senior Citizen's Roundup* on public access cable TV.

Empty Nest
(NBC, 1988–1996)

Cast: Richard Mulligan (Harry Weston), Kristy McNichol (Barbara Weston), Dinah Manoff (Carol Weston), Lisa Rieffel (Emily Weston), Park Overall (Laverne Todd), David Leisure (Charlie Dietz), Marsha Warfield (Dr. Maxine Douglas).

Basis: A doctor (Harry Weston) with two grown, live-at-home daughters (Barbara and Carol) struggles to cope with the daily pressures of life.

HAROLD "HARRY" WESTON

Father: Dr. Stanfield Weston (Harold Gould), a surgeon at Boston Community Hospital (has been married five times).

Place of Birth: Rochester, New York, in 1932.

Marital Status: Widower (his late wife Elizabeth, called Libby, passed away 18 months before the series begins; they were married for 32 years). Harry was attending medical school in New York when he met Libby. He proposed to her in Central Park, and their song was "How Much Is That Doggie in the Window."

Military Service: The navy (he was the unit's boxing champ and won the middle-weight trophy). He married Libby after his discharge.

First Girlfriend: Jean McDowall (Shirley Jones), whom he met in sixth grade.

Address: 1755 Fairview Road in Miami Beach, Florida (a 4,000-square-foot, two-story home with a three-car garage).

Phone Number: 555-3630.

Pet Dog: Dreyfuss.

Occupation: Pediatrician at the Community Medical Center in Miami Beach. He has a tenth-floor office (later the second floor [room 208] when the Greykirk Corporation purchases the building). The back wall in Harry's office reflects pictures of the children he treated over the years. There are 125 doctors in the building; Harry later retires to become partners with Dr. Maxine Douglas at the Canal Street Clinic. He also owns an interest in the Dade County Galleria.

Education: Bedford Medical School, Class of 1959. Harry hates germs, "and it's a miracle that I became a doctor." He has a Humpty Dumpty scale in his examining room and uses Star Bright bandages (Flintstones style) for his patients (purchased from Radacine Medical Supplies).

Mentor: Dr. Leo Brewster (Danny Thomas), who inspired him to become a doctor.

Hospital Parking Space: J-25.

Favorite Restaurants: Gerard's, Emilio's, and Bernadette's.

Favorite Coffee Shop: Marty's Coffee Shop.

Favorite Bar: Stubby's.

Favorite Holiday: Thanksgiving.

Favorite Singers: Mel Torme, Vic Damone, Lena Horne, and Dinah Shore.

Favorite Music: Jazz.

Favorite Musical Instrument: The saxophone (which he played at the Jazz Factory).

Favorite Sport: Golf.

Favorite Newspaper: Miami Examiner (in the opening theme, he is seen holding an issue of *TV Guide*). He also writes articles for the *Medical Journal*.

Radio Program: Hosts "Ask Dr. Weston" on WWEN (990 AM; Saturdays from 11 a.m. to 3 p.m.).

Family Crest: The Sword of Weston.

Quirks: Develops a nervous facial tic when women make a pass at him, walks Dreyfuss twice a day, puts out the garbage at 7 p.m. for next-day pickup, and can't eat a sandwich without pickles. Harry takes Dreyfuss to Pet Clinic when needed, and he considers eating white chocolate one of the biggest challenges of his life.

Teaching Tool: When Harry talks to children about seeing a doctor, he is "Dr. Feel Good," and "Germy" is his homemade sock puppet assistant.

Medical Issue: Rain affects his arthritis.

Vice: Smoked for 15 years but has given it up.

Awards: Voted Man of the Year by his alumni association (at Bedford University); the Humanitarian Award (and Hall of Fame recognition) from the Community Medical Center; Head of the Miami Pediatric Association.

Final Episode: Harry decides to sell the house and move to Vermont to teach medicine.

Relatives: Sister-in-law (Libby's sister), Susan (Lee Grant); niece, Amy (Cynthia Stevenson); British cousins, Basil and Baroness Daphne Weston (Richard

Mulligan). Not seen were Harry's eccentric cousin, Russell; aunts, Celia and Rosalie (who lives with 20 cats); cousin, Petey; and uncles, Sidney and Jim.

Flashbacks: Harry, as a boy (Christopher Pettiet); Jean, as a girl (Robin Lynn Heath).

Ghost Sequence: Libby, Harry's wife (Judith Marie Bergan).

CAROL OLIVIA WESTON

Year of Birth: 1958 (she mentions that her birthday comes on the anniversary of the French Revolution).

Relationship: Harry's eldest daughter (in her mid-thirties).

Marital Status: Divorced (from Gary [Adrian Zmed], who left her for a blonde named Rita; it caused her to have a nervous breakdown).

Address: An unspecified condo; she later lived with Harry (and Barbara) when she felt lonely and needed the company of her family.

Phone Number: 555-3630.

Bad Habit: Applying eyeliner while driving.

Dream: Open a self-help bookshop.

Character: Good with money, but "I can't sew," and "I laugh out too loud." She has "fat attacks" each spring and is a member of the therapy group Adult Children of Perfectly Fine Parents.

Bra Size: 36C.

Occupation: Assistant director of the University of Miami Rare Books Collection (after complaining that "a book fell on my thumb," she quit to open her own catering business, Elegant Epicure, in 1991). She also worked for Harry in public relations as the hospital's spokesperson and in 1995 became a reporter for the *Dade County Crier* at 111½ Blight Street (penned the advice column "Dear Aunt Martha"). She had 10 jobs before the series begins and quit the last one "because the air conditioning was too cold."

Education: Schools are not named. As a member of the high school glee club, she was told her singing could wake the dead and was voted "Most Likely to Drive Men into the Priesthood." In college, majoring in English (but said to possess a degree in philosophy), Carol worked at a hamburger stand, and "Childless Societies and Why They Die Out" was her anthropology class term paper.

Boyfriends: Difficult to find and tends to drop them abruptly. By 1993, Carol mentions she had 37 bad relationships. She did, however, marry (and later divorce) Patrick Arcola (Paul Provenza), an avant-garde, penniless sculptor with whom she had a son (F. Scott "Scotty" Weston) that she raised alone.

Musical Ability: The trumpet and guitar. As a child, she took piano lessons (Harry spent $3,500 so she could play "The Happy Farmer").

Favorite Poet: F. Scott Fitzgerald.

Childhood Memory: Her mother making hot cocoa with marshmallows to cheer her up, her father placing a paper bag over his head and calling himself "Paper Bag Man" to get her to laugh, and Harry singing the song "Davy Crockett" to stop her from crying. Carol (and Barbara) had a dog named Sergeant, and they were also Girl Scouts.

Term for Harry: When Carol calls him "Daddy Dear" (instead of just "Daddy"), Harry knows she is up to something.

Body Appearance: Unhappy with her butt (feels it sags).

Political Affiliation: Democrat.

Favorite Grocery Store: Value Size Discounts.

Final Episode: Carol marries her boyfriend, Kevin (David Mortin).

BARBARA WESTON

Year of Birth: 1962.

Relationship: Harry's middle daughter (mid-twenties). She moved back home after her unnamed apartment building was turned into a condominium.

Character: Perky, upbeat, terrible with money; tendency to plunge into the unknown without thinking first. Carol thinks that "Barbara's happiness and perkiness is disgusting."

Occupation: Police officer (then a sergeant) with the Miami Police Department (since 1983). Barbara originally wanted to become a pediatrician, then a ballerina, but chose police work because she felt it would be more rewarding for her.

Police Work: Her assignments included posing as a hooker to nab johns, a biker (to infiltrate a motorcycle gang), a drug pusher, and a nun. She was also injured (hit in the butt by a ricocheted bullet). She quit for a time to become a real estate agent when she felt the justice system was unfair (letting criminals off due to smart lawyers).

Award: The Medal of Valor for saving her partner's life during a case.

Dream: To become a lounge singer (she performed "Fever" at Open Mike Night at the Ocean Green Night Club in Miami).

Measurements: 34-23-34. She dislikes her lips, as she feels they are not full enough.

Nickname: Called "Barbie Barb" by Carol.

Book: She and Harry wrote the children's picture book *Jumpy Goes to the Hospital.*

Favorite Comic Strip: Beetle Bailey.

Hobby: Collecting back scratchers.

Deodorant: Zesty, the Official Antiperspirant of the Miss Junior Teen U.S.A. Pageant.

Summer Camp: Barbara and Carol attended Camp Weemawalk (Barbara was called "Swims Like Fish"; Carol was called "Stay in Her Tent").

Final Episode: Barbara, now living in Tucson, returns for Carol's wedding.

Note: Due to manic depression, Kristy McNichol left the series in 1992 with her absence explained as Barbara being on vacation or on various undercover police assignments.

EMILY WESTON

Relationship: Harry's youngest daughter (age 23; born in 1970). She was previously only mentioned and was first said to be attending a New York university, then "a college up North." She returns home in 1993 to work out her boyfriend problems.

Background: Emily attended the Mount Holyoke School for Girls but quit to work in a Vietnam medical clinic. She rode a moped over the Himalaya Mountains, went to Japan to work as a karaoke club waitress, and traveled to Italy to become a hand model. Here, the affections of an unwanted admirer forced her to return home. Emily called her father "Harry" (Carol and Barbara called him "Daddy") and in 1994 left to return to school.

LAVERNE TODD

Parents: Scarlet (Grace Zabriski) and Grit Higbee (Jim Haynie). Scarlet calls Laverne "Vernie." Grit is an auctioneer and the town judge (because he is "the only one who knows how to work a gavel"). Grace Zabriski first played Eva Barnett, the doctor who became the first woman Harry dated after Libby's death.

Occupation: Harry's hospital (and the clinic) receptionist/nurse. She took over the position in 1983 from Winifred McConnell (Barbara Billingsley), Harry's nurse for 20 years. She also does volunteer work at the Shady Pines Retirement Home.

Place of Birth: Hickory, Arkansas. To get to Hickory from Florida, Laverne takes a plane to Little Rock, then Dwayne's Plane to Hickory.

Maiden Name: Laverne Higbee.

Feud: Her family, the Higbees, and their neighbors, the Malloys, are in a prank war that began over 100 years ago.

Character: Laverne describes herself as "sassy and sexy and sometimes fun to be with."

Body Appearance: Feels her ears are too big.

Favorite Snack: Moon Pies (aka Scooter Pies) and coffee. She makes various jelly preserves when she becomes upset.

Favorite Newspaper: National Inquisitor.

Favorite Poet: Emily Dickinson.

Favorite Lipstick Shade: Passion Pink.

Husband: The often mentioned but rarely seen Nick Todd (Christopher McDonald); her keepsake from their first date is a hot dog wrapper from a ball game at Hickory Memorial Stadium; Nick opened a bar called Laverne's; Laverne lost Nick, a baseball player, when he joined the Osaka Hens, moved to Japan, and fell for a Japanese girl. He holds the record of being hit in the head 85 times by a pitched ball in one season.

Car License Plate: BGF5N7.

Pets: General Lee (cat); Leonard (iguana).

Belief: Ghosts and the supernatural.

Job Security: A secret decoder to unscramble her complex filing system.

Quirk: After attending a concert, she sings the songs the next day.

Musical Ability: Plays the organ (she was the stadium organist for the Arkansas Traveler's Double A's, a minor league baseball team). She can also perform magic and hypnotize people.

Final Episode: Laverne marries her boyfriend, Matt (Stephen Nichols).

Relatives: Aunt, Rheta (Doris Roberts); niece, Louella (Erika Flores); nephew, Wade (Joey Lawrence); ex-mother-in-law, Thelma "Mama" Todd (Ann Guilbert). Not seen are her cousins, Arleen and Tuppy; uncles, Ned, Ben, Herbert, and Walter (weighs 642 pounds); Aunt Edna; and twin nieces, Wilma and Winnie.

CHARLES "CHARLIE" DIETZ

Parents: Fred (Richard Stahl) and Ursula Dietz (Marian Mercer).

Brother: Dieter Dietz (Peter Scolari), manager of the Auto Delights car lot.

Relationship: Harry's neighbor (he briefly lived in Apartment 36 at the Beach Rise Complex).

Occupation: Fifth assistant purser on the luxury liner *Ocean Queen* (the ship docks at Fort Lauderdale; he has been with the company 10 years). On ship, he is called "Puck Boy" (has to clean the shuffleboard pucks). He mentions his first job as being a delivery boy and he attempted to breed race dogs with a greyhound named Amanda.

Childhood: Sent to a fat camp (even though he was thin); joined the church choir ("To get close to God and meet chicks").

Favorite Musical Group: The Bean Boys (sing songs about beans).

Character: An obnoxious, food-pilfering (from Harry's refrigerator) ladies' man.

Education: George S. Patton High School.

Dream: Become a stand-up comedian (he performed at the Laughter Rafter Club).

Favorite TV Show: Get Smart.
Favorite Game: Pool.
Membership: The Stallion Club; How to Meet Men (joined to meet the women who joined to meet men).
Favorite Bar: The Crotch Duster.
Passion: Strip clubs.
Favorite Eatery: The Weiner Shack.
Dumbest Thing Ever Done: Filling his water bed with helium, floating up to the ceiling, and breaking his nose.
Relatives: Son, Raymond (C.D. Barnes), from an affair she had 17 years ago.

OTHER CHARACTERS
Estelle Getty joined the cast in 1993 after the cancellation of *The Golden Palace*, reprising her role as the elderly Sophia Petrillo, now a regular visitor to the Weston home while residing at the Shady Pines Retirement Home.

Dr. Maxine Douglas is the owner of the Canal Street Clinic (located next to Ernie's Garage). In her five years at the clinic, she has seen over 30,000 patients, taken 11,000 blood samples, and looked at 4,000 X-rays. The clinic hours are from 9 a.m. to 8 p.m. on Mondays, Wednesdays, and Fridays and 2 p.m. to 7 p.m. on Tuesdays and Thursdays. She was born in New York City, has stage fright (can't speak to an audience), and lives in a house with the street number 9, and Taco Bell is her favorite eatery. She must have her coffee and donut each morning to start the day. Marla Gibbs played her mother, Josephine Douglas.

ORIGINS
A spin-off from *The Golden Girls*. The original 1987 pilot focused on the lives of Renee (Rita Moreno) and George (Paul Dooley), a middle-aged couple whose children have left home and who now seek a new meaning to life.

The Fall Guy
(ABC, 1981–1986)

Cast: Lee Majors (Colt Seavers), Heather Thomas (Jody Banks), Douglas Barr (Howie Munson).

Basis: A Hollywood stuntman (Colt Seavers) supplements his income with a more dangerous job: tracking down bail jumpers for the Los Angeles court system.

COLT SEAVERS

Place of Birth: California in 1939. He grew up in a rural area and became fascinated by the stunts he saw in movies. His father taught him how to hunt and track.

Education: The University of California, Los Angeles (where he met and befriended "Wild" Dan Wild, a famous stuntman who taught him the ropes).

Occupation: Hollywood stuntman (a member of the Fall Guy Stunt Association). He claims he makes money by "being killed, blown up, shot, punched, and being pushed off cliffs." He is also a bounty hunter for the Los Angeles criminal courts system. As Colt says, "Picture work is not like real work."

Character: Somewhat of a loner and claims to be the best tracker in the business.

Tan-and-Brown GMC 4-by-4 Truck License Plate: FALL GUY.

Weapon: A movie stunt gun (a Colt .45) with three-quarter-load blanks ("To impress people"). He also claims he uses "his charm" to impress the ladies.

Address: 22345 First Street (a home called "a shed in the woods"). A horseshoe hangs over the front door for luck.

Favorite Pastime: Soaking in his outdoor tub (smoking a cigar and playing with a yellow rubber duck).

Phone Number: 555-7015.

Favorite Bar: The Palomino Club.

Trait: Will not back down from a job; has to finish what he started.

TV Work: Model for Au Revoir jeans.

Stunt Doubled For: Clint Eastwood, Farrah Fawcett, Raquel Welch, Cheryl Ladd, Jaclyn Smith, Burt Reynolds, Bo Derek, Cheryl Tiegs, Robert Redford, and Sally Field.

Stunt Fee: $10,000.

Tracking Fee: $500 a day plus expenses (some cases involve Colt receiving only a percentage of the bail that was posted before a culprit skipped).

Bail Bondswomen: Samantha Jack (Jo Ann Pflug), nicknamed "Big Jack" and "Soapie" (because her life is like a TV soap opera); Teri Michaels (Markie Post), also known as Teri Shannon; and Pearl Sperling (Nedra Volz), all with Bond Street Bail (phone number 555-5000). Colt also worked for bail bondsman Edmond Trent (Robert Donner).

Complicating Colt's Life: Kim Donnelly (Kay Lenz), a beautiful but greedy insurance investigator; Kay Faulkner (Judith Chapman), the rival bounty hunter (lives at 3370 Cold Water Canyon); Charlene "Charlie" Heferton (Tricia O'Neal), "the world's most beautiful stuntwoman"; and Cassie Farraday (Dana Hill), "the rowdy little stuntwoman."

Theme Song: Although Lee Majors sings the theme ("The Unknown Stuntman"), some episodes credit the singer as "Colt Seavers."

JODY BANKS

Relationship: Colt's friend, a voluptuous stuntwoman who often takes chances to complete an assignment.

Birth Year: 1957.

Member: The Fall Guy Stunt Association.

Address: 146 Del Mar Vista (in the marina).

Measurements: 36-24-36.

Car License Plate: IGS 1267.

Ability: Can fly a plane, shoot a gun, skydive, and trick car ride.

Character: Colt's complete opposite when it comes to planning a stunt. Jody is much more cautious and figures on the path of least resistance to avoid injury. She often assists Colt on his court cases and does receive and even share what Colt makes. While alluring, Jody feels her looks are not always the key to solving a case; her stunt abilities are more of an asset.

HOWARD "HOWIE" MUNSON

Relationship: Colt's cousin.

Birth Year: 1949.

Occupation: Budding stuntman and Colt's business manager.

Education: Spent seven years in various colleges: Iowa State (specialized in Latin American culture), Yale University (campus boxing champion), Oklahoma

State (took accounting), Harvard University (majoring in business), Cornell University, Cal State (majoring in archaeology), Fresno State College, Segway Athletic Institute, Howard University, Penn State (taking mechanical engineering), and Northwestern University. He also served time in the Air Force Academy.

Ability: Can fly an airplane (doing so since high school) and pilot a helicopter and a boat.

Nickname: Called "Kid" by Colt.

Cooking Specialty: Turlinger chili (Jody claims it is too spicy).

Address: 1246 Allegro Drive (although at times he appears to be living with Colt).

Family Matters
(ABC, 1989–1997; CBS, 1997–1998)

Cast: Reginald VelJohnson (Carl Winslow); Jo Marie Payton France, then Judyann Elder (Harriette Winslow); Kellie Shanygne Williams (Laura Winslow); Darius McCrary (Eddie Winslow); Jaimee Foxworth (Judy Winslow); Telma Hopkins (Rachel); Jaleel White (Steve Urkel).

Basis: The events that befall the Winslows, an African American family living in Chicago: parents Carl and Harriette; their children, Laura, Eddie, and Judy; and Rachel, Harriette's sister. The program is a spin-off from *Perfect Strangers*.

CARL OTIS WINSLOW

Parents: Sam (deceased); Estelle "Mother" Winslow (Rosetta LeNoir).

Brothers: Calvin, Darryl, Frank, and an unnamed fourth brother.

Address: 262 Pinehurst Street. Carl mentions he bought the house in 1976, then in 1974, right before Eddie's birth.

Telephone Number: 555-6278 (later 555-0139).

Station Wagon License Plate: L95 541.

Occupation: Officer (later sergeant) with the Chicago Police Department, Metro Division of the Eighth Precinct. He was also the traffic reporter for the 4:00 p.m. news on WNTW-TV, Channel 13.

Assistant: Rex, the police dog that patrolled the streets with him.

Worst Day: His squad car running out of gas in the middle of a high-speed chase.

Car Code: 2-Adam-12.

Education: Vanderbilt High School, Class of 1969 (he first mentions Kennedy High School).

Front row: Jaleel White, Kellie Williams, and Jaimee Foxworth; back row: Darius McCrary, Reginald VelJohnson, and Jo Marie Payton. *ABC/Photofest. ©ABC*

Favorite Game: Pool. (Played at the Corner Pocket pool hall as a teenager and was known as "Rack and Roll Winslow." He is now a member of the department's bowling team, the Strike Force.)
Band: The singing group the Darnells.
Bank: The Investors Bank of Chicago.

HARRIETTE WINSLOW
Age: 37 (born in Chicago).
Maiden Name: Harriette Baines.
Occupation: Housewife. She was originally the elevator operator at the *Chicago Chronicle* (as seen on *Perfect Strangers*); she was later the newspaper's security director (held keys to 300 offices).

Education: Vanderbilt High School (where she and Carl first met). It is first mentioned that she and Carl have been married for 25 years, then 19, then 22 years.

Favorite Snack: Chocolate chip cookies.

Favorite Restaurant: Chez Josephine.

Childhood Memory: A scar on her left knee from falling off her tricycle.

EDWARD JAMES ARTHUR WINSLOW

Relationship: The eldest child.

Birthday: January 28, 1974 (later given as November 1976).

Education: Vanderbilt High School. (Not the smartest student. He is a member of the Muskrats baseball team and wears jersey 33.) Red and white are the school colors.

Trait: Takes after his father for his love of pool (known as "Fast Eddie Winslow" at the pool hall). He also believes that when it comes to women, "God smiled on the men in his family." He will not sleep without his Scooby-Doo night-light.

Occupation: Student. He worked as a waiter at the Mighty Weiner and later joined the police academy.

Best Friend: Waldo Geraldo Faldo (Shawn Harrison). He is dim-witted and after high school enrolled in culinary school to become a chef.

LAURA LEIGH WINSLOW

Relationship: The middle child.

Education: Vanderbilt High School (beginning with third-season episodes; she carried a *Punky Brewster* TV show lunch box to her unnamed grammar school).

School Activity: Cheerleader for the Muskrats basketball team; voted the 1992 Vanderbilt High Homecoming Queen. She also played Juliet to Steve Urkel's Romeo in the school's production of *Romeo and Juliet.*

Trait: Very pretty, fashion conscious, and bright (the smartest child).

Favorite Perfume: Rainbow Cloud.

Greatest Fear: The love of nerdy Steve Urkel (see below).

Occupation: Student. She attempted a business venture called the Winslow Babysitting Service (failed due to too many kids and no sitters).

After-School Hangout: LeRoy's, then Rachel's Place (where she works as a waitress).

JUDY WINSLOW

Information on Judy, the youngest child, is very limited, as she was dropped from the series (when Jaimee requested a salary increase) without explanation (as if she never existed). She attends an unnamed grammar school, is bright and pretty, and holds the record for selling 232 boxes of Girl Scout cookies. Valerie Jones played Judy in the pilot.

STEVEN "STEVE" QUINCY URKEL

Parents: Herb and Diane Urkel.

Relationship: A nerd who lives next door to the Winslow's. He is Carl's worst nightmare (always causing mishaps for him) and Laura's biggest fear (as he has an unrelenting crush on her, for he believes she is the most beautiful girl in the world). He always introduces himself as "Steven Q. Urkel."

First Meeting: He and Laura met in kindergarten; Laura took an instant dislike to him and made him eat Play-Doh; he believed it was love at first sight.

Trait: Steve's whole world revolves around Laura. He eats his lunch on a Laura place mat and has a photo of her on his desk and pictures of her in his school locker. By agreement, he walks 10 feet behind her at school and says, "I'm 98 percent brain and 2 percent brawn." Steve has a stay-away fund (relatives send him money so he will not visit), and after seeing Steve, people remark, "I thank God I never had children." Steve needs to wear his glasses, or he cannot see a thing.

Education: Same as Laura. At Vanderbilt High, he is a stringer for the school newspaper, the *Muskrat Times,* and equipment manager of the golf club. He is a straight "A" student with the exception of a "C" he received in home economics (when the yeast didn't rise in the bread he was making). He also worked as a (clumsy) waiter at Rachel's Place.

Musical Ability: Plays the accordion.

Favorite Music: Polka.

Favorite Snack: Anchovy paste on a dog biscuit (he says that as a child he ate a mouse); cheese is later mentioned as his favorite food.

Nickname for Carl: "Big Guy."

Catchphrase: "Did I do that?" He also has numerous terms of affection for Laura (e.g., "My Little Jell-O Mold" in the school lunch line, "My Little Crusader" when she stands up for something, or, what he says most, "Laura My Love").

Creations: A robot in his own image (the Urkel Bot) for the National Robotics Contest and the Laura Bot (made in Laura's image). He also created the Urk Pad (transports him from one place to another) and the Cloning Machine.

Award: The *Amateur Weekly* magazine award for creating the Transformation Machine (which changes Steve into the suave and sophisticated Stefan Urquette).

Car: The ultracompact Isetta 300 (two wheels in the back; one centered in the front), license plate P27 128 (then URK MAN); 1960 red-and-white BMW, plate P7C 128.

Play: Steve wrote "Farewell, My Laura," a 1940s-like murder mystery in which he played detective Johnny Danger.

Replacement Girlfriend: Myra Monkhouse (Michelle Thomas), Steve's romantic interest when he realized he could never have Laura. However, in the final episode, Laura returns to Steve, and they become engaged. It is at this time that Steve is chosen by the International Space Station to test his AGF 5000 (Artificial Gravity Flight) space suit. During the test, dubbed "Nerd Watch '98," Steve's lifeline becomes detached from the ship (*Explorer*), and Steve is last seen drifting into endless space.

Relatives: Cousin, Myrtle Urkel (Jaleel White); Aunt Oona from Altoona (Donna Summer). Mentioned was Steve's Uncle Cecil.

RACHEL

Relationship: Harriette's sister and the mother of Richie. She lives with Carl but "mysteriously" disappears from the series (seasons 5, 7, and 8) without explanation.

Age: 34 (three years younger than Harriette).

Place of Birth: Chicago (at St. Regis Hospital, as was Harriette).

Rachel and Harriette's Father: Jimmy Baines (Paul Winfield). Their mother, Darlene, is deceased.

Marital Status: Widow (her late husband was named Robert Crawford).

Full Name: In first-season episodes, her last name was given as Cochran, and Richie is an infant (Joseph and Julian Wright). For the second season, her last name was Crawford, and Richie was advanced three years in age (Bryton McClure).

Education: Vanderbilt High School.

Occupation: Freelance writer; later the owner of Rachel's Place, an eatery that became the after-school hangout (replaced LeRoy's after it burned down).

Relatives: Cousin, Clarence Baines (Shaun Baker).

Family Ties
(NBC, 1982–1989)

Cast: Meredith Baxter (Elyse Keaton), Michael Gross (Steven Keaton), Michael J. Fox (Alex P. Keaton), Justine Bateman (Mallory Keaton), Tina Yothers (Jennifer Keaton), Brian Bonsall (Andrew Keaton).

Basis: A family of six (parents Steven and Elyse) and their children (Alex, Mallory, Jennifer, and Andrew) struggle to cope with the incidents that affect their daily lives, especially Steven and Elyse, former hippies transforming into a suburban life.

OVERALL SERIES INFORMATION

Steven Keaton and Elyse Donnelly met as students at California's Berkeley College in 1963. They were called "flower children," and each shared the same political views as Democrats. They participated in 15 political demonstrations between 1966 and 1973, attended Woodstock in 1969, and were arrested three times for protesting government policies (they wanted to beautify America and ban the bomb). Later episodes change this: Steven, age 18, met Elyse, age 15, in high school (they married after she graduated—first said to be in 1962, then in May 1964).

Alex, the eldest Keaton child, was first said to have been born in a hut in Africa in 1965, when Steven and Elyse were serving in the Peace Corps; a Dr. Ellis delivered the baby. Next, he is said to have been born in California when his parents were living in a commune. (Steven and Elyse had contemplated naming him "Moonbeam." They chose the name Alex, as opposed to Steven, so that Alex would have his own identity.) In 1966, the family moved to Columbus, Ohio, and took up residence in an apartment on Rosewood Avenue (they moved into their series home [address not given] in 1968, when Alex was three years old).

Mallory was first said to have been born in California in 1967, when Steven and Elyse were students at Berkeley University (Steven had to leave Elyse's bedside to take a political science final exam right before Mallory's birth), then in Columbus, Ohio, in 1967 (delivered by a Dr. Waxman). Jennifer, delivered by a Dr. Rogers, was born in Columbus on November 7, 1972; Andrew was born in 1983 in Columbus.

STEVEN KEATON

Parents: Father, Jake (John Randolph), and May (Anne Seymour) Keaton.

Place of Birth: Buffalo, New York (later said to be Ohio), in 1945.

Childhood: Held a paper route; at the age of 18 worked in his father's dry-cleaning store (his father hoped to name the business Keaton and Son). He attended Camp Kiahoka during the summer.

Education: At Berkeley, he wrote a play called *A Draft Card for Burning* (in protest of the Vietnam War), was president of the south campus aluminum can recycling program, and edited the underground school political newspaper, *The Scavenger.*

Occupation: Manager of PBS station WKS, Channel 3 (614-555-6131, then 555-2131, is its phone number; he produced the science special *Oxygen, Our Favorite Gas*). He was offered but turned down the position of Midwest regional manager for PBS when it meant spending too much time away from his family.

Standing: Tina Yothers, Michael Gross, and Justine Bateman; sitting: Michael J. Fox, Brian Bonsall, and Meredith Baxter. *NBC/Photofest.* ©*NBC*

Character: Strong willed and totally devoted to his family. When family meetings are called to discuss problems, Steven brings it to order with a large soup ladle.

Family Car: Mentioned as being a Volvo.

Puppets: Steven uses Fluffy and Marv to entertain at his children's birthday parties.

Shoe Size: 13.

Favorite Meal to Prepare: Tuna noodle casserole.

Relatives: Brother, Robert Keaton (Norman Parker); niece, Marilyn Keaton (Tammy Lauren).

Flashbacks: Steven as a boy (Adam Carl); Steven as a college student (Michael David Wright); Steven's mother, May, when young (Maryedith Burrell); Steven's father, Jake, when young (Michael Aldredge); young Robert (Mark Marias).

ELYSE KEATON

Mother: Kate Donnelly (Priscilla Morrill). She and her husband, Charlie (not seen), divorced after 40 years of marriage in 1984.

Occupation: Freelance architect (she briefly held a job at the firm of Norvacks, Jenkins and St. Clair). The Cavanaugh Building in Columbus was the first building she designed.

Upbringing: Taught to think of a husband as the center of her universe, to live in his shadow, to wait on him hand and foot, and to satisfy his every desire. After meeting Steven, who treated her as an equal, she realized her parents were wrong.

Dream: To become a folk singer (she attempted to do so by performing at the Top Spot Café; two shows a week at $25 per week).

Support Group: While not named, devoted to helping distraught women.

TV Role: The Penguin Girl for Proper Penguin Frozen Foods.

Character: A loving mother who will sacrifice everything for her children. Her strict upbringing often challenges her disciplining her children, as she does not want what happened to her to happen to them.

Relatives: Sister, Michelle (Karen Landry; she is married to Marvin [Stuart Pankin], and they are the parents of Monica [Dana Anderson] and Marvin Jr. [Jeff B. Cohen]); brother, Ned Donnelly (Tom Hanks); aunts, Gertrude Harris, called "Aunt Trudy" (Edith Atwater), and Rosemary (Barbara Barrie).

Flashbacks: Elyse as a college student (Margaret Marx).

ALEXANDER "ALEX" P. KEATON

Education: Warren G. Harding High School (editor of the newspaper, the *Harding Hoorah* [which he wanted to change to the *Harding Herald*]); Leland College (where he majored in economics). He was president of the school's

Young Businessman's and Young Entrepreneur's Clubs. In grammar school (not named), he won the fourth-grade spelling bee with the word "Foreclosure."

IQ: 137 (two points lower than Mallory).

Shattered Hope: Not being chosen as the valedictorian for his 1984 graduating class at Harding. He achieved four "A's" and one "A minus," but his girlfriend at the time, Rachel Miller (Daphne Zuniga), achieved five straight "A's" and was chosen.

Trait: Worships money and prides himself on being different. He is hoping to become a captain of industry or a power broker.

TV Appearance: Alex (with Mallory as his teammate) appeared on the WKS-TV program *High School Quiz Off* (Steven hosted; Elyse designed the set). It was Harding High versus St. Mary's, and Alex's stage fright caused his team to lose.

Hero: President Richard Nixon (later George W. Bush). As a baby, Alex had a Nixon baby rattle.

Favorite Economist: Milton Friedman (Nobel Prize winner).

Favorite TV Channel: CNN (Cable News Network).

Political Party: The Young Republicans. He was also "Junior Mayor" for a week.

Favorite Strategy Game: Chess.

Favorite Childhood Song: "We're in the Money."

Award: The Matthews, Wilson, Harris and Burke Scholarship.

Favorite Newspaper: Wall Street Journal.

Radio Program: At Harding High, Alex hosted a program of jazz music on WHSH ("The Radio Station of Harding High and Parts of Ohio"); at Leland, Alex hosted "Syncopated Money" (music and business news on WLEL [Leland College Radio]).

Quirk: Carries his résumé with him at all times and has a collection of his report cards from nursery school through college. He refuses to watch TV soap operas "because they are demented." He sleeps with a Donald Duck nightlight; his vests reflect the initials "A.P.K."

Occupation: Student; clerk at Adler's Grocery Store; box boy at the Shop-a-Lot Supermarket; assistant at both the Harding Trust Company and the First Mercantile American Bank; production assistant at WKS-TV. In the final episode, Alex accepts a job offer from the Wall Street firm of O'Brien, Mathers and Clark.

Favorite Day of the Year: The first day of school.

Childhood: Alex first cried when he was five years old when he learned that his father worked for a nonprofit organization (he would tell his friends his father was a cowboy). As an infant, Elyse and Michael created a dollar-sign mobile that they placed over his crib to pacify him. His favorite story was "The Three Little Pigs" (he would fall asleep by page 5 as Elyse read it to him). When under stress, Alex suffers from insomnia.

Flashbacks: Alex as a boy (Chris Hebert).

MALLORY KEATON

Trait: Very pretty but much less studious than Alex. (She doesn't apply herself to her schoolwork and is thus a "C" student with algebra being her worst subject. Alex mentioned trying to teach Mallory long division and got a concussion from banging his head against the wall.) She is smart in her own way and claims to have a "fashion gift" (able to tell fabrics apart blindfolded; she mentions despising polyester).

Education: Warren G. Harding High School; Grant College (majoring in fashion design and a member of the Gamma Delta Gamma sorority). WGRW is the college radio station, and "Grant is conveniently located near all major highways."

IQ: 139 (two points higher than Alex).

Occupation: Student. She wrote the advice column "Dear Mallory" for the *Columbus Shoppers Guide* newspaper, held a job as salesgirl at a women's boutique called Alphabet Soup, and was an apprentice at David Campbell Fashions (where she designed a line of women's business clothes called "Dress for the Fear of Success").

Contest Winner: The Columbus *Express*–Ed Hamilton Modeling Agency Contest (photographed for the paper's annual mother–daughter modeling event).

Dream: To open a chain of women's boutiques called What's in Store.

Favorite Pie: Lemon meringue.

Childhood Memory: Mallory thought she was from another planet and hoped that her space mother would come back to Earth to find her.

Boyfriend: Nick Moore (Scott Valentine), a hoodlike environmental artist (creates art from junk). His greeting is "Heyyy," and he has a dog (Scrapper). His father, Joe (Nick Hedaya), owns a used-car lot (Joe Moore's Motors), and Nick later opens an art school for children. *Woman with a Half-Eaten Hamburger* was the first painting he sold. He previously worked as a stock boy (then salesman) at Gleason Brothers Shoes.

Flashbacks: Mallory, as a girl (Kaleena Kiff, then Bridgette Andersen).

JENNIFER KEATON

Trait: A tomboy who relished sports until she hit puberty and found an interest in boys, fashion, and makeup. As a child, she called Steven "Buddy."

Plush Toy: Sebastian (a cat).

Little League Team: The Leopards (coached by Alex).

Musical Ability: Attempting to learn the clarinet (another episode mentions piano). She also has an encyclopedic knowledge of baseball.

Affiliation: The Sunshine Girls, Troop 247, Patch 27.

Bands: The Permanent Waves, Keaton and the Kazoos, the New Keaton Minstrels, Keaton and Garfunkel, the Swinging Corporate Raiders (managed by Alex).

Favorite Magazine: Sports Illustrated (later *Seventeen*).

Favorite TV Channel: MTV (same for Mallory).

Favorite Pie: Apple.

Favorite Game: Checkers.

Dislike: Lima beans (same for Mallory).

Education: Randolph Elementary School; Thomas Dewey Junior High School; Harding High School; Leland College (she carries a 3.4 grade-point average). She works after school as an order taker at the Chicken Haven fast-food restaurant.

Summer Camp: Camp Dartmouth.

OTHER CHARACTERS

Andrew Keaton is the youngest of Steven and Elyse's children and is being groomed by Alex to follow in his footsteps (worship money). He attends Harper Preschool, is bright, and, like Alex, often dresses in a dress shirt and tie. His first doll as an infant was "Sassy Suzy" (which upset Alex, as he opposed boys having dolls).

Irwin "Skippy" Handelman (Marc Price) is Alex's best friend. He was born on March 5 and was adopted by Harry (Raleigh Bond) and Rose Handelman (Lois DeBanzie) after his birth mother, Elizabeth (Garn Stephens), was unable to care for him (being unmarried). He has a crush on Mallory (hopes to impress her with his fossil collection) and enjoys peanut butter and carrot sandwiches. His birth certificate reads "Baby Boy Doe." Tanya Fenmore plays his sister, Arlene Handelman (a pretty but klutzy girl who makes dresses for her pet turtles).

Ellen Reed (Tracy Pollan) was Alex's first college girlfriend; Lauren Miller (Courteney Cox), a psychology major at Leland, replaced her (they met when Alex volunteered to participate in her experiment on overachievers). Franklin Reed, Ellen's father, was played by Ronny Cox.

Full House
(ABC, 1987–1995)

Cast: Bob Saget (Danny Tanner), Candace Cameron (D.J. Tanner), Jodie Sweetin (Stephanie Tanner), John Stamos (Jesse), David Coulier (Joey Gladstone),

Lori Loughlin (Rebecca Donaldson), Andrea Barber (Kimmy Gibler), Mary Kate and Ashley Olsen (Michelle Tanner).

Basis: A widower (Danny) with three daughters (D.J., Stephanie, and Michelle) receives help in raising them from his brother-in-law (Jesse) and best friend (Joey).

DANIEL "DANNY" TANNER

Mother: Claire Tanner (Alice Hirson, then Doris Roberts).

Sister: Wendy Tanner (Darlene Vogel).

Address: 1882 Gerald Street in San Francisco, California.

Late Wife: Pam (Jesse's sister; killed in a car accident).

Family Dog: Comet.

Occupation: Cohost (with Rebecca Donaldson) of *Wake Up, San Francisco*, a daily half-hour early morning program on KTMB-TV, Channel 8. Danny was originally the Channel 8 sportscaster for *Newsbeat* and hosted the "We Love Our Children" telethon.

Jodie Sweetin, Bob Saget, Candace Cameron, John Stamos, Mary Kate/Ashley Olsen, and Dave Coulier. *ABC/Photofest.* ©*ABC*

Education: Golden Bay High School (where he was called "Dan Dan"); San Francisco University (hosted a campus TV show called *College Pop*).

Character: A neat freak. He attributes his excessive neatness to his fifth birthday, when his mother gave him a set of vacuum cleaner attachments; she called him her "special helper." He is also a health food fanatic and buys special, low-sodium pickles at Pickle Town and had a "friend" named Terry, the talking washcloth, as a child.

Car: A sedan (plate 4E11449) he calls Bullet.

Favorite Day: Friday (as it is "mop till you drop day").

Relatives: Nephew, Steve Tanner (Kirk Cameron); cousin, Melina Tanner (Mary Kate Olsen).

Flashbacks: Young Danny (Philip Glasser); Danny's wife, Pam (Christine Houser).

DONNA JO "D.J." TANNER

Relationship: The oldest of the children.

Education: Frasier Street Elementary School; Beaumont Junior High School; Van Allen Junior High School; Van Allen High School (editor of her un-named school newspaper).

Phone Number: 555-8722.

Favorite Pillow: "Pillow Person."

Eye Shadow: Passion Plum.

Occupation: Student. She worked as "The Happy Helper" for a photographer at Tot Shots in the mall.

Trait: Much like her father and neat until she discovered boys. She loves to shop at the mall, and at bedtime Danny would sing her the song "My Girl."

Dream: To own a horse (in the sixth grade, she had one named "Rocket").

Flash-Forwards: Adult D.J. (Melanie Nincz).

STEPHANIE JULIE TANNER

Relationship: The middle daughter.

Education: Frasier Street Elementary School; DiMaggio Junior High School. She carries a *Jetsons* TV show lunch box to school.

Trait: A tomboy (a member of the Giants Little League team; jersey 8). Danny called her "The Tanner Twister," as she threw "a curve ball like no other girl."

Favorite Doll: Emily.

Favorite Plush Toy: Mr. Bear.

Alternate Name: Dawn (which she used when schoolmates teased her as "Step-on-Me"); "Sneeze Burger" when she sneezed during the taking of class pictures.

Astrological Sign: Capricorn.

Scout Troop: The Honeybees.

TV Commercial: Appeared in "Oats Boats Cereal."

Catchphrase: "How rude."

Favorite Foods: Pizza and strawberry yogurt.

Favorite Book: Charlotte's Web.

Flash-Forwards: Adult Stephanie (Julia Montgomery).

JESSE

Parents: Nick (John Aprea) and Irene Katsopolis (Rhoda Gemignani, then Yvonne Wilder).

Name: First introduced as Jesse Cochran, then Jesse Katsopolis.

Ancestry: Greek (his real first name is Hermes, after his great grandfather). He was called "Zorba the Geek" at school until his mother changed it to Jesse.

Education: Golden Bay Union High School; State College. On his first day in grammar school (not named), he was the goldfish monitor and accidentally killed the fish when he took it for a walk without the bowl.

Occupation: Jesse originally worked with his father as a bug exterminator. He later joins Joey to create J.J. Creative Services (also called Double J. Creative Services), a commercial jingle writing company. He and Joey also work together as hosts of *The Rush Hour Renegades* on KFLH radio.

Idol: Elvis Presley.

Musical Ability: Sings and plays the guitar (in high school he had a band called both Disciplinary Action and Disciplinary Problem; his next bands were Feedback, Jesse and the Rippers, and Hot Daddy and the Monkey Puppets). He also has a contract with Fat Fish Records and performs at the Smash Club (transformed it into the New Smash Club when he inherited it).

Youth: Rode a motorcycle and was known as Dr. Dare (for taking dares).

Car: A Mustang (plate RDV 913) he calls Sally.

Catchphrase: "Have mercy."

Favorite Peanut Butter: Elvis Peanut Butter ("the chunka chunka kind").

First Girlfriend: Carrie Fowler (Erika Elenak), whom he met at the dentist's office and dated through high school. Their song was "Muskrat Love."

Wife: Rebecca Donaldson. Rebecca (Danny's TV cohost) and Jesse married on February 15, 1991, and honeymooned in Bora Bora. They first lived in Rebecca's apartment, then moved into a converted attic apartment in Danny's home.

Rebecca: Born on a farm in Valentine, Nebraska (where she had a pet cow named Janice). She gave birth to twins that she and Jesse named Nicholas and Alexander. Her engagement ring is inscribed with the song title "Love Me Tender," and the last "crazy thing" Jesse did before marrying was to go skydiving. Jesse wanted to get married at Graceland and Rebecca in Montana; they agreed on San Francisco.

Jesse's Relatives: Grandfather, Iorgos (Jack Kruschen); grandmother, Gina (Vera Lockwood); cousin, Elena (Jennifer Gatti).

Flashbacks: Young Jesse (Adam Harris).

Rebecca's Relatives: Mother, Nedra Donaldson (Lois Nettleton); father, Kenneth Donaldson (Don Hood); sister, Connie (Debbie Gregory); nephew, Howie (John Nunes); aunt, Ida (Dee Marcus).

JOSEPH "JOEY" GLADSTONE

Parents: Mindy (Beverly Sanders) and Colonel Gladstone (Arlen Dean Snyder).

Occupation: Stand-up comedian. He and Jesse form J.J. Creative Services, a commercial jingles company, and cohost *The Rush Hour Renegades* on KFLH radio.

TV Appearances: Star Search; a comedy pilot for a TV series called *Surf's Up* (starring Annette Funicello and Frankie Avalon, stars of several beach films of the 1960s). Joey played Flip, the surfer-dude mailman; Frankie and Annette owned a beachfront restaurant. When the live-action format was changed to a cartoon, Joey was the voice of Flip, the surfing kangaroo; Frankie and Annette were dolphins. Joey then made another pilot called *The Mr. Egghead Show* with Jesse as the Music Professor before hosting *The Ranger Joe Show* on Channel 8 (he had a hand puppet named Mr. Woodchuck and entertained kids from the Enchanted Forest; Jesse was Lumberjack Jesse).

Education: State College (where he was a member of the Chi Sigma Sigma fraternity with Jesse; their mascot was a seal).

Catchphrase: "Cut it out."

Car: A 1963 Rambler (plate JJE 805) he calls Rosie.

Flashbacks: Young Joey (Christopher Kent Hall).

KIMBERLY "KIMMY" LOUISE GIBLER

Relationship: D.J.'s best friend.

Education: Same schools as D.J. She writes the column "Madame Kimmy's Horoscope" for her grammar school newspaper. In second grade, she faked the mumps by stuffing two Hostess snack cakes (Sno-Balls) into her cheeks.

Character: Very pretty but mischievous and tends to get D.J. in trouble with her antics.

Nickname for Danny: "Mr. T."

Trait: "People say I look like Julia Roberts. I wish I was Madonna, she's rich." She cuts economics class because "I'm going to marry a doctor and hire a maid."

Pet French Poodle: Cocoa. She later calls the dog Sinbad.

Favorite Eatery: The food court at the mall.

Favorite Movie: Dirty Dancing ("for the kissing scenes").

Flash-Forwards: Adult Kimmy (Rhonda Shear).

MICHELLE TANNER

Relationship: Danny's infant daughter (when the series begins; eight years old when the program ends).

Education: Meadowcrest Preschool (where she was in charge of the class bird, Dave); Frasier Elementary School (played the Statue of Liberty in the school's production of *Yankee Doodle Dandy*; she was also "Officer Michelle" of the Polite Police).

Invisible Friend: Glen.

Goldfish: Frankie and Martin.

Favorite Breakfast Cereal: Honey Coated Fiber Bears.

Favorite Movie: The Little Mermaid.

Summer Camp: Camp Lakota (with D.J. and Stephanie); she was called "Trail Mix."

Catch Phrase: "You got it dude."

Character: Typical toddler; looks up to D.J. and Stephanie; often does what she is told (but when she has her mind set on something, she wants to get her way).

Flash-Forwards: Adult Michelle (Jayne Modean).

REBOOT

Fuller House (Netflix, 2016). D.J. (Candace Cameron), a veterinarian, is married to Tommy Fuller and the mother of three sons: 13-year-old Jackson (Michael Campion), seven-year-old Max (Elias Harger), and toddler Tommy Jr. (Dashiell and Fox Messitt). When Tommy, a firefighter, is killed in the line of duty, D.J. finds help in raising her children when her sister, Stephanie (Jodie Sweetin); her best friend, Kimmy (Andrea Barber); and Kimmy's teenage daughter, Ramona (Soni Nicole Bringas), move in with her (and in the same home in which she grew up). Stephanie is a disc jockey; Kimmy owns a party planning business. Danny (Bob Saget) and Rebecca (Lori Laughlin) moved to Los Angeles to host the TV show *Wake Up, U.S.A.*; Jesse (John Stamos) now composes music for the ABC series *General Hospital*; Joey is a Las Vegas stand-up comedian and is now married to Teri (Eva La Rue); and Jesse and Rebecca's twins, Nicholas and Alexander (Blake and Dylan Tuomy-Wilhoit), now operate a fish taco truck together.

Gimme a Break
(NBC, 1981–1987)

Cast: Nell Carter (Nell Harper), Dolph Sweet (Carl Kanisky), Kari Michaelsen (Katie Kanisky), Lauri Hendler (Julie Kanisky), Lara Jill Miller (Samantha Kanisky).

Basis: A singer (Nell) relinquishes her career to honor the last request of her dearest friend (Margaret) to help her husband (Carl) raise her three children, Katie, Julie, and Samantha.

NELL RUTH HARPER
Birthday: April 13, 1950.

Place of Birth: Alabama (she lived on Erickson Road and grew up in a musically inclined family, learning to sing and dance at an early age).

Mother: Maybelle Harper (Hilda Haynes, then Rosetta LeNoir).

Sister: Loretta Harper (Lynn Thigpen); also called Marie Harper.

Education: Etchfield High School (she appeared in the school's musical plays).

Occupation: Singer. Nell left home when she felt the time was right and began her show business career in small clubs for little pay and virtually no recognition.

Marital Status: Divorced from Tony Tremaine (Ben Powers).

Employer: Carl Kanisky, the widowed police chief of Glen Lawn, California. It is at Mr. Funky's nightclub, where Nell was performing and Carl and his wife Margaret (Sharon Spelman) chose to have dinner, that friends Margaret and Nell are reunited after a long absence. When Nell is fired for not sleeping with the club owner, Margaret invites Nell to stay with her. At this time, Margaret tells Nell that she is dying and asks her to help Carl care for her girls when the time comes.

Address: 2938 Maple Lane in Glen Lawn, California; also given as 2938 Wells Drive.

Phone Number: 555-8162 (later 555-2932).

Pet Goldfish: Gertrude (has the distinction of being killed several times but always comes back—from a gunshot to toxic water to vacuum cleaner scooping).

Carl Kanisky: At the stationhouse, Carl had a German shepherd named Rex. Before Carl passed, his father, "Grandpa" Stanley Kanisky (John Hoyt), also lived with him. Grandpa came to America from Poland on a ship called *Karkov*. Lili Valenty, Elvia Allman, Elizabeth Kerr, and Jane Dulo played Stanley's wife (Carl's mother), Mildred Kanisky (also called Emma Kanisky). Carl's brother, Ed Kanisky (called Uncle Ed), was played by Ed Shrum.

Nell's New Life: In 1985, after Carl's passing, Nell elects to study child psychology at Glen Lawn Junior College. Julie and Katie have since moved away, and Samantha was now being raised by Nell. Hoping for a change of life, Nell and Samantha move to Littlefield, New Jersey, where Nell acquires a job as an editor at the McDutton and Leod Publishing House, and Samantha enrolls in Littlefield College.

KATHERINE "KATIE" KANISKY

Relationship: Carl and Margaret's eldest child.

Education: Glen Lawn High School (also said to be Lincoln High School).

Rock Band: The Hot Muffins (Katie formed the group and they sang the song "I Can't Stop the Fire" at the Impromptu Club).

Club: The Silver Slippers sorority (its members are pretty but not the brightest of girls; as Julie says, "The biggest thing those girls have going for them are their bra sizes").

Dream: To become a fashion designer.

Dislike: Sports (she once tried to bowl and, according to her father, "threw herself down the alley").

Occupation: Student. Katie also had her own business, Katie's, a clothing store in the Glen Lawn Mall. In 1986, Katie moves to San Francisco to become a buyer for the Chadwick Department Store.

Quality: Always fashionably dressed, has perfect hair and makeup, but is a bit conceited.

Flashbacks: Katie, age 8 (Nicole Roselle).

JULIE KANISKY

Relationship: The middle daughter and the smartest child.

IQ: 160.

Education: Glen Lawn High School.

Talent: "I can hold my breath for two whole minutes underwater."

Character: Pretty but awkward and not sure of herself. She needs to wear eyeglasses and feels uncomfortable being plain and simple. Although she will not admit it, she is jealous of Katie and wishes she could be more like her (popular and beautiful). Katie feels that Julie dresses "like an awning on a pizza shop" and has no taste in clothes (Samantha thinks Julie buys her clothes at garage sales). She is sensitive and relaxes by reading.

Life Change: Julie impulsively marries Jonathan Silverman (Jonathan Maxwell), a delivery boy for Luigi's Pizza Parlor. After the birth of their daughter, "Little" Nell, they move to San Francisco to set up housekeeping.

Flashbacks: Julie, age six (Kari Houlihan).

SAMANTHA KANISKY

Relationship: The youngest of the daughters (her mother died when Samantha was a toddler and looks up to Nell as her real mother).

Education: Glen Lawn Elementary and High School. When she and Nell move to New Jersey, Samantha attends Littlefield College.

Trait: A tomboy (loves hockey and always accompanies her father to sporting events; the more bloody and violent, the better).

Favorite Movies: Horror and science fiction (she always cheers for the monster).

Nickname: Called "Baby" by Nell.

Dislikes: Loud music ("it makes my braces vibrate") but enjoys helping Nell cook, clean the house, and shop.

Imaginary Friend: Debbie Jo.

Flashbacks: Samantha, age four (Jeann Barron).

The Golden Girls
(NBC, 1985–1992)

Cast: Rue McClanahan (Blanche Devereaux), Betty White (Rose Nylund), Bea Arthur (Dorothy Zbornak), Estelle Getty (Sophia Petrillo).

Basis: Four women in their golden years (Blanche, Rose, Dorothy, and Dorothy's mother, Sophia) struggle to cope with life while sharing a house at 6151 Richmond Street in Miami Beach, Florida.

BLANCHE ELIZABETH DEVEREAUX

Father: Curtis "Big Daddy" Hollingsworth (Murray Hamilton, then David Wayne); her mother, Elizabeth Anne Bennett, is deceased. Curtis later marries Margaret Spencer (Sondra Currie).

Siblings: Sister, Virginia (Sheree North), and gay brother, Clayton Hollingsworth (Monte Markham).

Back row: Betty White and Rue McClanahan; front row: Bea Arthur and Estelle Getty. *NBC/Photofest. ©NBC*

Place of Birth: Atlanta, Georgia (where she lived in Hollingsworth Manor; she later mentions she was born in Virginia), in 1932.

Religion: Baptist.

Maiden Name: Blanche Hollingsworth. Marie is also given as her middle name.

Marital Status: Divorced from George Devereaux (George Grizzard). At the wedding, she and her father danced to the song "Tennessee Waltz."

Children: Unclear. Her daughters Rebecca (Shawn Scheeps, then Debra Engle), Charmayne (Barbara Babcock), and Janet (Jessica Lundy) are seen, but in dialogue, Biff, Doug, Matthew, and Skippy are mentioned as being her children.

Phone Number: 555-EASY (555-3279).

Occupation: Museum curator.

Character: The most flirtatious and sexiest of the women (she is proud that her initials spell "BED" and delights in showing cleavage). Blanche is known to have had many affairs and insists she is only 42 ("because living with women who look older than me makes it look possible"). She doesn't take offense to being called a "slut" and once a year tries on her red wedding dress; if it doesn't fit, she diets to regain her figure (her affairs prevented her from wearing white). Blanche originally shared her home with two old ladies she evicted because they were "sticks in the mud." She acquired Rose (first to respond), then Dorothy and Sophia, through a supermarket bulletin board ad.

Favorite Fictional Character: Scarlett O'Hara (from *Gone with the Wind*).

Favorite Meal: Tuna quiche (her "sensible meal" to keep her figure). In another episode, Blanche mentions that she dislikes tuna fish.

Favorite Dessert: Chocolate cheesecake.

Pageant Title: Citrus Festival Queen.

Model: The cover of *The Greater Miami Penny Saver* for Ponce de Leon Itching Cream.

College Sorority: The Alpha Gams.

Favorite Bar: The Rusty Anchor.

Relatives: Niece, Lucy (Hallie Todd); grandson, David (Billy Jacoby); granddaughter, Sarah (Robyn Faye Buckland); uncle, Lucas Hollingsworth (Leslie Nielsen); brother-in-law, Jamie Devereaux (George Grizzard); unseen granddaughter, Aurora (whom she sometimes calls Oreo).

Flashbacks: Blanche's mother (Rue McClanahan).

ROSE NYLUND

Date of Birth: 1930 (making her 55 when the series begins).

Place of Birth: St. Olaf, Minnesota. (A strange farming town in Minnesota known as "The Broken Hip Capital of the Midwest." "We revere our old people and put them on pedestals—but they fall off and break bones.") It has a make-out point called "Mount Pushover," and, according to Rose, its citizens do not believe in doctors or psychiatrists (Rose later says that St. Olaf is home to two world-famous psychotherapists, Sigmund and Roy); the town also has a famous explorer (Wrong Way Glookenflonken) and invented its own version of the game "Monopoly" called "Googen Spritzer."

Religion: Lutheran. Rose was originally a Baptist, but when her church refused to baptize her family's prize pig, Olga, they converted.

Parents: Rose's biological father was Brother Martin (Don Ameche), a monk. Her mother was Ingrid, a cook at the monastery. They had an affair; Ingrid became pregnant but died while giving birth to Rose. The infant Rose was placed in a basket with hickory-smoked cheese, beefsteaks, and crackers and placed on the doorstep of Alma and Gunter Lindstrom (who adopted and raised her). (In another episode, Rose mentions it was the Gierkeckibiken family; later, she says she was raised in an orphanage until she was eight years old, at which time she was adopted by the Lindstroms.) She also heard rumors that her father was a clown with the Ringling Bros. and Barnum & Bailey Circus. Jeanette Nolan appeared as Alma Lindstrom, Rose's adoptive mother.

Sisters: Lily (Polly Holliday), who is blind, and Holly (Inga Swenson).

Education: Rose first says St. Olaf High School (where she composed the school fight song "Onward St. Olaf"), then St. Gustav High School (where she studied pig Latin and was class valedictorian). She also says an illness (mono) prevented her from graduating. She next attended Rockport Community College (where she was a member of the Alpha Yams Farmer's sorority), then St. Paul's Business School.

Languages: English and Norwegian. Rose is supposedly descended from Vikings.

Childhood: Rose's mother called her "Twinkle Toes," and she had several pets: Rusty (a dog that saved her family from a fire), Larry (a mouse), Scruffy and Lindstrom (cats), and Lester (a pig who could predict Oscar award winners by wagging his tail).

Plush Toys: Fernando and Mr. Longfellow (teddy bears).

Pet Dog: Jake. Mr. Peepers, the cat that Rose had in the pilot episode, was given to a young boy after his cat died.

Inheritance: Baby, a 29-year-old pig she acquired after her Uncle Higgenblotter passed.

Allergy: Cats (although she previously had several).

Favorite Number: 12.

Favorite Radio Station: All-talk radio WXBC.

Beauty Pageants: The Little Miss Olaf Beauty Pageant (her talent was "rat smelling," and she lost 22 years in a row) and Miss Butter Queen of St. Olaf (lost when her churn jammed in the process of making butter); later crowned "St. Olaf Woman of the Year" (where she received a milk chocolate statue trophy).

Husband: Charlie Nylund, the owner of a tile grouting business. They married at the St. Olaf Shepherd Church, and its wedding march, "The Cuckoo Song," was used by movie comedians Stan Laurel and Oliver Hardy as their theme song. When Charlie died, Rose moved to Florida with her cat, Mr. Peepers.

Children: Daughters, Kirsten (Christina Belford, then Lee Garlington) and Bridget (Marilyn Jones). Her other children, Adam and Janella, are mentioned but not seen.

Occupation: Production assistant at WSF-TV, Channel 8, for the consumer affairs program *The Enrique Mas Show.* She is later associate producer of *Wake Up, Miami.* She first worked as a waitress at the Fountain Rock Coffee Shop, then as a counselor at an unnamed grief center. She is also a Sunshine Girls Cadet leader.

Character: The most naive of the women. Rose claims to always tell the truth. ("I lied only once to get out of class to see a movie. I'm sorry I did it because it must have been the day they taught everything—which explains why I am so dense.") Rose is most proud of the fact that she reached inside a chicken to aid in a breech birth (this would be impossible, as chickens lay eggs).

Therapy Group: An optimism meeting seen as "Create Your Own Happiness" but mentioned as "Create Your Own Miracles."

Favorite TV Show: Miami Vice.

Romantic Interest: Miles, a man in the FBI Witness Protection Program. His real name is Nicholas Carbone, and he is on the run from the Cheeseman, a mob boss (both roles played by Harold Gould).

Quirk: Places stickers of dead bugs on her car windshield as a warning for other bugs so they can avoid the same fate when she is driving.

Relatives: Granddaughter, Charlene (Bridgette Andersen); cousin, Sven (Casey Sander). Rose mentions Uncle Gustaf, who hanged himself after his horse beat him for the job of town water commissioner; and Uncle Arnold, who lives in Florida.

DOROTHY ZBORNAK

Place of Birth: Unclear: Said to be Brooklyn, New York (lived on Canarsie Street); then Sicily; and, finally, Queens, New York. Dorothy was first said to have been born in a hospital, then on a card table at her husband's lodge. As for breast-feeding, it is first mentioned being for two years, then not at all. Phil, Dorothy's brother, is first said to never have been breast-fed, later that he was until 12 years old.

Age: 53 (born in 1932); later said to be born in 1929, making her 56.

Parents: Sam and Sophia Petrillo.

Siblings: Sister, Gloria (Dena Dietrich, then Doris Belack). Her late brother, Phil Petrillo, a cross-dresser, was married to a woman named Angela (Brenda Vaccaro).

Religion: Roman Catholic.

Childhood Doll: Mrs. Doolittle.

Occupation: Substitute public school English teacher. She was the first one in her family to graduate from college and majored in U.S. history (she later says world history).

Maiden Name: Dorothy Petrillo.

Marital Status: Divorced from Stan Zbornak (Herb Edelman), a novelty items salesman who always said, "Hey, it's me Stan," when he entered a scene. Their wedding date was given as both June 1, 1949, and June 25, 1947; they divorced in 1983. As for their honeymoon, it is first said to have been in the Poconos, then Miami. Dorothy divorces Stan when he falls in love with a younger woman (Chrissy). Dorothy says her first pregnancy occurred in the back of a Studebaker; she later claims the car was a Nash. In the final episode, Dorothy marries Blanche's uncle, Lucas Hollingsworth (Leslie Nielsen), and moves to Atlanta to begin a new life.

Children: Daughter, Kate Zbornak (Deena Freeman, then Lisa Jane Persky); son, Michael Zbornak (Scott Jacoby), first said to be a member of the Boston Philharmonic Orchestra, then in a jazz band.

Character: The most outrageous of the four women with a tendency to lose her temper. She is usually the levelheaded one and tries to resolve the situations that arise from both her somewhat senile mother and Rose's attempts to deal with life.

Addiction: Gambling.

Dream: To become a stand-up comedian.

Favorite TV Show: Jeopardy (on which she became a contestant; she, Sophia, Rose, and Blanche also appeared on the game show *Grab That Dough*).

Stan's Relatives: Cousin, Magda (Marian Mercer); mother (Alice Ghostley); brother, Ted (McLean Stevenson).

Flashbacks: Young Dorothy (Lynnie Greene, then Jandi Swanson); young Stan (Richard Tanner).

Note: It is Dorothy who has the last line as the series ended. With Rose, Blanche, and Sophia by her side, she says, "You will always be my sisters, always."

SOPHIA PETRILLO

Year of Birth: 1906 (making her 79 when the series begins).

Place of Birth: Sicily.

Siblings: Brother, Angelo (Bill Dana), a priest; sister, Angela (Nancy Walker).

Marital Status: Widow (Salvatore "Sal" Petrillo was her late husband; they married in 1931, and Sal was mentioned as being an ice delivery man). It is mentioned that when Sophia lived in Italy, she had a prearranged marriage with a man named Guido (she broke off the relationship) and was engaged to a man named Giuseppe (whom she left at the altar). At some point (not clearly stated), she met Sal (dialogue makes it appear they came to America together). Sophia, who has gray hair, first mentions she was a blonde, then a redhead.

Second Husband: Max Weinstock (Jack Gilford). Max, the husband of Sophia's late friend, Esther, married Sophia in 1988. They continued the pizza/ knish stand business that Max and Esther started at the beach but realized that after the eatery caught fire, they married for all the wrong reasons and divorced.

Religion: Roman Catholic.

Favorite Actor: Sylvester Stallone (especially his *Rambo* movies "because he sweats like a pig and he never puts his shirt on").

Favorite Games: Bingo (which she plays at St. Genevieve's Church, later said to be St. Dominic's Church) and bowling (where, at the alley, she is known as "Dead Eye Sophia").

Character: The eldest of the women who is determined to be as independent as possible. It is not made clear what happened after Sal passed away. It is assumed that Sophia lived with Dorothy and that when Dorothy relocated to Florida, Sophia came with her. Apparently, Sophia was too old for Dorothy to care for and placed her in the Shady Pines Retirement Home. When the home catches fire, Sophia moves in with Dorothy (and Blanche and Rose). Sophia became senile as the series progressed and buys her shoes at Shim Shacks. When Sophia lived in Italy, she believed she was the most beautiful girl in her village. She claims to have put Sicilian curses on a number of people, but not actress Angela Lansbury, whom she admires. Sophia first says she never weighed over 99 pounds, then 100 pounds. When in Italy, however, she says she was determined to lose 200 pounds.

Occupation: Retired. She had a part-time job at the Pecos Pete Chow Wagon, then at Meals on Wheels, and was finally activities director for the Cypress Grove Retirement Home.

Nicknames for Dorothy: "Big Foot" and "Pussycat."

Quirk: When someone makes her angry, Sophia threatens to get even by her phrase "I will have my revenge; a Sicilian never forgets!" She claims that the use of Bengay ointment and oxygen makes her unable to think straight.

Relatives: Unseen cousins Monty and Carlotta.

Flashbacks: Sophia, age 50 (Estelle Getty); Sophia's mother (Bea Arthur); Sophia's husband, Sal (Sid Melton); young Sal (Kyle Heffner).

SPIN-OFF
The Golden Palace (NBC, 1992–1993). Following Dorothy's departure after marrying Lucas, Blanche, Rose, and Sophia pool their resources and purchase the Golden Palace, a 42-room hotel in Miami, as a means of helping them through their golden years. Blanche assumes the role of manager, Rose becomes the housekeeper, and Sophia, now in her eighties, becomes the kitchen manager. Sophia later joins the cast of *Empty Nest* (1993–1995; see entry) when *The Golden Palace* is canceled.

The Greatest American Hero
(ABC, 1981–1983)

Cast: William Katt (Ralph Hinkley), Robert Culp (Bill Maxwell), Connie Sellecca (Pam Davidson).
Basis: Schoolteacher Ralph Hinkley battles evil as a superhero when extraterrestrials grant him special powers to save the Earth from destroying itself.

OVERALL SERIES INFORMATION
Ralph, on a field trip with his students in Palmdale, California, and Bill Maxwell, an FBI field agent, are drawn to an open field (through their car radios) by forces from an unknown planet. While engulfed in a circle of light, an alien (John Zee) appears to tell them they have been selected to battle evil. Ralph is presented with a special suit to wear but loses the instruction book (dropping it when released from the light) and must now learn to become a hero through trial and error.

RALPH HINKLEY
Mother: Paula Hinkley (Barbara Hale).
Occupation: Special education teacher at Whitney High School.
Marital Status: Divorced from Alicia (Simone Griffeth) and the father of Kevin (Brandon Williams).
Address: A home on Meadow Lane.
Education: Union High School (college not mentioned).
Telephone Number: 555-4365 (later 555-0463).
Reason for Choice: The aliens believe that Ralph possesses integrity, a strong moral character, and a healthy idealism.

The Costume: Red tights with a black cape and silver belt; Ralph calls it "The Suit." It has a squarelike symbol on the front that presumably is a symbol of the alien society. The *Daily Galaxy* was the first newspaper to publish a picture of Ralph flying.

Powers: Ralph has numerous powers but learns of them only by accident; these include flight (he needs to take three steps to accomplish this), strength, invisibility, telepathy, speed, deflecting bullets, visions (called "Holographs" by Bill) that allow him to see past or future events associated with a case, the ability to shrink, and control over animals.

Name: Ralph has no official superhero name; he does call himself "Captain Crash" (for his inability to control his landings when airborne) and later "Captain Gonzo." He is just assumed to be "The Greatest American Hero."

Nickname: Called "Mr. H" by his students and Ralph by Bill.

Club: Ralph was a Boy Scout as a child; he now heads a Boy Scout troop.

Note: Ralph's last name was changed briefly to Hanley when John Hinckley Jr. attempted to assassinate then president Ronald Reagan.

WILLIAM "BILL" MAXWELL

Occupation: FBI field agent; assistant to Ralph.

Uncanny Ability: Being shot or kidnapped by the enemy.

Address: Varies. While not specifically assigned to Los Angeles, he appears to reside in a small, cluttered apartment at the Riverview apartment complex when in California.

FBI Car License Plate: 508 SAT (later 293 XU).

Favorite Snack: Milk-Bone dog biscuits.

Nickname for the Suit: "The Jammies."

Nickname for the Aliens: "The Little Green Guys."

Nickname for Women: "Skirts."

Worst Fear: Ralph's true identity being uncovered and his superiors discovering his secret crime-fighting activities; he calls this his "worst-case scenario."

Bill's Sustained Injuries: His hand (he is always a victim of Ralph's efforts to understand his powers and is forever saying, "Watch the hand, Raaalllph!").

The Discovery: The aliens inform Bill and Ralph that they were not the first to receive The Suit. It appears that a man named James Beck may have been the first (relieved of his duties when he used The Suit for self-gain). They also discover that the aliens' world has apparently been destroyed, and they have given Ralph The Suit to protect humanity, as the Earth is one of the last of the "garden planets."

Philosophy: "Life used to be so simple for me, an ordinary, card-carrying FBI agent trying to do the best job I know; doing everything by the book until they teamed me up with a schoolteacher named Ralph Hinkley." He also believes that "the job takes 110 percent of what you have 25 hours a day."

PAMELA "PAM" DAVIDSON

Birthday: September 25, 1955. She stands 5 feet, 9 inches tall and has dark brown hair and wears a size 9 shoe.
Parents: Harry (Norman Alden) and Alice Davidson (June Lockhart).
Address: An apartment at 2871 Bryer.
Occupation: Lawyer (first with the firm of Carter, Bailey and Smith, then Selquist, Allen and Minor).
Nickname: Called "Counselor" by Bill.
Car License Plate: 733 LBL (later 793 LAF).
Marriage: On January 6, 1983, Pam and Ralph wed (Pam handled Ralph's divorce and often questions her thinking when she places herself in danger by joining Ralph and Bill, especially since she has a tendency to be kidnapped by the enemy).

THE CHANGE

The time is 1986, and Ralph's identity as a superhero has been exposed. (In a rather vague sequence, Ralph saves the life of a girl who, in turn, thanks him as "Mr. Hinkley." Ralph is surprised—"How did she know?" [the viewer is never told].) This episode (seen only in syndication) leads to a pilot for *The Greatest American Heroine.*

The aliens have become upset that Ralph has become a celebrity and summon him, Bill, and Pam to Palmdale to tell them they must find another person for The Suit (so that crime can be battled in secret). Ralph suggests Bill, but the aliens refuse, as Bill was always meant to be an associate. As Ralph begins a search, he crosses the path of Holly Hathaway (Mary Ellen Stuart), a young woman devoted to helping others. She is the foster parent of seven-year-old Sarah (Mya Akerling), works in a day care center, and is the founder of the Freedom Life Foundation and owner of an animal shelter called Anything's Pawsable. She cares, is honest, and has a strong moral character. She is the girl Ralph chooses to replace him (as Bill says, "You did it to me Ralph, you picked a skirt, you paired me with Nancy Drew"; Pam's reaction: "She's not a skirt, she's a woman").

Holly faces the same problems as Ralph (he tried to convince the aliens to give Holly an instruction book but failed). Holly is never in a bad mood and has two pets named Churchill and Roosevelt, but what kind of pets? As Sarah told Bill, "You don't want to know." Holly drives a car with the plate 5Q8 HPO and believes their assignments will be fun. Although Bill insists, "They're not supposed to be fun," he does tell her as the episode concludes, "As I always said, we're gonna make a terrific team." It is also at this time that only Ralph, Bill, and Pam retain their memories, as the rest of the world will forget that Ralph Hinkley was "The Greatest American Hero."

Growing Pains
(ABC, 1985–1992)

Cast: Alan Thicke (Jason Seaver), Joanna Kerns (Maggie Seaver), Kirk Cameron (Mike Seaver), Tracey Gold (Carol Seaver), Jeremy Miller (Ben Seaver), Ashley Johnson (Chrissy Seaver).

Basis: Role-reversal comedy wherein a father (Jason) becomes a househusband while his wife (Maggie) returns to the workforce after raising their children (Mike, Carol and Ben).

JASON ROLAND SEAVER
Mother: Irma Seaver (Jane Powell).

Address: 15 Robin Hood Lane in Huntington, Long Island, New York (also seen as 15 Robin Lane).

Occupation: Doctor of psychology at Long Island General Hospital. He later operates from his home and volunteers at the community's free clinic.

Education: Boston College.

Rock Band: The Wild Hots.

Station Wagon License Plate: FEM 412 (later KMQC 487).

Childhood: Had Bud Collyer, 1950s TV game show host, as his imaginary friend ("who would come to my house and play games").

Marriage Year: First said to be 1968, then 1969.

MARGARET "MAGGIE" SEAVER
Parents: Ed (Gordon Jump) and Kate Malone (Betty McGuire).

Maiden Name: Margaret Malone (she is 13 months older than Jason).

Occupation: Housewife. Prior to her marriage, Maggie worked as a researcher for *Newsweek* magazine. For the series, reporter for the *Long Island Daily Herald*, reporter (as "Maggie Malone") for the TV news program *Action News* on Channel 19, and columnist ("Maggie Malone, Consumer Watchdog") for the *Long Island Sentinel*.

Education: Boston College (majored in journalism after switching from child psychology). It was here that Jason and Maggie first met.

Award: The 1989 "Working Mother of the Year Award."

MICHAEL "MIKE" AARON SEAVER

Relationship: The oldest child.

Education: Wendell Willkie Elementary School; Dewey High School; Alf Landon Junior College; Boynton State College.

Occupation: Student, then teacher (remedial studies), at the learning annex of the Community Health Center (at $100 a week). He previously worked as a paperboy for the *Long Island Herald* (200 customers on his route), waiter at World of Burgers, salesman at Stereo Village, car wash attendant, night man at the Stop and Shop convenience store, and singing waiter at Sullivan's Tavern. He also had aspirations to become an actor (starred in the Dewey High production of *Our Town*) and had his first professional acting job on the TV series *New York Heat* as Officer Bukarski (who was killed off; his closing theme credit read "Michael Weaver"). At Alf Landon, he was a member of the Drama Club and starred with his girlfriend, Kate McDonald (Chelsea Noble), in the play *The Passion.* He next appeared on the TV soap opera *Big City Streets.* Kate, who lived in Apartment 144, later became a model and appeared in the 1992 swimsuit edition of *Sporting Man* magazine.

Cars: Red convertible Volkswagen Bug (license plate BLA 395, later 6PU 570); blue sports car (plate 236R DKS).

Girlfriend: Julie Costello (Julie McCullough), a sophomore at Columbia University (majoring in child psychology). When she and Mike broke up, Julie quit school and became a waitress at the La Village Restaurant.

Flashbacks: Mike, age five (Victor DiMattia).

CAROL ANN SEAVER

Relationship: The second-born child.

Trait: Sensitive, smart, and pretty but wishes she could be thought of as "dangerous, provocative, and sexy; not the kind of girl who is voted recording secretary, left in charge of the class when the teacher leaves and immaculate."

Education: Dewey High School (where she was the 1988 Homecoming Queen and president of the Future Nuclear Physicists Club); Columbia University in Manhattan (takes the Number 1 IRT subway train to school).

Occupation: Student. Carol dropped out of Columbia in 1990 to work as a computer page breaker at GSM Publishing. She returned to Columbia in 1991 to study law and also works with Jason at the free clinic.

Boyfriend: Sandy (Matthew Perry); killed off in a drunk-driving accident.

Address: Carol first lived at home, then on campus (dorm room 436), before she chose to leave and commute (due to her roommate Brianne's tendency to bring home boyfriends and leaving her no place to sleep). Her bedroom wall at home reflects posters of movie comedians W. C. Fields, Laurel and Hardy, and the Marx Brothers.

Childhood: A member of the Happy Campers.

Medical Issue: Carol is said to be attending school in London (1991–1992) to allow Tracey Gold, suffering from anorexia nervosa (an eating disorder), to leave the series for treatment.

Flashbacks: Carol, age four (Judith Barsi).

Note: In the original unaired pilot, Elizabeth Ward played Carol.

BENJAMIN SEAVER

Relationship: The third-born child.

Middle Names: Hubert Horatio Humphrey.

Education: Wendell Willkie Elementary School; Dewey High School (where he had the potential to pick up where Mike left off as the worst problem student ever).

Imaginary Childhood Friend: Pirate Pete.

Girlfriend: Laura Lynn (Jodi Peterson), a pretty but bossy girl whom Ben tolerated but never really accepted; they met in 1989 and broke up the following year.

Occupation: Student. Ben held a job as a newspaper delivery boy and attempted to make money by managing a rap music group.

CHRISTINE "CHRISSY" SEAVER

Age: Six (the youngest child; born on October 26, 1988, at 12:30 a.m. and weighed 8 pounds, 4 ounces; played by twins Kristen and Kelsey Dohring). In 1990, she was advanced to the age of six. She was named Chrissy by Ben (after a dying man named Chris [Dick O'Neill], whom he met and befriended at the hospital where Chrissy was born).

Education: Parkway Preschool; Greenway Elementary School.

Favorite Bedtime Story: "Mr. Mouse."

Imaginary Friend: Ike (a 6-foot mouse who liked to drink beer; Kirk Cameron played Ike in costume, as Mike is Chrissy's hero and she envisioned him as Ike).

Plush Animals: Bertha Big Jeans (a bear); Papa Pig; Mr. Blow Hole (a whale).

Flash-Forwards: Chrissy, age 18 (Khystyne Haje).

FINAL EPISODE

Maggie acquires a job in Washington, D.C., as the executive director of media relations for an unseen senator. Jason, Ben, and Chrissy join her in Washington. Carol returns to the dorm at Columbia University; Mike remains in his apartment over the Seaver house garage (he mentions having "to break in new landlords").

TV MOVIE UPDATES

Growing Pains: The Movie (2000) reunites the family: Jason is practicing psychology in Washington, D.C., and has become the author of mystery novels called *Dr. Dick Hollister*; Maggie is the press secretary to an arrogant congressman; Mike is married to Kate McDonald (Chelsea Noble) and the vice president of the Genasse Advertising Agency; Carol, graduating third in her class at Columbia, is now a corporate lawyer; Ben is a real estate salesman; and Chrissy is a college film student who longs to become a singer.

Growing Pains: Return of the Seavers (2004) finds the family reuniting when Maggie runs for a seat in Congress as the Long Island representative and wins on the platform "Maggie Malone—I'm on Your Side."

SPIN-OFF

Just the 10 of Us (ABC, 1988–1990) features the character of Graham Lubbock (Bill Kirchenbauer), the coach at Dewey High School on Long Island, moving to Eureka, California, to coach the Hippos, the football team of Saint Augustine's, a Catholic high school that is nicknamed "Saint Augie's."

Graham is married to Elizabeth (Deborah Harmon), and they are the parents of Marie (Heather Langenkamp), Wendy (Brooke Theiss), Cindy (Jamie Luner), Connie (Jo Ann Willette), Sherry (Heidi Zeigler), J.R. (Matt Shakman), and infant twins Harvey and Michelle. The family dog is Hooter; the milk cow is named Diane.

Graham and Elizabeth met at a Catholic Youth Organization mixer and married in 1970. Graham held a job as a counter boy at the Burger Barn (under the name "Mitch"); Elizabeth volunteers at the food bank.

Marie, 18 years old, has set her goal to become a nun. She wears a size 34C bra and works at the Eurika Mission. She and her sisters formed the singing group the Lubbock Babes and perform at Danny's Pizza Parlor.

Wendy, 17, wears a size 5 dress, a size 34B bra, and a size 7½ shoe. She uses the lipstick shades Midnight Passion and Dawn at His Place and enjoys shopping at the mall.

Cindy, 16, wears a size 8 dress and a size 36C bra and held a job at the Eurika Fitness Center (at $8 an hour). She hosts "What's Happening, St. Augie's" over the school radio station, KHPO, and says "Hi-eee" for "hello" and "By-eee" for "good-bye."

Connie, 15, the most sensitive of the girls, wears a size 34B bra and a size 5 dress and hopes to become a journalist (she writes for the school newspaper, the *Herald-Gazette*). Her first job (at $4 an hour) was sweeping entrails at the MacGregor Slaughter House.

Sherry, 11, is the most intelligent child and strives for excellent grades; J.R. (Graham Lubbock Jr.), 14, loves horror movies, peanut butter, and playing practical jokes on his sisters.

Hill Street Blues

(NBC, 1981–1987)

Cast: Daniel J. Travanti (Frank Furillo), Veronica Hamel (Joyce Davenport), Michael Conrad (Phil Esterhaus), Bruce Weitz (Mick Belker), Barbara Bosson (Fay Furillo), Joe Spano (Henry Goldblume), James B. Sikking (Howard Hunter), Kiel Martin (J. D. LaRue), Betty Thomas (Lucy Bates), Taurean Blacque (Neal Washington), Charles Haid (Andy Renko), Ed Marinaro (Joe Coffey), Jon Cypher (Fletcher Daniels), Dennis Franz (Norman Buntz), Peter Jurasik (Sid the Snitch), Michael Warren (Bobby Hill).

Basis: An often realistic look at the men and women of a police precinct (Hill Street Station) and how they handle the daily pressures of the job, sometimes dealing with both professional and personal problems.

FRANCIS "FRANK" FURILLO

Frank, middle name Xavier and known by his trademark vests and waistcoats, is captain of Hill Street Station. After serving in the Korean War, he joined an unnamed police department where he rose to the rank of lieutenant. He is honest, has a somewhat superior attitude, and serves under Police Chief Daniels (a former inspector with the 23rd Precinct with whom he rarely agrees on policies). Frank, a recovering alcoholic, is divorced from Fay and later marries Joyce Davenport, a lawyer he affectionately calls "Counselor." Fay, the mother of Frank's troublesome son, Frank Jr., also remarries (a judge) and becomes the mother of a girl. Michael Durrell plays Frank's father, Joe Furillo.

JOYCE DAVENPORT

Joyce, a defense attorney, was originally seen as a public defender. She is Frank's second wife (married at the end of the third season) and first met Frank, just divorced from Fay, during a court trial. Their first date consisted of a free classical

Front row: Michael Conrad, Barbara Bosson, Daniel J. Travanti, Veronica Hamel, and Michael Warren; middle row: James Sikking, Taurean Blacque, Rene Enriquez, and Bruce Weitz; back row: Ed Marinaro, Betty Thomas, and Joe Spano. *NBC/Photofest. ©NBC*

musical concert and Frank buying a pizza afterward (wherein Joyce nicknamed him "Pizza Man"). Joyce, who stands 5 feet, 8 inches tall and measures 34-24-34, is a very independent woman who believes in pursuing justice within the limits of the legal system, although bending a rule or two is not foreign to her if it is beneficial to defending a client. It is later revealed that Joyce is unable to have children.

PHIL ESTERHAUS
Phil, middle name Freemason (apparently named after the Freemasons Society), is the desk sergeant who oversees the morning roll-call briefings (he concludes these with "Let's be careful out there"). While he tries to hide it, the pressures of the job do affect him (as he can be seen losing his temper). His car, a Buick, appears to be his most treasured possession, and although he would like to move up in rank (having passed the lieutenant's exam), situations prevent it from happening (such as budget cuts). Phil is divorced and during a romantic moment (with Grace Gardner) suffers a fatal heart attack (used to explain the character's absence when Michael Conrad died from cancer in 1983).

MICHAEL "MICK" BELKER
Mick, originally a detective, then a lieutenant, is rather daunting—small in size but very aggressive (he not only growls at suspects but also will bite them if they try to attack him; he claims that his father, who worked as a tailor, demonstrated the same attributes). He often works undercover and has a tendency to come off sounding nasty with remarks such as "hair bag" and threats to "rip out your kidneys." Although not seen, Mick has a sister named Luana (apparently just as arrogant) and finds his true love in Robin Tataglia (Lisa Sutton), an officer he later marries (they name their first child Phillip after Mick's dearest friend, Phil Esterhaus).

HENRY GOLDBLUME
Henry, first a sergeant, then a lieutenant, is the precinct's hostage negotiator. He prefers to do things his way and is often in conflict with his superiors, especially Frank Furillo. Henry served in the Korean War and joined the city's police force in 1969 (first being assigned to the Jackson Heights Precinct). He is right wing and tries to solve crisis situations with words rather than guns (it appears he is quite reluctant to even hold a gun). He is divorced from Rachel (Rosanna Huffman) and the father of three children. Rachel, who feared for Henry's life, ended their marriage when he was shot and her worst nightmare came true. In high school, Henry dreamed of becoming a writer and pursued that ambition when he chose to write of his work as a police officer.

ANDREW "ANDY" RENKO

Andy, a patrol officer called "Cowboy" by his partner (Bobby Hill), was born in Chicago and loved western movies and TV shows as a kid. He rides a motorcycle in his leisure time, speaks with a southern accent, and enjoys country-and-western music. He can be seen wearing a baseball cap with singer Waylon Jennings's name on it and has a wardrobe that is anything but policelike: a knit cap, a sleeveless leather jacket, a gray shirt, fingerless gloves, and a holster with a gun. He lacks administrative skills (e.g., he types with only one finger) and real social skills and is rather uncouth (especially with bathroom humor). Renko, who always calls his partner "Bobby Hill," feels he needs to rise in the ranks and is taking courses in law enforcement in college. Andy marries Daryl Ann McConnicke (Deborah Richter), and they become the parents of Laura Ann, but infidelity on both sides led to them divorcing. Morgan Woodward played Andy's father, John Renko, and Alley Mills played Andy's sister, Tracy Renko. His mother, Rose, is deceased.

ROBERT "BOBBY" EUGENE HILL

Bobby, an officer with the Jackson Heights Precinct, became Renko's partner on his transfer to Hill Street Station. He has training as a boxer (won two Golden Gloves championships and two Metro Police Department middleweight championships) and appears to have a slight gambling problem (cards and playing the lottery). He represented African American police officers as the temporary vice president of the Black Officers Coalition and is often hesitant about going undercover due to the extra stress and dangers associated with such assignments. Renko would react to cases they worked on with "Lordy, Bobby Hill"; he was said to drive a Camaro.

HOWARD HUNTER

Howard, a lieutenant, heads the precinct's Emergency Action Team. He often remarks about the downfall of society, perhaps stemming from his service as a covert operations marine during the Vietnam War. Hunter joined the police department in 1969, first as a sergeant at the Midtown Precinct. He was demoted to roll-call officer (ending sessions with "Dismissed!") when he showed questionable judgment in a fatal shooting case; his rank was restored after the case was reviewed and he was exonerated. Howard speaks his mind without thinking first (especially when referring to ethnic situations) and comes off as quite patronizing to his fellow officers. He is often at odds with Captain Furillo, as they rarely agree on anything, especially his attempts to upgrade the equipment that his unit utilizes.

LUCILLE "LUCY" BATES

Lucy, first an officer, then a sergeant, is often partners with Joe Coffey. She is somewhat of a rarity at the precinct, as she is virtually the only female officer with actual story lines that are in tune with her male counterparts. She is tough and tries not to let her issues as a female deter that image. Although Joe and Lucy form a "dog and cat" team (male being teamed with a female), they share a love–hate relationship, as they are often at odds with each other (stemming in part from the inner conflicts Lucy suffers as she patrols the streets). Lucy first replaced Esterhaus as the desk sergeant and serves as the roll-call officer in emergency situations. Although not married, Lucy is later seen adopting the child (Fabian) of a drug-addicted mother who could not care for him.

JOHN D. "J.D." LARUE
LaRue, a detective, shows great skill in solving cases but is a wreck when it comes to his personal life. He drinks and womanizes and risks his reputation (and job) by concocting get-rich-quick schemes that seldom work. His addiction to alcohol (and inability to quit) often places him in conflict with Furillo, a recovering alcoholic who sees LaRue as more of a threat to a case than a solution (he fears the day will come when LaRue will show up intoxicated and he will have to dismiss him).

NEAL WASHINGTON
Neal, a plainclothes detective, is a former professional football player whose career ended when he injured his knee. Although he is a competent detective, he is partners with LaRue and often involved in one of his fruitless schemes (although Neal admits he has learned a lot about undercover work through LaRue). Neal can be distinguished by the toothpick on the side of his mouth and his tendency to use the term "Babe" when referring to people. He can also be heard muttering "Ohhh, maaaannnnn" when LaRue causes them a problem; because of LaRue's constant flirtation with women, Neal calls him "Lover."

RAYMOND "RAY" CALLETANO
Ray, a lieutenant and Furillo's second in command, is a naturalized American citizen (born in Colombia). He joined the police force after serving as a marine during the Vietnam War, and his ability to speak and understand Spanish is a big asset when dealing with the Hispanic gangs in the city. In 1986, Ray is promoted to captain and assigned to the Polk Avenue Precinct. A short time later, he resigns to become a precinct instructor (teaching Spanish to rookies).

STANISLAUS JABLONSKI
Nicknamed both "Stan" and "Stosh," he is the sergeant who replaced Esterhaus as the roll-call officer. He previously worked at the Polk Avenue Station but was transferred to Hill Street due to an altercation with a female officer. He does not have the forcefulness that Phil possessed (no emotional bond with the precinct

officers; he ends sessions with "Do it to them before they do it to us") and appears to be a loner who lives with his dog, Blackie. Stan suffers a heart attack in the final season and is forced to retire (although he keeps in contact with the officers at Hill Street).

NORMAN "GUIDO" BUNTZ
Buntz, a lieutenant, is an expert marksman but often uses questionable tactics while on a case. He has a foul mouth (what NBC would allow at the time) and cuts corners when necessary. Buntz likes to encompass his street snitches for information, one in particular being Sidney Thurston, better known as Sid the Snitch (as he says, "I'm a snitch, it's what I do"). Buntz is often investigated by Internal Affairs, and his aggressive actions often infuriate Captain Furillo. It all came to a head when Buntz, angered at Chief Daniels calling for his dismissal, punched him in the face. This led to Buntz's firing but not the end of his career. With Sid by his side, they moved to California to become private investigators and partners in Norman Buntz Investigations (as seen in the 1987 spin-off *Beverly Hills Buntz*). Dennis Franz originally played the character of Detective Sal Benedetto, who was killed off in the first season.

JOSEPH "JOE" COFFEY
Joe, a veteran of the Vietnam War, is a patrol car officer and partners with Lucy Bates. While they work well together (and Lucy seems to be attracted to him), she opposes his off-duty activities of frequenting clubs and bars. Joe's character is a bit unusual in that he was originally killed in a shooting that was later changed to sustaining severe injuries.

OTHER CHARACTERS
Detective Harold "Harry" Garibaldi (Ken Olin), originally with the Midtown Precinct, is heavily in debt to loan sharks, bends the rules to get things done, and is hoping to become a lawyer (attending school at night).

Detective Patricia "Patsy" Mayo (Mimi Kuzyk), transferred from the Midtown Precinct, is totally dedicated to her job and goes strictly by the book (more so than her partner, Garibaldi). She was transferred back to Midtown in the sixth season.

Officer Tina Russo (Megan Gallagher) is new to the precinct (1986) and being mentored by Belker for work in his undercover unit. Unlike normal police officers who offer money for information, Tina offers sexual favors.

Mayor Ozzie Cleveland (J.A. Preston) was originally the commander of the Midtown Precinct and president of the Black Officers Coalition before winning the race for mayor. He grew up in a poor section of the city and has a particular hatred for the gangs and drug dealers that are destroying his city.

Officer Leo Schnitz (Robert Hirschfeld) is the overweight, blind-without-his-glasses booking officer. He is married, but after his wife leaves him, he slims down and elopes with fellow officer Celeste Patterson (Judith Hansen), who, like him, dresses in khaki. Leo was originally attracted to desk officer Natalie Deroy (Ellen Blake).

Grace Gardner (Barbara Babcock), the widow of Sam Gardner (a chief of detectives), works with the police department to improve the quality of Hill Street Station. She is drawn to Phil Esterhaus, and it is a tryst with her that causes his heart attack and death. Grace, deeply affected by what happened, believes that becoming a nun (Sister Chastity) will cleanse her. Her erotic desires force her to leave to become a field representative for a contraceptive company.

Jesus Martinez (Trinidad Silva) is a warlord and head of the Diablos street gang. He also works with Furillo as sort of a snitch and later enrolls in law school (with forged documents) to become a paralegal (and an adviser to Furillo). Tommy Mann (David Caruso) was the leader of the Shamrock gang; Abdul Hussein (Bobby Ellerbee) led the Blood gang.

Captain Jerry Fuchs (Vincent Lucchesi), Furillo's former drinking buddy, was in charge of the Midtown Vice Squad and Special Narcotics Unit before his transfer to Hill Street. He was born in New York City (his accent is still reflected) and is tough, although his fellow officers show little respect for him. He quit to begin his own private investigative practice when he was found to be corrupt.

Alan Wachtel (Jeffrey Tambor) is an unscrupulous (if not sleazy) lawyer whose home away from home appears to be Hill Street Station (he attended law school with Joyce Davenport and was in the top percentage of his class). Alan was, in a way, confused by his sexual status and wore women's clothing to find his true gender identity. He later becomes a judge but turns cynical.

Irwin Bernstein (George Wyner) is the assistant district attorney who becomes part of Frank Furillo's Commission on Corruption. He eventually leaves the position to begin a private law practice in Los Angeles.

Note: The title refers to the blue uniforms most city police officers wear. An exact location is not given (although it is said that the state bird is the swallow). Press material only says "a large midwestern city"; by the TV station that is mentioned, WREQ, Channel 6, the "W" in the call letters indicates that it is located east of the Mississippi (call letters beginning with "K" normally indicate west of the Mississippi). The phone number given for the Hill Street Station is 555-8161.

Hunter

(NBC, 1984–1991)

Cast: Fred Dryer (Rick Hunter), Stepfanie Kramer (Dee Dee McCall).

Basis: The son of a mobster (Rick Hunter) distances himself from his family to battle crime as a detective with the Los Angeles Police Department.

RICHARD "RICK" HUNTER

Place of Birth: Los Angeles on February 3, 1941.

Social Security Number: 991-02-2042.

Address: 5405 Ocean Front Drive (Los Angeles); 1229 Riverside Drive (San Diego).

Telephone Number: 619-555-0142 (San Diego).

Police ID Number: 179.

Badge Number: 89.

Precinct: Detective with Division 122 of the Los Angeles Police Department (LAPD) (also called Central Division, Metro Division, and the Parker Center Police Station); lieutenant with the Robbery-Homicide Division of the San Diego Police Department (SDPD).

Car Code: 1-William-56 (in Los Angeles; also given as 1-William-156 and L-56); 930-Sam (San Diego).

Car: 1978 green Dodge Monaco (plate 1ADT 849); 1990 silver Ford LTD Crown Victoria (plate 21Q 1584).

Nickname: "The Head Hunter" (for his relentless pursuit of criminals).

Character: Tough and honest and not afraid to use his gun. He takes cases too personally and likes to do things his way—not what the law calls for.

Catchphrases: "Works for me" (when he collars a suspect); "The worst part of your day is not when I show up but when I come back" (said to suspects).

Snitch: Sporty James (Garrett Morris) supplies Hunter with street information and owns the shady Sporty James Enterprises.

Relatives: Rick's Uncle John (Lee Patterson); Uncle Jilly, a bookie (not seen).

DEE DEE MCCALL

Birthday: September 6, 1956.

Occupation: Detective sergeant with Division 122 of the LAPD; detective with the Robbery Homicide Division of the SDPD.

Nickname: "The Brass Cupcake" (for her strict adhesion to the rules; she does mention that she "likes bubble baths, soft clothing, and frilly things on her bed" despite her nickname).

Partner: Rick Hunter.

Address: 8534 (then 1721) Mezdon Drive in Los Angeles (a large metal machine gear hangs on the wall behind her bed); 808 McKenzie Street in San Diego.

Car Code: 1-Adam-43 (also given as Charles Albert 420 and L-59; all Los Angeles); 930-Sam (San Diego).

Badge Number: 794 (also given as 358).

Red-and-Silver Car License Plate: 1HYQ483.

Hobby: Writing songs and baking cakes.

Favorite Plush Animal: Tom Dewey (a teddy bear).

Expertise: Picking locks (carries a set of lock picks in her purse and a concealed knife in her boot).

Tragic Event: Raped (as seen in the 1985 episode "Rape and Revenge").

Marital Status: Widow (Steve McCall [Franc Luz] was her husband). In 1979, when Dee and Steve were rookies, Steve was killed "by a punk at a routine stop." This changes when Dee Dee mentions that in 1982, when she was a rookie and Steve was a homicide cop, he was killed during a murder investigation. In 1990, Dee Dee marries Dr. Alex Turner (Robert Conner Newman), a college professor and old flame.

HUNTER'S OTHER PARTNERS

Joann Molinski (Darlanne Fluegel) is teamed with Hunter in 1990 after Dee Dee leaves the force. Like Hunter, she is tough and has a never-ending drive to bring criminals to justice. She resides at 4535 North Sheridan in Los Angeles, and her car license plate reads 2GEE 645. Her badge number is 1836, and R-21 is her police car code. Six months later, however, Joann is killed (shot three times) by the psychotic Loren Arness (Ellen Wheeler).

Christine Novak (Lauren Lane), a detective who prefers to be called Chris, becomes Hunter's partner in 1991. She is divorced from Al Novak (Robin Thomas) and the mother of Allie (Courtney Barilla). Allie attends the Worster Avenue Grammar School and lives with her mother at 6341 West Beverly Drive in Los Angeles. Chris's police car code is R-30 Charles, and she and Allie shop at a store called One Life.

HUNTER'S SUPERIORS

Lester Cain (Michael Cavanaugh, then Arthur Rosenberg) was the first captain, an older, by-the-books commander. Captain Dolan (John Amos) replaced him; Captain Wyler (Bruce Davidson) replaced Dolan, and Chief Charles Devane (Charles Hallahan) replaced Wyler.

TV MOVIE UPDATES

The Return of Hunter (1995) finds Hunter, now a lieutenant with the Parker Division of the LAPD, on a personal vendetta to find Jack Valko (Miguel Ferrer), a madman who killed his fiancée, Vickie Sherry (Beth Toussaint).

Hunter: Return to Justice (2002). Dee Dee has rejoined the force (but as a sergeant with the Juvenile Division of the SDPD). Hunter has become a loose cannon (involved in three justified fatal shootings) and is reunited with Dee Dee to investigate a series of murders that appear to be linked with Roger Prescott (Sam Hennings), Dee Dee's fiancé (no mention is made as to what happened to Alex, the man she married in 1990).

REBOOT

Hunter (2003 TV series). Following the death of his partner, Lieutenant Rick Hunter resigns from the LAPD to become partners with Sergeant Dee Dee Mc-Call in the Robbery and Homicide Division of the SDPD; Captain Gallardo (Mike Gomez) is their superior. Rick and Dee's car code is 930-Sam; Rick's license plate is first seen as 9999042, then E9999028; Dee Dee, who teaches music to children at the Juvenile Center in her spare time, has the license plate 9999027, and her badge number is 794.

It's a Living
(ABC, 1980–1982; Syndicated, 1985–1989)

Cast: Susan Sullivan (Lois), Barrie Youngfellow (Jan), Ann Jillian (Cassie), Gail Edwards (Dot), Wendy Schaal (Vickie), Louise Lasser (Maggie), Sheryl Lee Ralph (Virginia), Crystal Bernard (Amy), Marian Mercer (Nancy), Paul Kreppel (Sonny).

Basis: Incidents in the lives of a group of waitresses (Lois, Jan, Dot, Vickie, Maggie, Amy, and Ginger) who work at Above the Top, a thirteenth-floor restaurant (owned by Pacific Continental Properties) that features "Sky High Dining." The program was originally titled *Making a Living*.

LOIS ADAMS
Year of Birth: 1942 in Minnesota (she mentions being a Scorpio).

Husband: Bill (never seen); the mother of Amy (Tricia Cast) and Joey (Keith Mitchell).

Address: 8713 Mercer Street.

Measurements: 36-28-34. She has blonde hair and wears a size 10 dress and a size 7 shoe.

Prior Job: Secretary in Minnesota before moving to California when Bill, a salesman, received a job promotion.

Hobbies: Art and reading.

KATIE LOU "CASSIE" CRANSTON
Year of Birth: 1950 in Missouri.

Marital Status: Single. She uses the name Cassie so people will not think of her as a hick.

Bra Size: 36C. She is blonde, has blue eyes, and stands 5 feet, 8 inches tall.

Address: Sun Palace Condominium.

Education: Beth Grammar School; Kansas City High School.

Dream: Becoming rich by marrying into wealth (her reason for moving to California).

Character: Very sexy and loves to flaunt her breasts in low-cut uniforms. She cannot cook but tells men, "I'm a terrific cook" ("making toast" is her specialty).

Volunteer Work: Reading to senior citizens at the Willow Glen Rest Home.

JANICE "JAN" HOFFMEYER

Year of Birth: 1948 in Philadelphia.

Parents: Will (Richard McKenzie) and Phyllis Frankel (Georganne Johnson).

Education: Temple High School (Class of 1968) and Berkeley College (Class of 1972; during a Vietnam War protest, she was arrested for mooning a cop).

Marital Status: Divorced from Lloyd Hoffmeyer (Dennis Dugan) and the mother of Ellen (Lili Haydn, then Virginia Keene). In 1985, Jan marries Richard Grey (Richard Kline), divorced from Cindy (Maura Soden) and the father of Charlie (Andre Gower).

Character: "I plan to do more with my life than hand out menus." She hopes to become an attorney and is attending the North Los Angeles School of Law. She earns extra money (for Ellen's ballet lessons) by producing elegant, handwritten invitations.

Pet Cat: Ralph.

DOROTHY "DOT" HIGGINS

Year of Birth: Detroit in 1952.

Mother: Harriet Higgins (K Callan); she has a dog named Scrappy.

Education: Detroit High School; Baxter College (majoring in theater).

Stage Work: Bye Bye Birdie (as Kim); *The Garden of Countess Natasha* (as Natasha); *Esmeralda* (a play about the history of the Philippines).

Television Work: Made her debut in a commercial for Autumn Years dog food; appeared in spots for Le Stiff hair spray; sang "My Buddy" to a dog on the "Adopt a Pet Telethon," and played three roles on the TV soap opera *All My Sorrows* (a nun; the nun's sister, Esmeralda; and Esmeralda's sickly triplet, Juanita).

Pets: Mr. Puss (cat), Pardon (dog), and Mouse (a mouse).

Newspaper Fame: A caricature of her appeared as "Betty Spaghetti" in the comic strip "Billy Bonkers."

VICTORIA "VICKIE" ALLEN

Birthday: July 2, 1954, in Pocatello, Idaho.

Father: Emmett Allen (Richard Schaal).

Height: 5 feet, 10 inches tall.

Address: 102 North Brewster Place, Apartment 304.

Pet Parakeet: Squeaky.

Character: A bit unsure of herself and the most sensitive of the waitresses. She is also somewhat clumsy (lacks confidence) and is best friends with fellow waitress Dot.

AMY TOMPKINS

Birthday: September 30, 1961, in Snyder, Texas.

Address: The Carrie Nation Hotel for Women in Los Angeles (Ginger is her roommate).

Measurements: 34-25-34; she is 5 feet, 4 inches tall and has brown hair and wears a size 7 shoe.

Education: Middleton Elementary School; Snyder High School.

Pet Goldfish: Cletus and Oscar.

Member: A.G.O.A. (American Gun Owners Association). She has a chrome-plated .357 Magnum that was given to her by her father with the words "Keep your chin up and your skirt down" (she hides the gun in her "pink jammy bunny with a zipper in its tummy").

VIRGINIA "GINGER" ST. JAMES

Birthday: December 30, 1956, in Buffalo, New York.

Education: Buffalo High School.

Measurements: 34-26-36. She stands 5 feet, 7 inches tall and has dark brown hair and wears a size 8½ shoe.

Character: The only featured African American waitress. Her teenage years were difficult, as she was slow to develop and became jealous of girls with fuller figures. To attract boys, she stuffed her bra with socks but was caught and called "Booby Soxer." She flirts with patrons and at one point had a wealthy admirer name his yacht after her (*Ginger Snaps*).

Dream: To become a fashion designer.

Relatives: Unnamed grandmother (Eyde Bryde).

MARGARET "MAGGIE" MCBIRNEY

Birthday: April 11, 1939, in Ohio. She is the oldest of the waitresses.

Marital Status: Widow. Her late husband, Joseph, a salesman for Kitchen Help Dishwashers, was her everything. She is now living in a somewhat depressed state, as all she has are the memories of her life with Joseph.

Address: 1417 Brooke Avenue.

Character: Attractive but seemingly not interested in starting a new relationship (she tends to restrain herself if a man shows interest in her).

NANCY BEEBEE

Place of Birth: South Philadelphia in 1939.

Position: Restaurant hostess.

Prior Job: Ballerina, then waitress at Above the Top.

Character: Always elegantly dressed (adds an air of sophistication to the restaurant) but snobbish and often finds herself disciplining her waitress staff for their antics.

Husband: Howard (Richard Stahl), the restaurant's top chef. Howard, born in Trenton, New Jersey, enjoys fishing on Oregon's Rogue River and has a pet dog (Bluto) and two fish (Ike and Mamie).

Relatives: Nancy's sister, Gloria Beebee (Linda G. Miller); cousin, Grace Beebee (Kelly Britt); Howard's daughter, Lori Miller, from a prior marriage (Sue Ball).

SONNY MANN

Parents: Rose (Nita Talbot) and Irv (Paul Kreppel) Manischewitz.

Brother: Buddy Manischewitz (Donnelly Rhodes).

Place of Birth: Reno, Nevada. He changed his real last name (Manischewitz) to Mann, as it is better sounding for his budding career as a lounge singer; he calls himself "The Singing Sex Sensation."

Occupation: "One Man Entertainment Center" (as he calls himself) at Above the Top.

Idol: Singer Jack Jones.

Character: Obnoxious at times, as he not only hits on women but also stages elaborate shows when record producers are restaurant patrons.

Membership: The Bullwinkle the Moose Fan Club (from the TV series *Rocky and His Friends*).

Prized Collection: Franklin Mint All Nation Dolls.

Book: Mann to Man: A Man's Guide to Picking Up Girls. When no publisher would touch it, he had 750 copies printed by a vanity press.

Nightclub Performances: Vinnie's Romper Room and the Play Pen Lounge at Chuck's Game Room in Las Vegas.

Pet Dog as a Kid: Buster.

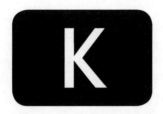

Kate & Allie

(CBS, 1984–1989)

Cast: Susan Saint James (Kate McArdle), Jane Curtin (Allie Lowell), Ari Meyers (Emma McArdle), Allison Smith (Jennie Lowell), Frederick Koehler (Chip Lowell), Sam Freed (Bob Barsky).

Basis: Two divorced women, Kate (the mother of Emma) and Allie (the mother of Jennie and Chip), attempt to rebuild their lives as single mothers while sharing an apartment to save on expenses in New York's Greenwich Village.

KATHERINE "KATE" MCARDLE

Place of Birth: New York City on August 14, 1946.

Mother: Marian Hanlan (Marian Seldes).

Maiden Name: Katherine Hanlan.

Ex-Husband: Max McArdle (John Heard), an actor now living in California.

Occupation: Housewife. She later works for the Sloane Travel Agency.

Measurements: 36-27-34. She has brown hair and wears a size 5½ dress and a size 8½ shoe.

Education: New York University. She was a radical college student during the 1960s (attended Woodstock in 1969, protested government policies, and burned her bra).

First Meeting: She and Allie met at the orthodontist's office as kids.

Bank: Holland Savings Bank (375-70-60-572 is her savings account number).

Habit: Smoking (which she is trying to break).

Quirk: Always gives Allie a purse on her birthday.

TV Appearance: She and Allie appeared on *The Dick Cavett Show* with the topic "Combining Households to Save Money."

Pretense: Although Kate and Allie are not lesbians, they pretended to be such a couple when a new landlord took over the building but wanted couple-only tenants.

ALLIE LOWELL

Full Name: Allison "Allie" Julie Charlotte Adams Lowell.

Place of Birth: New York City on September 6, 1947. She stands 5 feet, 5½ inches tall.

Parents: Joan (Rosemary Murphy, then Scotty Bloch) and Dr. Ed Adams (Robert Cornthwaite).

Maiden Name: Allison Adams.

Education: Lexington High School. She returned to school (Washington Square College) to study art history.

Ex-Husband: Charles Lowell (Paul Hecht), a doctor now living in Connecticut. He is married to Claire (Wendie Malick) and is the father of Stuart. Allie and Charles were planning to name their firstborn child (Jennie) Tiffany (if a girl) or Brooks (if a boy).

Second Husband: Robert "Bob" Barsky, a former football player turned sportscaster for WNDT-TV, Channel 10, in Washington, D.C. (he commutes between New York and Washington and does the "Sports Update" for the *11 O'Clock News*). When Allie and Bob move into Apartment 21C on West 55th Street, Kate joins them when Emma enters college. As a kid, Bob was called "Mickey Pants" (he was playing baseball [left field] when a mouse ran up his pants leg; he dropped his pants in front of everyone to let the mouse escape). Bob's mother, Eileen Barsky, was played by Elizabeth Parrish.

Occupation: Housewife. Part-time jobs: bookstore salesclerk; 9th Street Cinema box office cashier, law firm receptionist, selling posters at a museum gift shop, and volunteer at Channel G, a Manhattan cable station run by a woman named Eddie Gordon (Andrea Martin). In 1988, Kate and Allie formed their own company, "Kate and Allie Caterers" (which they operate from their apartment).

Quirk: Always gives Kate a sweater as a gift.

Habit: Eating too much chocolate.

THE CHILDREN

Emma Jane McArdle, Kate's daughter, wears a size 5 dress, is quite studious, and attends Lexington High School. She is accepted into both Columbia University and the University of California, Los Angeles (UCLA), and chooses to attend Columbia in Manhattan. In 1987, she decides to attend her dream school, UCLA, and relocates to California.

Jennifer "Jennie" Lowell, Allie's eldest child, attends Lexington High School (later Columbia University; lives in dorm room 512). She is a bit more rebellious than Emma and works after school at a French diner called Le Bon Croissant. She is fashion conscious and would like to dress like Madonna, but Allie has forbidden that. As a teenager, Jennie felt she had a boyish figure and wished for larger breasts.

Chip Lowell, Allie's youngest child, attends Parkside Elementary School. He has a dog (Tristan) and a cat (Iggie) and loves animals but became a bit morbid when he opened a pet cemetery in his backyard. He considers Alan Thicke (star of the series *Growing Pains*) to be America's greatest actor and earned money by delivering bagels to the neighbors. Brad Davidson played Chip as an adult in flash-forwards.

Knight Rider
(NBC, 1982–1986)

Cast: David Hasselhoff (Michael Knight), Edward Mulhare (Devon Miles), William Daniels (voice of K.I.T.T.).

Basis: A lone crusader (Michael Knight) battles crime and corruption with the aid of K.I.T.T., an indestructible, talking car of the future.

MICHAEL KNIGHT

Real Name: Michael Arthur Long.

Place and Year of Birth: Reno, Nevada, in 1949.

Military Service: Joined the Green Berets when he turned 20; served a three-year tour of duty in Vietnam (working in counterintelligence).

Occupation: Detective with the Nevada Police Department (after his military discharge), then undercover detective with the 11th Precinct of the Los Angeles Police Department (when relocating to California in 1982; he was also said to be with the Las Vegas Police Department).

Badge Number: 8043.

Address: 1834 Shore Road.

Life Changer: During an assignment, Michael is shot in the face and left for dead in the desert. He is found by Wilton Knight (Richard Basehart), a dying billionaire and the owner of Knight Industries. Specialized surgery saves Michael's life, and his face is reconstructed to look like Wilton's face when he was young. He is given a new identity (Michael Knight) and a mission: bring to justice criminals who believe they are above the law as part of the Foundation for Law and Government. Devon Miles is its head (drives a Mercedes-Benz convertible). Richard Basehart also narrates the opening theme.

Signature Look: Maroon T-shirt, blue jeans, and a black leather jacket.

K.I.T.T. (KNIGHT INDUSTRIES TWO THOUSAND)

Car Type: Black Pontiac Trans Am.

License Plate: KNIGHT.

Engineers: Bonnie Barstow (Patricia Richardson) and April Curtis (Rebecca Holden).

Car Serial Number: Alpha Delta 227529.

Ability: To speak through ultrasophisticated and elaborate microcircuitry.

Features: Molecular-bonded body; programmed to protect human life and avoid collisions. Long-range tracking scopes, turbo boost, normal and auto driving capabilities; superpursuit mode. A third-stage aquatic synthesizer allows it to ride on water (developed by April); analysis through a minilab; road detection through red flashing grill lights. When on the road and not in use, K.I.T.T. is housed in the Roving Knight Industries portable lab, a black-with-gold-trim, 18-wheel truck (distinguished by a chess knight symbol), plate 1U1 3265.

Mobile Unit: SID (Satellite Infiltration Drone), a bugging device that can go where the car cannot (developed by Bonnie).

Prototype: K.A.R.R. (Knight Automated Roving Robot), an evil car (voiced by Peter Cullen). Wilton designed it to be "the car of the future" but neglected to incorporate a program to respect life. It is now self-servicing with only one goal: to survive at any cost.

Enemy: Goliath, a seemingly indestructible truck that was built by Wilton's genius son, Garthe (David Hasselhoff), a man who is seeking to kill Michael because he is a living-and-breathing insult to his likeness.

Nickname: Michael calls K.I.T.T. "Buddy."

PILOT FILM UPDATE

Knight Rider 2000 (1991). It is the year 2000, and the Foundation for Law and Government (FLAG) and Knight Industries have become the Knight Foundation, an independent corporation that assists various police departments.

Foundation Head: Devon Miles.

Chief Operative: Michael Knight. Although Michael had retired in 1990 (operating a bass-fishing charter service), he returns to help Devon. Michael now lives in a house by the lake and drives a classic 1957 Chevrolet.

K.I.T.T.

Upgrade: The Knight Rider 4000. The original K.I.T.T. was dismantled, and his parts were sold off; all but one memory chip were recovered to rebuild K.I.T.T.

Cost: $10 million.

Features: A three-liter, 300-horsepower engine that operates on nonpolluting hydrogen fuel refined from gases emitted in algae fields. It can go from 0 to 300 miles per hour in a matter of seconds and detect odors and immobilize criminals with sonic beams. A collision factor analyzer alerts Michael when it is safe to run a red light or speed through traffic. Virtual reality presents an enhanced simulation of the road's topography; a thermal expander can heat the air in the tires of pursuing cars and explode them. Digital sampling allows K.I.T.T. to analyze voice patterns and duplicate them exactly.

New Agent: Shawn McCormick (Susan Norman). During a case investigation, Shawn, an officer with the Metropolitan Police Department, is shot in the head. An operation saves her life, and a computer chip is used to restore her memory. Shawn, however, quits the force when she learns she will be relegated to desk duty and applies for a position at the Knight Foundation. She is hired (and teamed with Michael) when Russell "Russ" Maddock (Carmen Argenziano), the designer of the Knight 4000, discovers that Shawn carries K.I.T.T.'s missing memory chip (which was sold to a trauma hospital). Adam 20-20 was her police car code.

REBOOT 1: TEAM KNIGHT RIDER (1997–1998)

Michael Knight retires from the Knight Foundation, and TKR (Team Knight Rider) is formed: Kyle Stewart (Brixton Karnes), Jenny Andrews (Christine Steele), Erica West (Kathy Tragester), Duke DePalma (Duane Davis), and Kevin "Trek" Sanders (Nick Wechsler). The team is based in *Sky One*, a large cargo plane controlled by a sexy-voiced computer (Linda McCullough). It also incorporates five talking vehicles: Dante (Ford Expedition sport-utility vehicle; driven by Kyle and voiced by Tom Kane), Kat (motorcycle driven by Erica; voiced by Andrea Beutner), Domino (Ford Mustang GT; driven by Jenny and voiced by Nia Valdaros), Beast (Ford F-150 truck; also called "Attack Beast"; driven by Duke and voiced by Kerrigan Mahan), and Pluto (motorcycle; driven by Trek and voiced by John Kissir).

Kyle leads the team, a former CIA operative who was called "America's James Bond." He was hired as the team leader when his cover was exposed.

Jenny, a tough ex–marine sergeant, was raised in a military family and fought in the 1991 Gulf War.

Erica, a blonde with a mysterious past, is an expert con artist who, after serving three years in prison, was released to Kyle to use her skills to help TKR.

Duke, born in Chicago, fought his way out of the slums to become a small-time boxer, then a police officer. He was recruited for his connection with the common man.

Kevin, nicknamed "Trek" for his obsession with *Star Trek*, has an IQ of 200, graduated from the Massachusetts Institute of Technology at the age of 12, and joined TKR because it intrigued him.

REBOOT 2: KNIGHT RIDER (2008)

K.I.T.T. has been upgraded to the Knight Industries 3000 (voice of Val Kilmer) by scientist Charles Garinman (Bruce Davison). He is assisted by his daughter,

Sarah (Deanne Russo), a 24-year-old PhD candidate at Stanford University. She drives a silver Ford Escape (plate 6EX 1928).

Driver: Michael "Mike" Traceur (Justin Bruening), a 23-year-old ex–Army Ranger (later called Michael Knight to keep his past a secret). Michael was born on June 10, 1983; weighs 185 pounds; and stands 6 feet, 3 inches tall.

K.I.T.T. Improvements: Morphing abilities (change color and shape), super-pursuit mode, advanced attack mode, turbo boost (allows K.I.T.T. to become airborne), underwater capability, grappling hook, offensive missiles, parachute (to stop safely at high speeds), immobilizing dart gun, sonic wave inhibitor, a 3-D generator (presents a holographic image), and a self-destruct program.

K.I.T.T.'s Morphing Identities: Hero, a Ford Mustang Shelby GT 500 KR that appears as any ordinary car; *K.I.T.T. Attack*, a high-speed version of *Hero* that transforms into an attack vehicle; and *K.I.T.T. Remote*, a driverless version of *Hero*. In this series, K.I.T.T. refers to K.A.R.R. ("Knight Auto-Cybernetic Roving Robot Exoskeleton"). It is revealed that K.A.R.R. killed seven people before it was taken off-line.

Note: Knight Rider 2010 is a 1994 pilot film that is believed to be a spin-off from *Knight Rider* but is a separate entity. Two brothers, Jake (Richard Joseph Paul) and Will McQueen (Michael Beach), use a specially equipped 1969 Ford Mustang to battle crime. Hannah (voice of Heidi Leich) is the onboard computer that assists them.

Life Goes On
(ABC, 1989–1993)

Cast: Patti LuPone (Libby Thatcher); Bill Smitrovich (Drew Thatcher); Kellie Martin (Becca Thatcher); Monique Lanier, then Tracey Needham (Paige Thatcher); Chris Burke (Corky Thatcher); Mary Page Keller (Gina Giordano).

Basis: Dramatic incidents in the lives of the Thatchers, a Catholic family living in Glen Brook, Illinois: parents Libby and Drew and their children, Paige, Becca, and Corky.

ELIZABETH "LIBBY" THATCHER
Place of Birth: Illinois in May 1949 (she is a Taurus; stands 5 feet, 2 inches tall; has dark brown hair; and wears a size 7 shoe).

Parents: Sal (Al Ruscio) and Teresa Giordano (Penny Santon).

Maiden Name: Libby Giordano.

Address: 305 Woodridge Road.

Telephone Number: 555-1967.

Education: Marshall High School; Glen Brook Junior College.

Occupation: Housewife. Libby was originally a singer and actress (worked under the name Libby Dean; starred in a production of *West Side Story*). She is later an account executive at the Berkson and Berkson Advertising Agency; her boss, Jerry Berkson (Ray Buktenica), calls her "Libs." Martin Sporting Goods was her first account.

Favorite TV Soap Opera: Forever and a Day.

Pet Dog: Arnold ("The Semi-Wonder Dog").

Car License Plate: JNE 734 (later RAH 207).

Quirk: Programs the automatic coffeemaker to activate at 6:55 a.m.; sets the clock alarm to wake her and Drew first at 7:00 a.m., then 6:45 a.m.; buys mostly No Frills products at the supermarket.

Clockwise from left: Patti LuPone, Bill Smitrovich, Kellie Martin, Monique Lanier, and Christopher Burke with Arnold (dog). *ABC/Photofest.* ©*ABC*

Relatives: Cousins, Angela Giordano (Gina Hecht) and Gabrielle "Gaby" Giordano (Patti LuPone).

ANDREW "DREW" THATCHER
Place of Birth: Illinois on May 16, 1947.
Father: Jack Thatcher (Pat Hingle).

Brother: Richard Thatcher (Rick Rosenthal).

Occupation: Operates the Glen Brook Grill; originally employed by the Quentico Construction Company.

Education: Marshall High School. Drew married Katherine Henning after graduating, and they became the parents of Paige. They divorced several years later.

First Date with Libby: The Glen Brook Drive-In to see the movies *Curse of the Swamp Creature* and *Curse of the Stone Hand* in Drew's old Plymouth. They dated, married, and became the parents of Becca and Corky; Paige came to live with them. On May 5, 1991, Libby gives birth to a son whom she and Drew name Nicholas James Thatcher.

Dream Car: An Austin-Healey 3000.

Relatives: Cousin, Frances (Claire Berger).

Ghost Sequence: Drew's grandfather (Bert Remsen).

PAIGE THATCHER

Natural Mother: Katherine Henning (Lisa Banes).

Nickname: Called "Button" by Drew.

Pet Rabbits: Sammy and Matilda.

Hobby: Painting.

Occupation: The original Paige (Monique Lanier) worked as a receptionist at the Matthews Animal Hospital but left home at the end of the first season. When the new Paige (Tracey Needham) returned in November 1990, she moved back in with her parents but seemed to lack direction. She worked at several temporary jobs before enrolling in acting class at Glen Brook Community College. When this failed, she became a waitress at the family diner, then a "cross worker" (doing what is necessary) at Stollmark Metal Industries.

Love: A roustabout sculptor named Michael Romanov (Lance Guest). They married, moved to Europe, and divorced 10 weeks later when Michael chose work over Paige and left her stranded in Bulgaria. She returned home and found work at the Darlind Construction Company. Michael called her "Gus."

Flashbacks: Paige as a girl (Jenna Pangburn).

REBECCA "BECCA" THATCHER

Age: 15 (born on October 16, 1974). She has brown hair and weighs 85 pounds.

Regret: Small breasts (in the opening theme, Becca looks sideways into a mirror and says, "Come on, where are you guys already?"). Life changed a year later when she did develop and Paige called her "a major babe." It also made her realize she was not the "ugly duckling" she thought she was.

Education: Marshall High School (editor of *The Underground Marshall*, the school's alternative newspaper; also a member of the debate team and the gymnastics team); Brown University (studying medicine); Harvard Medical School.

Talent: Writing (at one point, she hoped to become a journalist).

Ability: Dancing (took ballet lessons from Lillian Doubsha [Viveca Linford], a world-famous ballerina).

Character: Bright, pretty, often self-conscious, always willing to help others.

Boyfriend: Jesse McKenna (Chad Lowe), an artist who was HIV positive. He painted a picture of Becca in the nude—and displayed it at the Glen Brook Bookstore.

Best Friend: Maxine "Maxie" Maxwell (Tanya Fenmore). Maxie is physically more developed than Becca but a bit flaky and boy crazy. Just the opposite is Rona Lieberman (Michele Matheson), a girl with a gorgeous face and figure (the envy of Becca and Maxie) who uses her beauty to become the best at everything.

Beauty Pageant: Becca, under the sponsorship of the Glen Brook Savings Bank, entered the Tri-State Teenage Miss Pageant; she was crowned third runner-up and received a $5,000 scholarship. Rona, who has been entering beauty pageants since she was a child, won first runner-up and a $10,000 college scholarship.

Favorite Breakfast: French toast with whipped cream.

Flashbacks: Becca as a child (Heather Lind).

CHARLES THATCHER

Year of Birth: 1971.

Nicknames: "Corky" and "The Cork."

Medical Condition: Has Down syndrome (one of the first such characters [real life too] to be featured on a TV series).

Education: The Fowler Institution; Marshall High School (although older than other students, Corky became "one of the guys," proving that even with a handicap, he could become a part of society and do what other kids do—from playing drums to running for class president). It was his decision to enter a mainstream school, and as a result, his grades suffered, especially in math.

Occupation: Student. He had a paper route, worked at the family diner, and was an usher at the Glen Rock Theater (earning $165 every two weeks).

Accomplishment: The Glen Brook 50K Bike Race (wore number 277). Although he came in last, it was a victory for Corky, as he was able to accomplish something.

Favorite Sandwich: Ham and cheese on whole-wheat bread; sliced turkey on raisin bread.

Girlfriend: Amanda Swanson (Andrea Friedman), a girl also suffering from Down syndrome. They impulsively married, and while she attended college, they lived on what Corky earned as an usher.

ANGELA "GINA" GIORDANO

Relationship: Libby's younger sister (brought on in 1990–1991 to help Libby care for her family during her pregnancy).

Daughter: Nine-year-old Zoe (Leigh Ann Orsi).

Husband: Dennis Rydell (Drew Pillsbury), from whom she is separated (deserted her when he learned she was pregnant).

Quirk: Impressed by people who can cook.

Occupation: Housewife and owner of an unnamed cheesecake business.

MacGyver
(ABC, 1985–1992)

Cast: Richard Dean Anderson (Angus MacGyver), Dana Elcar (Peter Thornton), Elyssa Davalos (Nikki Carpenter).

Basis: A lone survival expert and scientific genius (MacGyver) uses his unique skills to perform seemingly impossible missions for the Phoenix Foundation.

ANGUS "MAC" MACGYVER

Place of Birth: Mission City, Minnesota (also said to be in Missouri).

Birthday: January 23, 1951 (also given as March 23). On his tenth birthday, Mac received a chemistry set that piqued his interest in science; he recalls his mother saying, "He would either come up with a formula that would improve the world or blow up the house trying to do so." It took him years to perfect a nonalcoholic eggnog drink.

Name Note: MacGyver originally had no first name and was called "Mac" or "MacGyver," as that was what he preferred. In the 1991 episode "Goodnight, MacGyver," his first name is revealed to be Angus. In a preproduction press release, "Stacey" was listed as Mac's first name. His grandfather, Harry Jackson, calls him "Bud."

Occupation: Agent (troubleshooter) for the Phoenix Foundation for Research, an organization involved in environmental issues and foreign affairs; he previously worked for Western Tech, U.S. intelligence, the Department of External Services (DXS), and The Company. Because of the nature of his job, Mac says, "I'm sort of a repairman."

Education: Mission City High School (where he met his first girlfriend, Ellen Stewart [Mary Ann Pascal]); Western Technical College (spent summer vacations working as an usher at Met baseball stadium, but he also says he worked as a rigging slinger at an Oregon logging camp).

Languages: American Sign Language, Russian, Italian, German, Spanish, and French.

Home: A houseboat (Marina Slip 22, Meridian Dock 1, Santa Louisa, California); a loft over a Los Angeles hardware store owned by sculptor Melvin Krasney; the Griffiths Observatory; an apartment above the Coney Island stand in Venice Beach.

Phone Number: 555-8990.

Foster Child: Sue Ling (not seen; adopted as a child through the Asian Orphan Foundation; she was killed during the student protests in China in Tiananmen Square).

Favorite Sports: Ice hockey and automotive racing.

Musical Ability: The guitar.

Cars: Jeep Cherokee Chief (plate IRJQ 104); Jeep Grand Wagoneer; Jeep Wrangler CJ7; 1946 Ford Truck (plate 21AB 345); 1957 Chevy Nomad (plate 2ASB 795).

Food Preference: Vegetarian. He will not drink coffee but likes tofu.

Favorite Movie Genre: Westerns.

Alias: Dexter Fillmore, a nerdy character he uses to fool people.

Dislike: Firearms. In 1963, Mac (Sean Wohland) and three friends, Neal (Marc Reid), Chuck (Gregory Togel), and Jesse (Dustin Hyland), found a gun. Neal aimed it at a hawk in a tree and was about to shoot it when Mac knocked the gun out of his hand. The gun hit the ground and discharged, killing Jesse. Mac has since been reluctant to use a gun; it is only in the pilot episode that Mac is seen firing a rifle at the enemy.

Ability: To take unrelated items and make them into something: "It's not necessarily what I bring along with me; it's what I find along the way." He is also an expert in Morse code, military signal flags, mountain climbing, hang gliding, and skydiving.

Favorite Survival Items: Duct tape ("it has a million uses") and a Swiss army knife.

Mac's First Telecast Assignment: Seeking a downed air force jet in central Asia.

Twist: In "The Stringer" (April 25, 1992), the series' supposedly final episode, Mac meets Shawn A. Molloy (Dalton James), a photojournalist and the son he never knew he had, while investigating a case involving smuggled goods. Shawn is the son of Kate Molloy (Lisa Savage), Mac's college girlfriend (a photojournalist killed during the democratic movement in China). Mac learns that the "A" in Shawn's name stands for "Angus," and the locket he carries has a picture of his mother and a man who was unknown to him until now—MacGyver. After completing the assignment, Mac leaves the Phoenix Foundation to spend time with his son. The actual final episode, "The Mountain of Youth," aired on May 21, 1992, and was unrelated to the above episode.

Terminology: The steps Mac takes to resolve situations are called "Mac-Gyverisms," although all the scientific principals involved are not shown (to prevent real-life copycat situations).

Charity Work: The Derpin Society (to save sea otters).

Relatives: Grandfather, Harry Jackson (John Anderson), lives in Missouri.

Flashbacks: Mac, as a boy (Sean Wohland, then Shawn Donahue); Mac's father, James MacGyver (Phil Redrow, then Martin Milner); Mac's mother, Ellen MacGyver (Sheila Moore); Harry's wife, Cindy Jackson (Jan Jordan). Mac was raised by his mother and grandfather (who taught him the art of fair play) after his father (James) and grandmother (Cindy) were killed in a car accident on a stormy night. Mac first mentions this happened when he was seven years old, then 10 years of age.

PETER "PETE" THORNTON

Occupation: The deputy chief of the Department of External Affairs in 1980 (when he first met MacGyver); he resigned in 1986 to become the director of operations for the Phoenix Foundation (has security clearance 1A); it was at this time that Pete asked MacGyver to join him as a troubleshooter.

Birthday: December 18, 1933.

Ex-Wife: Connie Thornton (Linda Darlow, then Penelope Windust), an archaeologist.

Son: Michael Thornton (T. Scott Coffey).

Military Service: The Vietnam War.

Character: Stubborn, tolerant of MacGyver's actions, will not break the code of the Phoenix Foundation unless there is no other choice. In the first episode, Dana Elcar plays Andy Colson, the government agent for whom Mac works. It is through Pete's questioning of Mac that we learn how Mac does what he does: "Well, it comes down to me against the situation. I don't like the situation to win." Pete also says that when a rescue team is needed, "the team is MacGyver and only Mac."

Car License Plate: IRK 1567.

Medical Issue: In 1991, Dana Elcar was diagnosed with the eye disease glaucoma; Pete was also said to have the same condition.

NICOLE ANNE CARPENTER

Occupation: Agent for the Phoenix Foundation.

Place and Date of Birth: Washington, D.C., on May 30, 1959.

Nickname: Nikki.

Address: 2723 Forster Lane, Apartment 206, Los Angeles, California 90068.

Telephone Number: 818-555-3082.

Measurements: 36-24-34. She has brown hair and stands 5 feet, 10 inches tall and weighs 105 pounds.

Marital Status: Widow (although she never mentions this; always remarks that she is divorced).

Late Husband: Adam Carpenter (killed in a car bombing on March 14, 1985). Nikki worked as an investigator for a Senate subcommittee in Washington and uncovered incriminating evidence; she believes the bomb was a mob hit and meant to kill her.

Security Clearance: Level 6.

Driver's License: Type 2; expires October 5, 1989.

Training: Nikki mentions that she attended law school and has police training; it also appears she worked for an insurance company at one point. About working with Mac, she says, "I'm a professional, and you make things up as you go along." She also carries a gun, something that displeases MacGyver.

Note: Two TV movies were produced after the series ended: *MacGyver: Lost Treasure of Atlantis* and *MacGyver: Trail to Doomsday.*

REBOOT

MacGyver (CBS, 2016). Lucas Till is Angus "Mac" MacGyver, a resourceful troubleshooter for the Phoenix Foundation (now under the direction of Matilda "Matty" Webber [Meredith Eaton]; she replaced Patricia Thornton [Sandrine Holt] after 12 episodes when Patricia was found to be a double agent for a terrorist organization). George Eads is Jack Dalton, Mac's friend and field operative, a former Delta Force soldier; and Tristin Mays is Riley Davis, the foundation's technical specialist.

Magnum, P.I.
(CBS, 1980–1988)

Cast: Tom Selleck (Thomas Magnum), John Hillerman (Jonathan Higgins), Larry Manetti (Rick Wright), Roger E. Mosley (T.C. Calvin).

Basis: Thomas Magnum, a Hawaii-based private detective, solves crimes of the most deadly nature (murder) but also enjoys the good life, providing security for Robin Masters, a mysterious pulp writer who lives on a fabulous estate.

THOMAS SULLIVAN MAGNUM IV

Place of Birth: Detroit, but grew up in Tidewater, Virginia.

Birthday: Unclear. He is said to be 34 when the series begins, making his birthday coincide with his driver's license date of January 5, 1946, but he is also said to be born on August 8, 1944, and in 1945 and 1947.

Father: Thomas Magnum III, a navy aviator killed in the Korean War (in 1951); his grandfather is Captain Thomas Sullivan Magnum I (Howard Duff);

Clockwise from top: John Hillerman, Roger E. Mosley, Tom Selleck, and Larry Manetti. *CBS/Photofest. ©CBS*

Catherine Peterson (Gwen Verdon) is his mother, and Frank Peterson (David Huddleston) is his stepfather. It is said that Thomas had a half brother (Joey) who died in Vietnam.

Late Wife: Michelle (played in flashbacks by Marta DuBois).

Education: The U.S. Naval Academy (where he played quarterback on the football team; both the Class of 1967 and the Class of 1968 are given).

Languages: English, French, and Vietnamese.

Military Service: Navy SEAL with the VM02 (Marine Corps Helicopter Observation Squadron 02) in Da Nang during the Vietnam War. He next served as an intelligence officer and resigned in 1979 (after 12 years of service) as a lieutenant commander ("I woke up one morning and realized I was 33 and never 23"). He wears a Cross of Lorraine ring from his time in Vietnam, and in the final episode, Magnum relinquishes his job at Robin's Nest to return to naval intelligence (with the rank of commander).

Occupation: Owner of Thomas Magnum Investigations. He also worked temporarily as the house detective for the Hawaiian Gardens Hotel (but was angered because he wasn't allowed to carry a gun). As a kid, Magnum's first job was delivering newspapers for the *Tidewater Daily Sentinel* (earned $12 a week plus one cent for each paper he sold). He hates being called a private eye or a private detective; he prefers private investigator. It was after his hitch in the navy that he established his business but was also, in a way, a beach bum, with few clients and no money; six months later, he secured the job for Robin Masters.

Address: The guesthouse on Robin's Nest (Robin Masters Estate) on Concord Road on the north shore of Hawaii (later said to be on 1429 [then 1541] Kalakaua Avenue). He lived previously at 11435 18th Avenue, Honolulu, HI 96816. "Rosebud" is the password to the estate's computer system.

Fee: $200 a day plus expenses for his investigation services (he will lower it to $175 a day if he sees a client is strapped for money).

Author: Writing a book called *How to Be a World-Class Private Investigator* (the rules of which he often relates to the audience while on a case).

Exercise: Swimming, playing tennis, running, and volleyball. He exercises his mind by attempting the *New York Times* Sunday crossword puzzle.

Favorite TV Series: Hogan's Heroes.

Favorite Movie: Stalag 17.

Favorite Sport: Baseball (Magnum is often seen wearing a Detroit Tigers baseball cap with Al's Automotive and Muffler King as a sponsor) or a U.S. Navy SEAL cap. He is also a fan of football and softball. He is fond of a red "Jungle Bird" Hawaiian shirt and wears a Rolex watch that belonged to his father.

Awards: Navy Cross, Purple Heart, Surface Warfare Pin, National Defense Service Medal, Vietnam Gallantry Cross, and the Republic of Vietnam Campaign Medal.

Favorite Music Groups: Blondie, Jefferson Starship, and Styx. He also has audio-cassettes of Bach and Beethoven (to show Higgins he has some class).

Favorite Bar: The King Kamehameha Club (located on Old Pali Road).

Favorite Drinks: Old Dusseldorf beer; scotch on the rocks.

Cars: A red Ferrari 308 GTS with the license plate ROBIN 1 (but also seen as 5GE 478 and 308 TTS); a red Audi 3000 (plate ROBIN 2).

Phone Number: 555-2131.

Quirk: Hangs his head when he becomes frustrated. He also acts like a big brother to the girls he meets and hates to be called "Tommy."

Weapon: A Colt Government Model .45 ACP M-1911 handgun (which he used in Vietnam). A Colt Government Model 9-mm Parabellum is used in firing scenes.

Childhood: Magnum was a fan of western star Roy Rogers's movies and pretended to be a hero to keep his neighborhood safe from outlaws.

Catchphrase: "I know what you're thinking" (addressing the audience through narration about a situation he just encountered).

Relatives: Cousins, Karyn (Julie Cobb) and Billy (Brandon Call); aunt, Phoebe Sullivan (Barbara Rush).

Flashbacks: Thomas as a boy (R.J. Williams); Thomas's mother (Susan Blanchard); Thomas's father (Robert Pine).

JONATHAN QUAYLE HIGGINS III

Place of Birth: England in 1920. He claims to be the second son of the Duke of Perth and is himself the Baron of Perth.

Position: Major Domo of Robin's estate (which he calls "Robin's Nest"). In 1957, he ran a hotel called the Arlington Arms, which catered to the rich and famous.

Education: The Eton School and Sandhurst Academy (a military college). He also claims to have a 1947 doctorate in mathematics from Cambridge University.

Military Service: MI-5 and MI-6 (British intelligence) during World War II; a sergeant major in the British army's West Yorkshire Regiment (awarded the Victoria Cross).

Author: Writing a book called *Crises at Suez*, which recalls his war experiences as a survival expert. He was a prisoner during the war and helped build the famous Bridge on the River Kwai (a model of which also appears in his office).

Hobbies: Building model bridges and painting. He created his own blend of tea called Lady Ashley Tea and enjoys doing the *Times of London* Sunday crossword puzzle.

Catchphrase: "Oh my God!" (usually when reacting to something Magnum has done).

Ham Radio Call Letters: NR6DBZ.

Guard Dogs: Apollo and Zeus (Doberman pinschers that patrol the estate grounds and that he calls "The Lads"—and that are not particularly fond of Magnum).

Activity: Chairman of the board of the King Kamehaneha Club; chairman of the Honolulu branch of the Britannic Seaman's Fund charity.

Secret: Thomas believes (is 99 percent sure) that Higgins is actually Robin Masters ("But it is that 1 percent that could mean disaster").

Cars: A GMC station wagon (plate ROBIN 3).

Mobile Car Code: N6DBZ.

Weapon of Choice: A British Webley Mk-VI .455-caliber revolver (from his service with the British army).

Relationship: Magnum claims that between him and Higgins, it "consists of arguing, yelling and constant, long boring stories and constant not knocking on my door."

Quirk: Rambles when asked a question.

Relatives: Jonathan's half brothers, Father Paddy MacGuinness (an Irish priest) and Don Luis Monqueo, heir to the throne of Costa De Rosa in South America (John Hillerman); niece, Jilly Mack (Sally Pontig). Unseen (all by the same father but different mothers): Albert Stanley Higgins, Elmo Ziller (owns a rodeo in Texas), Soo Ling (Chinese), Elizabeth Whitefeather (Native American), and Catoomba Noomba (African).

Flashbacks: Jonathan as a boy (Robert Mederros III).

ORVILLE WILBUR "RICK" WRIGHT

Relationship: Magnum's friend. He has numerous underworld connections and helps Magnum by obtaining street information.

Place of Birth: Chicago.

Military Service: Same unit as Magnum; he was a weapons expert.

Occupation: Owner of Rick's Place, a disco-themed nightclub (later the manager of the King Kamehameha Club). The club is also called Rick's Cafe Americain (based on the café from the film *Casablanca*).

Cars: A Datsun and a Mercedes-Benz.

Relatives: Sister, Wendy (Alice Cadogan).

THEODORE "T.C." CALVIN

Relationship: Magnum's friend.

Military Service: Chopper pilot in Vietnam (same unit as Magnum). He graduated from college in 1968, then joined the navy.

Occupation: Runs the Island Hopper Helicopter Service (rates are $100 an hour).

Helicopter: Various models of the Hughes 500D.

Van: A Volkswagen Caravelle.

Air Code: Bravo 516. Prior to the war, T.C. was a Golden Gloves boxer (also said to have been a football player).

Favorite Beverages: Milk, juice, soda, or coffee; he avoids alcoholic drinks.

Trait: Calls Higgins "Higgy Baby" and was the only character to call Higgins by his first name.

Marital Status: Divorced from Tina (Fay Hauser) and the father of Bryant (Shavar Ross).

ROBIN MASTERS

Robin, seen from the back only (Bruce Atkinson), is voiced by Orson Welles. The Home for Wayward Boys is his favorite charity. Thomas (jersey 4), Rick (jersey 17), and T.C. (jersey 32) are members of Robin's softball team, the Paddlers. Robin's first published story was "The Last Days of Babylon." Visitors to the estate must sign "The Robin's Nest Guest Book." *The Serpent's Wisdom* is one of the books mentioned as being written by Robin (whom Higgins calls "Mr. Masters").

Mama's Family
(NBC, 1983–1984; Syndicated, 1986–1990)

Cast: Vicki Lawrence (Thelma "Mama" Harper), Ken Berry (Vinton Harper), Dorothy Lyman (Naomi Harper), Eric Brown (Buzz Harper), Karin Argoud (Sonja Harper), Allan Kayser (Bubba Higgins), Beverly Archer (Iola Boylen).

Basis: A cantankerous old woman (called Mama) struggles to retain the position she once had (the guiding light of her family) despite the fact that her children (Ellen, Eunice, and Vinton) are grown and leading their own lives.

THELMA MAE "MAMA" HARPER
Place of Birth: Raytown U.S.A. (founded by James Ray and known as a state for "Farming, Industry, and Pork"). It was Sam Lincoln, a somewhat unstable man, who got the Auto Club to place Raytown on their road maps. Most businesses or areas of the town start with "Ray" (e.g., K-Ray Television, Ray Lake, St. Ray's Hospital, and Ray-Mart).

Maiden Name: Thelma Crowley (she is in her sixties when the series begins).

Address: 1542 Ray Lane (also given as 1542 Ray Way). The house was originally a brothel called Ma Beaudine's and was located at 10 Decatur Road. There are two plastic pink flamingos on the front lawn that Mama has named Milly and Willy.

Marital Status: Widower (her late husband, Carl, earned a living as a dockworker; he called her "Snooky Ookems" and passed away in 1973 in his favorite place, the bathroom).

Occupation: Housewife. Prior to her marriage, Mama was hostess at a USO (United Serviceman's Organization) canteen (of Raytown) during World War II. After raising her children, she became a receptionist at the Raytown Travel Agency, then a consumer consultant ("Ask Thelma") and checker at Food Circus. She attempted to market Mother Harper's Miracle Tonic (a cold remedy with a touch of vanilla extract and 35 percent alcohol that intoxicated users).

Education: Gilmore Junior High School; Raytown High School (where she was called "Hot Pants," a false, loose reputation created by a boy who couldn't have his way with her).

Childhood: Thelma was jump-rope champion of the second grade (and called "Watermelon Bottom"). She developed at an early age (now wears a 44D bra) and has become nagging and demanding. She was also a drum major-ette and lived on a farm (where she helped deliver the calf of a cow named Rita Rose).

Activities: Teaches ballet to retired people at the Raytown Senior Center; member of the Raytown Community Church League; founder of M.O.P. (Mothers Opposing Pornography).

Political Career: Ran for mayor in 1984 and defeated Mayor Alvin Tutweiller (Alan Oppenheimer); she quit when it became overwhelming for her.

Favorite Magazine: Ladies' Circle.

Favorite Perfume: Obsession.

Favorite Recipe: Million Dollar Fudge.

Favorite Hair Salon: The Beauty Spot.

Favorite Drink: Beer (it is the only thing that calms her or, as she says, makes her "stay lit").

Favorite Oven Cleaner: Easy-Off.

Favorite Store: Neidermeyer's Department Store.

Favorite Movies: Detective films of the 1930s and 1940s.

Favorite Dessert: Rhubarb pudding.

Clothing: Partial to flower-print dresses.

Addiction: The TV shopping channel K-Ray Teleshopper.

Hobby: Her rose garden (hopes to win the Crystal Thorne Award for her Herbert Hoover Roses).

Car: Mama first mentions she doesn't drive (due to a 1946 accident in which she left the house in a sedan and came home in a convertible). In 1984, she is seen purchasing a sedan that she calls "Blue Thunder" with the license plate GAH 320.

Pageant Title: First Runner-Up in the Lovely Be Lady Grandma U.S.A. Pageant.

Most Valuable Possessions: A diamond broach and the silver dinnerware left to her by her mother.

Family Tradition: Her children learning to tap dance because "there ain't a Harper who can't sing and dance."

Quirk: A stare she calls "The Look," which forces people to tell the truth; has a temper that often gets her into trouble.

Relaxation: Knitting.

Catchphrases: "Horse Pucky" and "Ut, Oh."

TV Shows: Jeopardy (where Mama won a Hawaiian vacation). With Vint, Naomi, Ellen, and Buzz, she appeared on *Family Feud* and lost (Sonja was strangely absent from this episode ["Family Feud"]).

Relatives: Cousins Lydia (Vicki Lawrence), Ruth (Annie O'Donnell), and Flor-ence (Debra Duggan); sister, Effie, who "has papers to prove she is crazy" (Dorothy Van); aunt, Gert (Imogene Coca); brother-in-law, Roy Harper

(Murray Hamilton). Unseen was Mama's "Crazy" Uncle Oscar, the owner of a car rental business who thought he was a pirate (Mama inherited his parrot, Captain Petey); Aunt Penelope, Uncle Baxter, and Uncle Willie (a flasher).

Flashbacks: Thelma as a young woman and Thelma's mother (Vicki Lawrence).

VINTON "VINT" HARPER

Relationship: Thelma's only son. Mama mentions that Vint was born in a hen-house, not a hospital.

Birthday: Given as April 23 in one episode, March 10 in another.

Birth Weight: 8 pounds, 2 ounces (he was 22 inches long).

Education: Edgar Allan Poe High School.

Occupation: Locksmith for Kwick Keys (owned by the Bernice Corporation).

Wife: Naomi Oates. His ex-wife, Mitzi, left him and the kids (Sonja and Buzz) for a job in Las Vegas as a cocktail waitress. Vint and Naomi had planned on operating a trailer park in Arizona after marrying, but the man with whom they entrusted their money ($5,000) stole it. They were then forced to move in with Mama (Vint and Naomi occupy the basement). Vint mentions that he, Sonja, and Buzz first moved in with Mama when his chinchilla farm fell through (due to mange).

Allergy: Allergic to strawberries. He also has sinus problems.

Hobby: Collecting *TV Guide* magazine (dates back to 1958; the issue with a caricature of Mister Ed on the cover is his favorite).

Club: The Mystic Order of the Cobra Club.

Bowling Team: Oak Park League (he believes the key to winning is "the thumb hold").

Favorite Hangout: Bigger Jigger Bar.

Favorite Eatery: Burger Barn.

Favorite Breakfast Cereal: Dino Puffs (for the surprise toy dinosaur in the box).

Favorite Card Game: Poker (he is a member of the Poker Pals).

Childhood: Teased at school for carrying a Binky Bunny lunchbox (made by Mama). He had a pet rabbit (Fluffy) and a paper route and was a Cub Scout and a member of the Raytown Little League. He had a 9 p.m. curfew at age 16 and a snake collection and dreamed of becoming a firefighter ("a hook-and-ladder man").

Quirk: After Mama took Vinton to see the movie *Pinocchio*, he now touches his nose when he lies to make sure it has not grown.

Talent: After winning a talent contest for dancing at the Bigger Jigger, Vinton attempted to break into show business as Vinnie Vegas.

Insurance Policy: Mutual of Raytown.

Flashbacks: Vinton as a boy (David Friedman).

NAOMI HARPER

Relationship: Vinton's second wife (married in 1983) but Naomi's fifth husband; Tommy Ray (also called Tommy Lee), Bill, Leonard, and George are her prior husbands.

Maiden Name: Naomi Oates.

Education: Edgar Allan Poe High School (where she met Vinton).

Occupation: Checker (then assistant manager) at Food Circus. She also wrestled briefly as "Queen Bee" in the Women's Wrestling League (Vinton was her ringside attendant, the Bee Keeper). She also attempted a catering business (Naomi's Catering) wherein she used day-old food from a local deli. Naomi can't cook, and Mama believes her idea of a balanced meal is "a chili dog in each hand."

Reputation: Known as "the sexiest woman in Raytown." Mama believes Naomi is the kind of girl whom mothers fear their sons will marry. Because of her sexy attire and flamboyant reputation, Mama believes she is not a respectable member of her family.

Nickname: Called "Skeeter" by Vinton.

Favorite Magazine: Instant Beautiful.

Favorite Eatery: The Java Stop (a truck stop café) off Route 32.

Pet Dog: Marlon (named after her favorite actor, Marlon Brando).

Favorite Candy: Red licorice whips.

Clothing: Partial to the color yellow (especially in dresses).

Final Episode: Naomi gives birth to a girl she and Vinton name Tiffany Thelma Harper. Just prior to the birth, Vinton and Naomi moved into a decrepit mobile home parked in Mama's driveway.

Relatives: Ex-husband, Leonard Oates (Jerry Reed).

OTHER CHARACTERS

Sonja and Buzz Harper are Vinton's children (by Mitzi) and are attending Edgar Allan Poe High School. Sonja, age 17, is named after her cousin, Sonja ("a schoolteacher for 35 years who went berserk and set the gym on fire"); she has a midnight curfew and has a wardrobe that is mostly unflattering (being that she is pretty, she is seen in sweatpants and loose-fitting blouses). Her favorite activity appears to be talking on the telephone. Mama's advice to her regarding boys: "Don't marry a locksmith." Sonja entered and won the 1984 Miss Rayteen Beauty Pageant.

Vinton Harper Jr., nicknamed "Buzz," has a 1:00 a.m. curfew and is somewhat girl crazy. His favorite sports are basketball and bowling, and he is a member of the school's debate team. He and Sonia were dropped in 1985 without explanation.

Iola Lucille Boylen is Mama's longtime friend and neighbor, a spinster who lives with her never-seen, overweight, and domineering mother. She is a member of the Pepperpot Playhouse Theater Company and enjoys knitting, sewing, and arts and crafts (she makes artworks from washed clothing lint [acquired from the local Laundromat lint traps]). Her ideal mate is an "understanding, decent, loving, handsome, successful blue-eyed man in the medical profession." She always says "Knock Knock" before opening the front door and entering Mama's house (she calls Mama "Thelma"). She is also the editor/publisher of the local newsletter, the *Gourmet Gazette*. She claims to be allergic to hamsters in one episode but later says she raised hamsters for 10 years. *The Wild and the Wonderful* is her favorite TV soap opera, and she is partial to the color pink.

Ellen Jackson (Betty White) is Thelma's firstborn daughter and married to Bruce, a man she leaves for cheating on her; she is later seen in the company of the town's mayor, Alvin Tutweiller. Ellen, a society woman (voted "Woman of the Year" by the Raytown Country Club), drives a Cadillac Seville. As a child, Ellen had a Storybook doll collection (which Vinton broke on her). Amy O'Nell plays Ellen as a child in flashbacks.

Eunice Higgins (Carol Burnett), Mama's neurotic daughter, is a walking nervous wreck and married to Ed Higgins (Harvey Korman), a hardware store owner. Ed calls Thelma "Mama Harper"; Mama would call Eunice "Missy" when she became angry at her. Eunice calls Naomi "a bleach-blonde bimbo." Tanya Fenmore and Heather Kerr played Eunice as a girl in flashbacks.

Fran Crowley (Rue McClanahan) is Thelma's younger sister, a spinster who writes "a column for the local paper that is thrown on the porch." Yellow roses are her favorite flower, and she has been writing a novel for 20 years that Mama calls "smut." Fran attends the First Methodist Church, is partial to rhinestone jewelry, and is frowned on by Mama when she drinks beer ("Because you can't hold your hooch"). Although Fran thinks she is perfect, she is high strung and easily excitable. She saved Thelma's life when they were children (on a Campfire Girl Scout trip when Thelma fell into a lake), and the Raytown Home for Wayward Girls is her favorite charity. Fran was written out when she died after eating a roast beef sandwich and choking on a toothpick in the bathroom at the Bigger Jigger bar.

Bubba Higgins is Mama's grandson (Eunice and Ed's son). Bubba, a delinquent, was arrested for stealing a car and placed in juvenile hall (called reform school by Thelma) for 14 months. Ed and Eunice, unable to take Bubba with them (as he is not allowed to leave the state), move to Florida, leaving Thelma to care for him. He attends Raytown Junior College and, like Vinton, believes he is a ladies' man.

Note: The program is a spin-off from sketches on *The Carol Burnett Show*.

Married . . . With Children
(Fox, 1987–1997)

Cast: Ed O'Neill (Al Bundy), Katey Sagal (Peggy Bundy), Christina Applegate (Kelly Bundy), David Faustino (Bud Bundy), Amanda Bearse (Marcy Rhoades), David Garrison (Steve Rhoades), Ted McGinley (Jefferson D'Arcy).

Basis: Life with an uncaring, self-centered family of four: parents Al and Peggy and their children, Kelly and Bud.

OVERALL SERIES INFORMATION

The Bundy's reside at 9674 (also seen as 9764) Jeopardy Lane in Chicago, Illinois (555-2878 is their phone number). Buck (then Lucky) is their pet dog. Al created a male Bundy chant ("Hooters, hooters. Yum, yum, yum. Hooters on a girl who's dumb"), and "Whoooa, Bundy!" is the family cheer. They also live by a motto: "A Bundy never wins, but a Bundy never quits," "When one Bundy is embarrassed, the rest of us feel good about ourselves," and "When you are going to lose, lose big."

For Thanksgiving, the family celebrates with its traditional meal, a pizza (called "The Bundy Turkey"); Labor Day finds the Bundy BBQ and Bundy Burgers ("last year's grease and ashes for this year's burgers"). The 1989 episode "I'll See You in Court" (canceled before its February 19 airing) is "The Lost Episode," as it did not air on Fox but only in syndication for the first time in 2002 on FX (Al and Peggy's involvement in a motel sex tape was considered too risqué to air). Teresa Parente had the recurring role of Miranda Veracruz de la Jolla Cardinale, the TV news reporter.

ALVIN "AL" BUNDY

Place of Birth: Chicago on November 7, 1948.

Parents: Unnamed father (Cliff Bemis, then Ed O'Neill) and mother (Gita Isak).

Occupation: Salesman at Gary's Shoes and Accessories for the Beautiful Woman (in the New Market Mall); his boss is a woman named Gary (Janet Carroll). Al's failed moneymaking attempts include a $50,000 investment in the "Dr. Shoe" telephone hotline (555-Shoe; the episode title, "976-Shoe," reflects a different phone number), TV pitchman for Zeus Athletic Shoes, security guard at Polk High School, counter "boy" at Burger Trek fast food, and Al Bundy's House of Sole (selling 1970s-style shoes).

Yearly Salary: $12,000.

Company Newsletter: Shoe News. In an attempt to get his name in print, Al teamed with Kelly to produce a movie called *Sheos* (Kelly misspelled "Shoes"). The National Endowment for the Arts gave Al $10,000, and he produced *A Day in the Life of a Shoe Salesman*—a disaster that got him in *Shoe News* but with the headline "Big Idiot Makes Movie."

Worst Fear: Nightmares about feet ("and the fat women attached to them"). To make matters worse, he was selected to judge the Ugly Feet Contest of 1990.

Education: Polk High School (voted "Most Valuable Player of 1966" as a member of the football team; he prides himself on scoring four touchdowns in one game against Andrew Johnson High School).

High School Hangout: Johnny B. Goods, fast-food hamburgers (where Al mentions he first met Peggy, also a student at Polk High).

Pride and Joy: His collection of *Playboy* magazines (a male family legacy).

Greatest Moment: Named "The Greatest Football Player" at Polk High in 1995. The scoreboard was dedicated to him and the field renamed "Al Bundy Field."

Refuge: The "cold, white, and soothing restroom" in the garage (where he has a Ferguson toilet and considers it his escape "from pantyhose and women"). It ended when Peggy took interior decorating classes at the Cook County School of Design and turned it into "a frilly pink nightmare."

Obsession: Big-breasted women.

Organization: NO'MAM—the National Organization of Men Against Amazonian Masterhood.

Hangout: The Jiggly Room of the Nudie Bar.

Reading Matter: TV Guide and the girlie magazine *Big 'Uns.*

Favorite TV Shows: Psycho Dad, Tube Top Wrestling (mythical), *The Avengers,* and *The Three Stooges.* When *Psycho Dad* (a western) was canceled for being too violent, *Friends* became his favorite TV show "because if you watch through binoculars, you can see that Jennifer Aniston (Rachel) isn't wearing a bra."

Favorite "Hooter Classic" Movies: Breast Monsters from Venus and *Planet of the D-Cups.* Real movie favorites are the westerns *Hondo* and *Shane.*

Favorite Songs: "Duke of Earl" and "Anna."

Favorite Food: Turkey (but he never gets it) and Weenie Tots ("nature's most perfect food," as Al claims; it is a frankfurter rolled in bread and fried in lard).

Favorite Dessert: Cheesecake (but only made by Hans from Chuck's Cheese Bowl).

Favorite Drink: Although Tang (the orange drink) is mentioned, Al is most often seen drinking his favorite alcoholic beverage—Girlie Girl beer.

Car: A run-down 1974 Dodge Dart (license plate F3B-259, later 61-CS2).

Favorite Activity: Sports (member of the baseball team Chicago Cleavage [Al's jersey: 38DD] and the New Market Mallers softball team; here, Al wore jersey 14; Peggy, jersey 11; Kelly, jersey 10; and Bud, jersey 00). He also enjoys bowling at Jim's Bowl-a-Rama (where Peggy holds the record for bowling a perfect 300 game).

Regret: "The day I said I do" (referring to marrying Peggy, whom he considers "my red-haired plague").

1989 Exchange Student Fiasco: Hoping to earn $500 a month by hosting a foreign exchange student, the Bundys were sent Yvette (Milla Jovovich), a gorgeous, intelligent French girl who became fixated with Kelly's lifestyle and was soon withdrawn from the program when she began failing courses at Polk High, including French. Kelly, who felt Yvette was a threat to her standing at school, called her "Y-vette."

Property Owner: A toxic dump called Lake Chikomicomico.

The Bundy Curse: In 1653, Shamus McBundy, an ancestor of Al's who lived in the town of Lower Uncton in England, angered a witch by calling her fat and ugly. In retaliation, she cursed the town to always remain in darkness (while its sister town, Upper Uncton, would always remain in the light). Al and Bud are the last remaining Bundys, and only their deaths can lift the curse and return Lower Uncton to the light.

Relatives: Uncle, Eugene Bundy (Charlie Brill); aunt, Heather Bundy (Karen Lynn Scott). Not seen was Al's Uncle Stymie.

MARGARET "PEGGY" BUNDY

Place of Birth: Wanker County (first said to be in Wisconsin, then Milwaukee), a community founded by her ancestors. She was born on April 12.

Father: Ephraim Wanker (Tim Conway). Her grossly overweight mother, who has to be transported from place to place on a flatbed truck, is not named or seen but is voiced by Kathleen Freeman. Al did catch a glimpse of Peggy's mother at one time and went temporarily blind.

Maiden Name: Margaret Wanker.

Childhood: Although Peggy, who is also called Peg, mentions she never had a Barbie doll while growing up (her parents would not allow it), she later contradicts herself by saying that she had no real friends, only her Barbie dolls.

Education: Polk High School.

Occupation: Housewife (although she doesn't cook, clean, or care for the kids). She worked at Muldin's Department Store (to earn money to buy a VCR) and created the comic strip "Mr. Empty Pants" (based on Al's lack of money) for *Modern Gal* magazine (she ended the strip when Al was killed by a falling meteor shaped like a woman's shoe). Peggy also operated a phone sex line ("1-900-Yummy . . . You're Cookin' with Butter") from her bedroom.

Because Peggy does not cook, Al has to beg for leftovers at the local pizza parlor and eat Tang sandwiches. On the rare occasions when Al has food to take to work, he carries a *Charlie's Angels* lunchbox. Because there is a lack of dinner plates in the house, Al must share the dog's food bowl. His bank checks also depress him, as they say, "Mrs. Peggy Bundy and the Nameless Shoe Salesman." When Kelly and Bud were growing up, they thought Al was the dim-witted handyman. To make up for this, Peggy has instituted "Make-Believe Daddy Day" on Friday afternoons (wherein she uses a sock puppet to represent Al to convince her children that Al is really their father).

Another Mouth to Feed: When Peggy's cousin Ida Mae (Linda Blair) and her strange husband Zemus Wanker (Bobcat Goldthwait) come for a visit in 1992, they depart without their five-year-old son, Seven (Shane Sweet), leaving Al and Peggy to care for him. The concept did not work, and Seven just disappeared without explanation (his picture is only seen on a milk carton as a missing child).

Favorite Activity: Spending Al's hard-earned money; eating bonbons while watching TV (especially *The Oprah Winfrey Show*); smoking cigarettes; staying married to Al (she knows giving him a divorce will make him happy, but she won't do that); attending Troy's, the local male strip club.

Goal: To somehow make Al romantic (as he avoids intimacy with her).

Bra: Perfect Figure (Model 327) 36-C bra.

Stuffed "Pet" Parrot: Winky.

Anniversary Gift: Peggy always gives Al a necktie (they were married in 1972, although other episodes place the marriage in 1966 and 1967).

The Pregnancy That Never Happened: Sixth-season episodes find Peggy becoming pregnant (to reflect Katey's real-life pregnancy); Al considered her a "Pregasaurus" and called her "Pregzilla." In October 1991, when Katey Sagal suffered a miscarriage, the story line was dropped and explained as Al's dream.

Relatives: Cousins, Effie Wanker (Joey Lauren Adams), Eb Wanker (William Sanderson), Otto Wanker (Effie James Haake), and Irwin Wanker (King Kong Bundy); triplets Milly, Elena, and Eadie (Milly, Elena, and Eadie Del Rubio). Not seen were Peggy's cousins Hootie (half man, half owl) and Possum Boy.

KELLY BUNDY

Place of Birth: Chicago.

Birthday: November 25, 1971 (the eldest child). She first says she was born in February (while an Aquarius, she says, "I'm an aquarium"), then November 27.

Measurements: 34-25-34. She has blonde hair and wears a size 6 dress and a size 7 shoe.

Education: Polk High School, the Larry Storch School of Modeling (named after actor Larry Storch of *F Troop* fame), and an unnamed modeling school where she got tension headaches from smiling but was cited as "a natural leg crosser" ("I can do it at will"). Kelly attended high school only as a means for meeting friends and supplying pens and pencils for the family; she is quite dense and has to write her name on the palm of her hand to remember who she is.

Talent: Using her beauty to manipulate people. Kelly could sing, and Al saw this as an opportunity to make money by pairing Peggy and Kelly as "Juggs—The New Mother and Daughter Singing Duo."

Wardrobe: Tight jeans, miniskirts, and low-cut blouses. She has a tendency to give the neighborhood men (and boys) a thrill by dressing with her window shades up.

Exercise: Classes at the Northside Aerobics Studio.

Occupation: Hussy. She began her work career at the age of five when Peggy put her to work selling kisses. She was then a roller-skating waitress at Bill's Hilltop Drive-In; representative as Miss Weenie Tots hot dogs; the Allanti Girl (model for a foreign sports car; she acquired the job by jiggling her breasts in what she calls "The Bundy Bounce"); Verminator Girl (model for an insect spray; she lost the job when she refused to wear a skimpy Verminator bikini) at Chicago TV World Theme Park (mistakenly called "TV Land" in one episode); model for Easy-Off Jeans; window "display" model at the Kyoto Bank (in a bikini with the bank slogan "Check Out Our Assets"); spokesgirl for Ice Hole Beer ("The Micro-Brewed Beer"); Rock Slut in a Gutter Cats music video; actress in a TV commercial for Romantic Roast Instant Coffee; Waist-A-Way Diet Drink representative; and actress (dressed as a sexy dog) for Hungry Puppy Dog Food and host of the cable access show *Vital Social Issues with Kelly* (which dealt with topics like "Slut of the Week," "Bad Perms," and "Hunks"). When the NBS network picked up Kelly's show (and changed the vital issues to things like drinking milk and reading books), it was cancelled when ratings declined (replaced by a *Star Trek* spoof called *Shoe Trek*. Other "top notch" shows carried by NBS include *The Homeless Detective, Tugboat Danger, Me and the Shiska, Black Cop/White Girl* and *Ellen and Her Dog Spike).* Kelly was also as an intern as the Weather Bunny Girl for the Channel 8 "Action News" program. When her stunning good looks boosted ratings she was paid a salary ($1,000 a week) and given a raise to $250,000 a year despite the fact that she didn't know where "East Dakota" was. She lost the job when she couldn't read the teleprompter. She was also a waitress at an unnamed restaurant that was soon closed by the Board of Health. She got the job because she knew what a plate was, what a table was and that you bring the plate to the table, not vice versa.

Favorite Article of Clothing: A see-through blouse (which she can never find—
"It's see-through," she says).

Favorite Food: Veal.

Nickname: "Pumpkin" (as called by Al). Al can recall doing only two things for
Kelly: carrying her home from the hospital (although he left her on the car
roof) and buying her ice cream when she was 10 years old.

Note: Tina Caspary played Kelly in the unaired pilot version.

BUDRICK "BUD" FRANKLIN BUNDY

Place of Birth: Chicago on January 22, 1976.

Education: Polk High School (a member of the soccer team, the Reepers; he
wore jersey 9); Trumaine College (a member of the Gamma Gamma Sigma
Pi fraternity).

Occupation: Student. He held jobs as an instructor with the department of motor
vehicles (fired for being a go-getter and trying to help people); Kelly's agent
(when she became a model); apprentice chimney sweeper; volunteer for the
Virgin Hotline (phone number 1-800-ZIPP UP).

Favorite TV Shows: Dateless Dude Late Night Theater and *Star Trek* reruns ("to
get a glimpse of Klingon Cleavage," as said by Kelly).

Reading Matter: Boudoir (a girlie magazine).

Nickname: "Rat Boy" and "Toad Boy" (as called by Kelly).

Favorite Clothes: Cowboy pajamas.

Aftershave Lotion: Open Sesame.

Greatest Ambition: To acquire a girlfriend by any means possible (everything
always fails, including his pretending to be the street rapper Grand Master B).

Becoming a Man: When Bud turned 18, Al initiated him into manhood by taking him to the Nudie Bar (a tradition in the Bundy family).

Note: Hunter Carlson played Bud in the unaired pilot version.

MARCY RHOADES

Place of Birth: Chicago.

Occupation: Loan officer at the Kyoto National Bank.

Address: Given only as Jeopardy Lane (Al's neighbors).

Fear: Speaking in public. As a child, she was at school giving a speech when a
roach started climbing up her leg. She screamed, took off her dress, and
"revealed my Hey, Hey We're the Monkees panties." She was teased for the
rest of the school year.

Childhood Pets: Winkems (dog) and Gringo (cat). She also had a cuckoo clock
she called Petey and an invisible friend named Jennifer.

Nickname: Called "Chicken Legs" by Al (refers to her slim stature, tendency to put her hands on her hips when she is angry, and her small bustline, which, Al says, "are not breasts, just nuggets").

Organization: To battle Al's degrading-to-women NO'MAM, Marcy formed FANG (Feminists Against Neanderthal Guys).

Relatives: Niece, Amber (Juliet Tablak).

First Husband: Steve Rhoades, a loan officer at the Leading Bank of Chicago (they were married on Valentine's Day). When Steve loaned Al the $50,000 to start Dr. Shoe, he was fired and first became a cage cleaner at Slither's Pet Emporium, then a forest ranger at Yosemite National Park (at which time he left the series). Steve was a member of his high school band, the Tuxedos, and called Marcy "Angel Cups"; she called him "Sugar Tush." He and Marcy were vegetarians and had a yearly tradition: "On the first sunny day in May, we go to the beach to shake hands with Mr. Sunshine."

Second Husband: Jefferson Millhouse D'Arcy, a con artist now on parole after he was caught stealing money from investors in a scam. In 1991, Marcy attends a banking seminar and becomes a party animal, waking up the next morning in a bed with Jefferson, a man she married at Clyde's No Blood Test Needed Chapel. Jefferson called Marcy "Bon Bon Bottom"; she called him "Cinnamon Buns." While Jefferson had numerous cons to make money, he is most noted for his and Al's efforts to establish the Church of NO'MAM (based on the organization Al created) as a way to avoid paying taxes. It failed when Marcy exposed Reverend Al as a fraud. Jefferson was simply following in the footsteps of his gigolo father and felt he was too handsome to work (he preferred living off Marcy's salary). He first claimed to be a former criminal who was now in the FBI's Witness Protection Program, then a former CIA undercover agent (with the code name "Bullwinkle"). Jefferson says he was expelled from the CIA because he could not fulfill an assignment: kill Fidel Castro, who was allegedly a friend of his.

Relatives: Mandy, Marcy's identical twin cousin (Amanda Bearse).

Matlock
(NBC, 1986–1992; ABC, 1992–1995)

Cast: Andy Griffith (Ben Matlock), Linda Purl (Charlene Matlock), Julie Sommars (Julie March), Nancy Stafford (Michelle Thomas), Kari Lizer (Cassie Phillips), Don Knotts (Les Calhoun), Kene Holliday (Tyler Hudson), Clarence Gilyard Jr. (Conrad McMasters).

Basis: The cases of Ben Matlock, a southern, down-to-earth criminal lawyer based in Atlanta, Georgia.

BENJAMIN "BEN" LAYTON MATLOCK

Place of Birth: Mount Harlan, Georgia. His father owned a gas station.

Marital Status: Widower.

Daughters: Charlene and Lee Ann.

Birth Sign: Gemini.

Education: Harvard Law School; a doctorate degree from Baxter University.

Business: Ben Matlock: Attorney-at-Law (originally called "Matlock and Matlock" when Ben worked with Charlene, who left in 1987 to begin her own practice in Philadelphia). Ben previously worked as a public prosecutor. Lori Lethan plays Charlene in the pilot.

Fees: Ben is known "for his high prices ($100,000 a case) and his high rate of successfully defending clients" (most often at the Fulton County Courthouse).

Home Address: 618 Mill Pond Road.

Office Address: Matlock and Matlock, Atlanta, Georgia 30303.

Sedan License Plate: RAF 285.

Office Phone Number: 555-9930.

Quirk: Doesn't trust police labs ("They're not working for my clients").

Award: Voted 1991 "Man of the Year" by the Atlanta Chamber of Commerce.

Wardrobe: White suits. It began in 1969 when a case brought Ben to Los Angeles, and eating bad fish made him ill. He was taken to Community General Hospital and met Dr. Mark Sloan (Dick Van Dyke), a resident intern (from the series *Diagnosis: Murder*) who convinced him to invest his life savings ($5,000) in the newest music form: eight-track tapes. The system never caught on (replaced by audiocassettes), and Ben lost everything; wearing cheap white suits off the store rack was all he could afford.

Favorite Snack: Hot dogs and grape soda.

Steadfast Rule: No smoking in his office ("Not even my best paying clients").

Biggest Complaint: Paying taxes ("I owe thousands and thousands of dollars").

Hobby: Collecting old coins (his rarest is an 1804 silver dollar).

Wake-Up Time: 5 a.m. each day ("It's the best time for thinking").

Musical Ability: Singing (sang with a church choir) and playing the guitar.

Least Favorite Newspaper: Informer (it reports his cases and hampers his chances of freeing his clients).

Gift: Known as a great storyteller and how to appeal to a jury.

Lost Case: Ben can brilliantly argue the cases of other people but not for himself. He tried to sue a woman who sold him a used refrigerator (for $68.42) that broke down but lost, as it was an "as is" sale.

Relatives: Nephew, Irwin Bruckner (Billy Mumy), a genius who works for the Mansbridge Institute; aunt, Elsie (Anne Haney); cousin, Diana Huntington (Christina Pickles); uncle, Bink (Kay E. Kuter).

Flashbacks: Ben's father, Charlie Matlock (Andy Griffith); Ben in 1956 (Steve Witting).

OTHER CHARACTERS

Julie March is the prosecuting attorney with the Atlanta district attorney's office. She was born in Nebraska and claims to be an expert on jewelry. She considers herself to be one of the best legal minds in the South while Ben calls her "the wildest, most ruthless prosecutor they [the state] have." He claims that Julie makes the best fried chicken he ever had—even better than what his mother used to make. Ben and Julie enjoy a movie or play on Friday nights; she left to become a prosecutor for the Los Angeles district attorney's office.

Michelle Thomas joins Ben's firm after his daughter, Charlene, leaves. She is as shrewd and cunning as Ben but is not as visibly credited as Ben on the office door ("B.L. Matlock—Attorney-at-Law" appears in large letters, while "Michelle Thomas—Attorney-at-Law" appears in smaller letters under his).

Les Calhoun, who says, "Call me Ace," is Ben's neighbor. Les, patterned a bit after Don Knotts's character of Barney Fife on *The Andy Griffith Show*, is a nervous chap who is now retired. He made plastic eyelets for sneakers and "ate chop suey and wore lizard skin shoes every day." He calls Ben "Benjie" and "Benge." He loves to shop for Christmas presents and claims, "I've got great taste in everything."

Cassie Phillips is Ben's law clerk. She was attending the University of Chicago when she interviewed Ben Matlock, a guest lecturer, for the school newspaper and became so impressed that she decided to become an attorney. After graduating, she enrolled in the Baxter Law School in Atlanta and asked Ben for a job.

Tyler Hudson was Ben's first investigator. He was a stock market investor, named "Young Atlanta Businessman of the Year," and won $2,000 in the Junior Chamber of Commerce Chili Bake-Off. He was replaced by Conrad McMasters, a deputy with the Atlanta Police Department who doubled as Ben's investigator. Carol Huston appeared briefly in 1994 as Jeri Stone, the private detective Ben hired as his investigator when Conrad left.

In the final first-run NBC episode "The Assassination" (May 8, 1992), Brynn Thayer appeared as Ben's daughter, Lee Ann McIntyre (no mention is made of Charlene). Lee Ann is a prosecutor in Philadelphia who comes to Atlanta to visit her father following a legal separation from her husband, Peter. She helps her father defend a client and decides to remain in Atlanta.

"Tonight, look who's coming to ABC" preceded the ABC premiere of *Matlock* on November 5, 1992 (with the episode "The Vacation"). Ben and Lee Ann have formed a partnership and operate a firm called "Matlock and McIntyre" in Atlanta. Lee Ann and Peter (whom Ben calls "the jerk") are still separated, and she uses her married name, although Ben is trying to convince her to use his last name.

While on vacation in Wilmington, Ben meets Cliff Lewis (Daniel Roebuck), a recent law school graduate, at the Food Lion supermarket. Cliff is the son of Billy Lewis (Warren Frost), Ben's old nemesis from Mount Harlan. (Billy blames Ben for breaking the heart of his sister, Lucy. Billy claims that Ben dated her for eight years then dumped her; Ben claims that they mutually agreed to separate.) When Cliff, a member of the Mount Harlan Volunteer Fire Department, is set up on a false murder charge and Ben clears him, he is hired by Ben to assist Conrad as his legman.

Matt Houston
(ABC, 1982–1985)

Cast: Lee Horsley (Matt Houston), Pamela Hensley (C.J. Parsons).

Basis: Matt Houston, the son of oil-rich Texas parents, turns private investigator to do what he enjoys most—solving crimes.

MATLOCK "MATT" HOUSTON

Parents: Natural father, Virgil Wade (Lloyd Bridges); adoptive father, Bill Houston (David Wayne). Bill's wife, Elizabeth, is not seen.

Place of Birth: Texas on May 15, 1955.

Education: Texas A&M University (quarterback on the football team). He apparently played professional football at one time, as he was voted "All State, All City" champion.

Business: Houston, Inc. (also called Houston Industries), in Los Angeles (located first at 100 Century Plaza South, then 200 West Temple Street, 90012). It oversees many operations from diamond mining to soybean futures. Matt moved to California to oversee his family's offshore oil drilling operations and then, after acquiring his private investigator's license, established Houston Investigations.

Ranch: The Houston Cattle Ranch (he purchased it, the former Landers Ranch, from movie star Ramona Landers [Janet Leigh]).

Oil Company Business Car: A Rolls-Royce (plate COWBOY 1).

Investigative Work Car: The *Excalibur* (plate 21 VE 124).

Investigative Fees: $500 a day plus expenses. He says, "I like to ask the questions. That's how I know I'm a detective."

Yacht: Endeavor.

Hughes Helicopter ID: N1090Z.

Home: Penthouse apartment at Houston, Inc.

Charitable Work: Donated a wing at the Children's Hospital.

Telephone Numbers: Home: 555-2922; Office: 555-3141; P.I.: 555-6728.

Favorite Sport: Football.

Favorite Eatery: Mama Novelli's Restaurant (owned by Rosa Novelli [Penny Santon], the mother of Vincenzo "Vince" Novelli [John Aprea], the Southern California Police Department lieutenant whom Matt assists).

Childhood Trauma: Kidnapped and held for $50,000 ransom. He was rescued after five days but terrorized by his kidnapper, who pointed a gun filled with blanks at him.

Relatives: Uncle, Roy Houston (Buddy Ebsen), a former police detective turned private investigator; cousin, Will (Michael Goodwin).

C.J. PARSONS

Relationship: Matt's lawyer, business associate (oversees Matt's corporate matters), lover, and occasional assistant in his investigative work. She uses Matt's office computer, "Baby," for her research (when she signs on, the computer, believing it is Matt, says, "Hi Boss").

Place of Birth: Texas on October 3, 1950.

Education: Harvard School of Law.

Address: 8766 West Beverly, Apartment 3C. In Texas, she lives "five miles down the road from Matt."

Car: Usually rides with Houston; in Texas, she drives "Matt's brown and white Ford Lariat" (plate COWBOY 9).

Telephone Number: 555-9080.

Measurements: 34-24-34. She has brown hair and stands 5 feet, 7 inches tall.

Miami Vice
(NBC, 1984–1989)

Cast: Don Johnson (Sonny Crockett), Philip Michael Thomas (Ricardo Tubbs).

Basis: Sonny Crockett and Ricardo Tubbs's investigations as undercover detectives with the Miami-Dade County Police Department (also called the Miami, Florida, Police Department).

JAMES "SONNY" CROCKETT

Place of Birth: Florida (although he is seen wearing a University of Kansas T-shirt) in 1949. The Texas Rangers were his inspiration to become a law enforcer.

Education: University of Florida (wore jersey 88 as a member of the Gators football team).

Military: Sonny had a promising career as a professional football player, but "I traded the whole thing in for two years in Nam" (he volunteered in the early 1970s; another episode mentions that he was a football player but that his career ended when he injured his knee). He then attended rookie school and was first assigned as an instructor. He worked his way up to the Robbery Division; four years later, he was transferred to the Vice Squad and finally to the Organized Crime Bureau.

Undercover Name: Sonny Burnett, an enterprising businessman (who could be a drug dealer one week, an outlaw the next). "I'm trying to get by on four hours of sleep a day. I go undercover for weeks at a time. It's disastrous on a marriage, hell on the nervous system."

Wardrobe: Pastels and bright colors (making the character one of the biggest fashion icons of the 1980s). He also had his signature "two-day stubble" look (as he seldom had a chance to shave after a stakeout).

Address: Lives on an Endeavor sailboat he calls the *Saint Vitus Dance.* He also has a 39-foot Chris Craft Stinger offshore racing boat (later a 38-foot Wellcraft Scarab).

Problem: Gambles and drinks. He prefers to do things his way and has been suspended for misconduct. Once assigned a case, Sonny will not request backup or submit progress reports (he fears that department leaks could compromise his cases).

Sailboat Mate: Elvis, the former alligator mascot of the Gators football team (he was benched for biting a player and "works" as Sonny's watchdog). Elvis shows his teeth when strangers appear, ticks (swallowed a clock), and is high at times (ate a bag of LSD).

Car: A Ferrari Daytona Spyder, then a Ferrari Testarossa.

Bank: The Dade County Federal Bank.

Ex-Wife: Caroline (Belinda J. Montgomery). They are the parents of six-year-old Billy (Clayton Barclay Jones). Sonny later dates Detective Gina Navarro Calabrese (Saundra Santiago), then Caitlin Davies (Sheena Easton), whom he marries.

RICARDO TUBBS

Position: Sonny's partner (as Sonny says about himself and Ricardo, "We're just tollbooths on a highway when it comes to bustin' drug dealers").

Place of Birth: The Bronx, New York.

Occupation: Detective with the Armed Robbery Unit of the New York Police Department, Bronx Division (another episode claims he was with the Narcotics Division). It is said that while working here, his brother, Rafael (also a cop), was killed by the drug lord Esteban Calderon (Miguel Pinero) and that Ricardo, seeking the culprit, tracked him to Florida, where he met Sonny, who was seeking the same man. After successfully capturing the killer, Ricardo was offered and accepted the opportunity to work with Sonny, first in vice, then for the Organized Crime Bureau. Ricardo's prior New York partners were Valerie Gordon (Pam Grier) and Clarence Batisse (Victor Love).

Undercover Name: Ricardo "Rico" Cooper (to protect his identity). In the pilot, it was Teddy Prentiss; his alias was also given as Richard Taylor.

Nickname: Called "Rico" by Sonny (Ricardo claims that his name stands for "tough, unique, bad, bold, and sassy").

Marital Status: Single.

Address: An apartment on Linden Avenue.

Car: A 1964 Cadillac Coupe de Ville convertible.

Character: Not as aggressive as Sonny and careful during case investigations. He has a calmer approach when it comes to questioning suspects (just the opposite of Sonny's more violent tactics). He will use a gun only when necessary (unlike Sonny, who will use a gun when he feels the need to) and often finds himself in trouble for following Sonny's unorthodox methods; he does it, however, because they are partners and somebody has to cover Sonny's back.

Bank: The Security Central Bank of Florida.

Moonlighting
(ABC, 1985–1989)

Cast: Cybill Shepherd (Maddie Hayes), Bruce Willis (David Addison), Allyce Beasley (Agnes DiPesto), Curtis Armstrong (Herbert Viola).

Basis: A former model (Maddie) and a private detective (David) join forces to solve crimes.

MADELYN "MADDIE" HAYES

Parents: Alexander (Robert Webber) and Virginia Hayes (Eva Marie Saint).

Place of Birth: Chicago on February 4, 1951 (also mentioned as October 11, 1951).

Address: 88 East Oak Avenue, Chicago.

Pet Sheepdog: Sport.

Occupation: Model, then owner of Blue Moon Investigations in Los Angeles. She began modeling as a child and ventured into adult fashion, gracing the covers of such magazines as *Vogue, Glamour, Vanity Fair*, and *Mademoiselle*. While Maddie is beautiful, she is often seen by her legs only as she walks to her office.

Bruce Willis and Cybill Shepherd. *ABC/Photofest. ©ABC*

Television Work: Spokesgirl for Blue Moon Shampoo.

Measurements: 34-25-36. She has blonde hair.

Life Changer: Maddie lost everything when her business manager embezzled her
    funds. She was left with only one of her holdings, City of Angels Investiga-
    tions, and was about to sell it when agency employee David Addison sweet-
    talked her into keeping it (and making him her partner to recoup losses).
    She renamed it Blue Moon Investigations (but it is also called the Blue
    Moon Detective Agency).

Regret: "No one calls. No one comes in and it's bankrupting me." She also com-
    plains about the clients they do get (hookers or people with psychological
    problems).

First Profit: $2,035.76.

Character: A constant worrier—not only about how she looks but also about
    how to keep her sanity as a detective. She has to be in control of a situation,
    or she falls apart (babbles and acts incoherently). She had placed herself
    above everyone else, but the sleazy clients the agency attracts have made her
    soft and vulnerable to their causes.

Nickname: Called "Blondie Blonde" by David.

Car License Plate: 280018.

Religion: Although Maddie is seen celebrating religious holidays (like Christmas), she mentions that she is an atheist.

Relatives: Cousin, Annie Charnock (Virginia Madsen); she is married to Mark (James Stephens).

Note: Mary-Margaret Humes was originally cast as Maddie Hayes.

DAVID ADDISON JR.

Father: David Addison Sr. (Paul Sorvino); his mother, Irma, is deceased; his father later married a woman named Stephanie.

Brother: Richard Addison (Charles Rocket).

Birthday: March 23, 1956 (also given as November 27).

Place of Birth: Philadelphia (where he lived on Bainbridge Street).

Occupation: Private detective (he was originally a bartender but figured he could make more money as an investigator).

Character: David is immature, deceitful, and totally distrustful of people. He is optimistic about everything but jokes constantly and makes lewd sexual jokes.

Habit: Singing whenever the opportunity arises (even when there is no opportunity).

Obsession: Money (he will take whatever cases he can even if it displeases Maddie).

Address: An apartment at 46 LaPaloma Drive.

Car License Plate: 2900LB.

Catchphrases: "Do bears bare?" and "Do bees be?"

Favorite Music: Rhythm and blues.

Favorite Sport: Bowling.

Dislikes: Foreign films and seafood.

Note: Harley Venton was originally cast as David.

OTHER CHARACTERS

Agnes DiPesto, the agency's receptionist, answers calls in rhyme, for example, "Blue Moon Investigations. Get in some trouble, we'll be there on the double"; "Blue Moon Detective Agency. If persons are missing; if objects are lost, we'll find them for you at a reasonable cost"; and "Blue Moon Detective Agency. Wife a philanderer, don't worry, we'll handle her." She lives at 633 Hope Street, Apartment 723. Her romantic interest is Herbert Viola, the agency's bookkeeper and sometimes assistant to Maddie and David on cases. Imogene Coca played Agnes's mother, Clara DiPesto.

Note: In the black-and-white episode "The Dream Sequence Always Rings Twice," Maddie dreams she is a 1940s singer named Rita Adams at the Flamingo Club (she sings the song "Blue Moon"); David is seen as a cornet player named Chance McCoy. The episode "Atomic Shakespeare," a parody of *The Taming of the Shrew*, finds Cybill as Katarina and Bruce as Petruchio, the gentleman of Verona who sets out to tame the shrewish Katarina.

Mr. Belvedere
(ABC, 1985–1990)

Cast: Christopher Hewitt (Lynn Belvedere), Bob Uecker (George Owens), Ilene Graff (Marsha Owens), Tracy Wells (Heather Owens), Rob Stone (Kevin Owens), Brice Beckham (Wesley Owens), Michele Matheson (Angela).

Basis: A staunch British butler (Lynn Belvedere) takes on the challenge of his life when he becomes the housekeeper to the disorganized Owens family: parents George and Marsha and their children, Kevin, Tracy, and Wesley.

LYNN ALOYSIUS BELVEDERE

Mother: "Mumsey" Margaret Belvedere (Sylvia Kauders).

Place of Birth: Stonehedge, England (where he lived on Higby Road).

Education: The Pennington School.

Curse: Once every seven years, Lynn is affected by the Stonehedge Curse, a force that makes him bounce back and forth between himself and someone else; the cure is to wait it out or return home and dance around the statue of Stonehedge, the town's founder.

Treasured Item: A $750,000 Faberge Egg (a present from a sheikh for saving his life).

Occupation: Housekeeper (but he also says butler). He previously worked as a housekeeper for Gandhi and Queen Elizabeth II and as a valet for Winston Churchill.

Awards: Medal for climbing Mount Everest; winner of the Pillsbury Bake-Off cooking contest; named "Housekeeper of the Year" by *World Focus* magazine.

Book: An American Journal: The Suburban Years (his experiences in America).

Vices: Junk food (enjoys Ding Dongs and Scooter Pies; shops at Donut World); smoking cigars.

Final Episode: Lynn marries Louise Gilbert (Rosemary Forsythe), an animal behaviorist he met at a Laundromat. He leaves the Owenses to help Louise with a gorilla census for the University of Boutari in Africa. Lynn mentions that he left his weekly diaries (which he is seen writing at the end of each episode) at the Owens home with the hope of one day retrieving them. He never did.

Relatives: Cousin, Galen Belvedere (David Rappaport).

Flashbacks: Lynn as a boy (Trevor Thiegen).

GEORGE OWENS

Address: 200 Spring Valley Road, Pittsburgh, Pennsylvania (Beaver Falls).

Education: Cleveland High School.

Occupation: Host of "Sports Page" (later called "Sports Rap") on radio station WBK-AM (phone number 555-2222); sports anchor of WBN-TV, Channel 8 *Metro News*; columnist for the "Sports Beat" column of the Pittsburgh *Bulletin.* He was originally said to be a construction worker.

Nickname for Mr. Belvedere: "Big Guy."

Favorite Dinner: Meatloaf, potato logs, and creamed corn.

Favorite Snack: Pork rinds and Spam dip.

Favorite Activity: Shopping at Lumber-Rama.

Childhood: Played pinball machines at the arcade on First Avenue (stayed out until midnight, then sneaked back into his room).

Fear: Flying. To overcome it, George closes his eyes and pretends he is on a bus.

Favorite Eatery: McSwarley's Restaurant.

Membership: The neighborhood watch "Happy Guys" (with Lynn).

Vice: Smokes cigarettes.

MARSHA LEIGH OWENS

Place of Birth: Pittsburgh, Pennsylvania.

Maiden Name: Given as both Cameron and McClellan.

Education: University of Pittsburgh (majored in law; ranked 76 out of 278 students; spent $30,000 on tuition; passed the bar exam in July 1987).

Occupation: Lawyer with the firm of Dawson, Metcalfe and Bach; a year later, she became a Legal Hut attorney but quit when she found it unfulfilling (unable to help the underdog) to become "Babs," a waitress at the Beaver Falls Diner. George mentions he hired Lynn so that Marsha could begin her law career.

Favorite Dinner: Lobster thermador.

Car: A never-seen white Porsche she calls "Wolfgang."

Wedding Date: Varies. Mentioned as September 2, 1967; September 17, 1967; then only as in 1968. They honeymooned at the Altoona Motor Lodge, room 14.

Note: In one episode, Ilene Graff played Marsha's double, a dangerous criminal named Sharon Witt.

KEVIN OWENS

Relationship: The eldest child (born in 1967). George and Marsha contemplated calling him either Moon Shadow (if a girl) or Moondoggie (if a boy). But when the baby was born, "he looked like a Kevin."

Education: Van Buren High School; University of Pittsburgh (where he lives in Apartment 5 next to a sewage treatment plant because the rent is cheap).

Occupation: Student. He worked part-time at Mr. Cluck's Fried Chicken and as a salesman for Phil's Friendly Motors (a used-car lot).

Band: The Young Savages (played drums).

Childhood: Developed an allergy to raisins and was an Eagle Scout.

HEATHER OWENS

Relationship: The middle child (born in 1969).

Nickname: Called "Kitten" by George.

Education: Van Buren High School (cheerleader for the football team, first called the Bulls, then the Beavers). She is an average student and is happy with "B" and "C" grades.

Occupation: Student. She worked after school at Traeger's Records (a music store).

Favorite Breakfast: Kellogg's Corn Flakes.

Hair Parlor: Synder's Beauty Salon.

Boyfriend Issues: When Heather loses a boyfriend and becomes depressed, eating Rocky Road ice cream and shopping at the mall will get her back to normal.

Alias: At the age of 16, Heather felt she needed a more sophisticated name and called herself "Bianca." She also dyed her brown hair blonde to experience something different. She was whistled at, had doors opened for her, and received free food "from the guy in the cafeteria." She returned to her former self when she felt she was becoming someone she was not.

Character: A bit klutzy but yearns to look sophisticated and alluring, not cute as her mother says, "with green eyes, a little button nose, and an adorable smile."

WESLEY OWENS

Relationship: The youngest child.

Education: Conklin Elementary School; Allegheny Junior High School; Beaver Falls Junior High School (wore jersey 31 on the school football team).

Pets: Spot (dog); Captain Nemo (snake); Inky (hamster).

Sport: The Colts Little League team (coached by George).

Club: The Junior Pioneers (Group 12) scout troop; attended Camp Chippewa.

Favorite Sandwiches: Tuna fish and marshmallow spread on white bread; bologna and marshmallow spread on raisin bread.

Nickname: Called "Wesman" by George and "Master Wesley" by Lynn.
Trait: Mischievous; enjoys annoying his neighbors, the Hufnagels. Teresa Ganzel plays the only Hufnagel to be seen, the gorgeous Giselle.
Film: Made a home video about Lynn he called *The Housekeeper from Hell.*
Moneymaking Scheme: Selling Heather's bras over the Internet, claiming they belonged to Madonna.
Expertise: Playing cards, especially gin rummy.
Forbidden: Joining George at Lumber-Rama (for using a leaf blower to "to blow up ladies' skirts").

ANGELA
Relationship: Heather's best friend.
Last Name: Rarely mentioned but called Gilbert, Jostakovich, or Shostakovich.
Trait: As Heather says, "Being blonde and pretty are about the only assets Angela has."
Hobby: Collecting clothes hangers.
Education: Van Buren High School (a cheerleader for the Beavers football team). She works after school with Heather at Traeger's Records.
Association: The Iron Maidens, a community group that reads to the elderly.
Beauty Pageant: The Miss Beaver Falls Beauty Pageant (won with a ventriloquist act using a dummy patterned after Mr. Belvedere).
Inability: To remember Lynn's last name (calls him names like "Mr. Bell Ringer," "Mr. Beer Belly," "Mr. Belly Button," "Mr. Bumper Sticker," and "Mr. Beaver Dam").
Ability: Believes she possesses psychic powers and was possessed by the spirit of Lars Frederickson, a Swedish dairy farmer who was also "The Healer of Mankind."

Murder, She Wrote
(CBS, 1984–1996)

Cast: Angela Lansbury (Jessica Fletcher), William Windom (Dr. Seth Hazlitt), Tom Bosley (Amos Tupper), Ron Masak (Mort Metzger).
Basis: Jessica Fletcher, a mystery novelist and amateur sleuth, solves crimes to acquire story material.

JESSICA BEATRICE FLETCHER
Place of Birth: New England.
Siblings: Four brothers and a sister; only Marshall (a doctor) and Martin are mentioned.

Address: A Victorian home at 698 Candlewood Lane, Cabot Cove, Maine 03041 (also mentioned as being on Candlewood Road; her address is seen as "Mrs. Jessica Fletcher, R.F.D. #3, Cabot Cove, Maine"). In Manhattan episodes, where Jessica moves to be closer to her publisher, she lives at the Penfield Apartments (Apartment 427) at 941 West 60th Street; 212-124-7199 is her phone number.

Maiden Name: Jessica McGill. She is often called "J.B. Fletcher."

Heritage: Irish (only mentioned that her mother came from Ireland).

Childhood Memory: Skinny-dipping in the lake behind the family house.

Education: Cabot Cove High School; Boston University (majoring in education, but journalism is mentioned; she was a member of the Delta Alpha Chi sorority).

Hobbies: Gardening, jogging, cooking, and helping with local charities.

Quirks: Will not drive a car (dislikes it and will not get a license; she rides a bicycle around Cabot Cove). She rarely drinks, but when she does, it's a glass of wine.

Late Husband: Frank Fletcher (whom she met as a coworker at the Applewood Playhouse). They had a faithful marriage but no children. He passed away from natural causes in the early 1980s and had established the Cabot Cove Democratic Society. He was also an army navigator during the Korean War (at which time Jessica lived in San Diego). To always have Frank near her, Jessica wears a pendant near her heart that contains his picture. Frank enjoyed smoking a pipe.

Occupation: An English teacher at Cabot Cove High School, but after 19 years, she quit to become a writer (Jessica mentions that during a college semester break, she became interested in writing when she worked as a reporter for a newspaper wire service; an unsolved murder in the neighboring town of Bay Harbor inspired her to write mystery novels). In New York, she teaches a criminology course at Manhattan University and a creative writing course at the Inner City High School; she does volunteer work for the Museum of Cultural History and the Library Foundation.

Jessica's Publishers: Coventry House; Sutton Place Publishing; Consolidated Publishers (all in New York City). Most of her books are a "Murder of the Month" book club selection; six were mentioned as being on the *New York Times* best-seller list.

Jessica's Fictional Characters: Damian Sinclair, the jewel thief; and Inspectors Dison and Gelico.

Expertise: Poisons (due to her research). She can also speak Chinese.

Catchphrase: "I think I know who the killer is. Now to prove it!"

Substitute: In episodes that do not feature Jessica, her former flame and reformed jewel thief Dennis Stanton (Keith Michell), now an agent for the Consolidated Casualty Insurance Company in San Francisco, is seen.

Relatives: Nieces, Victoria "Vicki" Brandon-Griffin (Genie Francis; a real estate broker for Precious Premises, Inc.), Pamela Crane McGill (Belinda J. Montgomery; the daughter of Jessica's brother, Marshall McGill), Nita Cochran (Alice Krige), Carol Donovan (Courteney Cox), Tracy McGill (Linda Grovernor), and Jill Morton (Kristy McNichol); nephew, Grady Fletcher (Michael Horton); cousins, Emma McGill (Angela Lansbury; a British lounge singer), Calhoun "Cal" Fletcher (Peter Bonerz), Ann Owens (Shirley Jones), George Owens (Robert Walker), and Abby Benton Freestone (Lynn Redgrave); aunt, Mildred (Penny Singleton); brother-in-law, Neil Fletcher (Jackie Cooper). Mentioned were Jessica's Aunt Harriet; great aunts, Sarah and Amanda; great uncle, Henry; and a nephew, Johnny Eaton.

JESSICA'S BOOKS

The Corpse Danced at Midnight (her first book; became a best seller that led to her career as a mystery novelist); *Ashes, Ashes, Fall Down; The Belgrade Murders; Calvin Cantebury's Revenge; A Case and a Half of Murder; The Corpse at Vespers; The Corpse Danced at Midnight* (made into a book on tape for the blind); *The Corpse Wasn't There; The Crypt of Death; The Dead Must Sing; Dirge for a Dead Dachshund; The Killer Called Collect; A Killing at Hastings Rock* (made into a virtual reality game); *The Launch Pad Murders; Lover's Revenge; Messengers of Midnight* (also called *Messenger at Midnight;* made into a movie); *Murder at Midnight* (Jessica's favorite book "because I didn't know who the killer was until the last 12 pages"); *Murder at the Asylum; Murder at the Digs; Murder at the Ridge Top; Murder Comes to Maine; Murder in a Minor Key; Murder in White* (produced as a London stage play); *Murder on the Amazon; Murder Will Out; Runaway to Murder; Sanitarium of Death; The Stain on the Stairs; Stone Cold Dead; The Triple Crown Murders; The Umbrella Murders; The Uncaught; The Venomous Valentine; Yours Truly, Damian Sinclair.*

OTHER CHARACTERS

Dr. Seth Hazlitt, called "Doc Hazlitt," has been practicing medicine for 37 years and lives in a 120-year-old house. He is a widower and set in his ways and can be a bit grouchy at times. He has a natural curiosity about life and a penchant for talking. He claims Cabot Cove leads the nation in the sale of live bait. He and Jessica have been friends for a long time, and together they enjoy fishing off his boat, the *Cavalier.* He drives a car with the license plate 6006, and when in Boston, he enjoys meals at the Clams 'n' Claws restaurant. He plays pool at Haggerty's Pool Hall, served as a corporal during World War II, and will not practice in a big city due to his being kidnapped by mobsters when he was in Boston. His birthday is only mentioned as on "the 21st."

Amos Tupper was the original town sheriff. He drove a bus before joining the police department and is a bit inept at his job (better at talking and eating).

He was replaced by Sheriff Mort Metzger when Amos retired and returned home to Kentucky to be with his family. Mort, who calls Jessica "Mrs. F," was a former Los Angeles Rams football player whose career ended when he injured his knee. He then became an officer with the New York City Police Department but quit because "I couldn't handle the politics." He relocated to Maine "because I like it here." His wife is named Adele (not seen), the Joshua Peabody Inn is his favorite eatery, and he drives a patrol car with the number 103 and the license plate 0170702. Ron Masak originally played the character of Lieutenant Meyer.

Note: In Cabot Cove, the newspaper is the *Gazette* (established in 1822; also seen as the *Globe Gazette*), the Cabot Cove Bus Lines (later, the Tri-County Bus Lines) services the town, and other businesses are the Light House Motel, the Navarro Inn, the Cabot Cove Bus Works, and the Cabot Cove Depot (an eatery). The Cabot Cove Cemetery dates back to 1710. Leticia is the unseen telephone operator; the town population is 3,560. Four TV movies also appeared: *Murder, She Wrote: South by Southwest* (1997); *Murder, She Wrote: A Story to Die For* (2000); *Murder, She Wrote: The Last Free Man* (2000); and *Murder, She Wrote: The Celtic Riddle* (2003).

Murphy Brown
(CBS, 1988–1997)

Cast: Candice Bergen (Murphy Brown), Faith Ford (Corky Sherwood), Joe Regalbuto (Frank Fontana), Charles Kimbrough (Jim Dial), Grant Shaud (Miles Silverberg), Robert Pastorelli (Eldin Benecky), Pat Corley (Phil).

Basis: Incidents in the life of Murphy Brown, a journalist and anchor of the Washington, D.C.–based television newsmagazine series *F.Y.I.* (For Your Information). Her coworkers are Jim Dial, Corky Sherwood, Frank Fontana, and Miles Silverberg.

OVERALL SERIES INFORMATION

F.Y.I., broadcast from Studio 6A (from a set called "The Window on America"), premiered on September 21, 1977, and has been honored by the Museum of Broadcast Arts for 15 years for journalism excellence (it first aired at 10 p.m., then 9 p.m.). It is assumed to be broadcast by CBS.

The gimmick is to exasperate Murphy by assigning her a different (and rather strange) secretary in virtually every episode (she had a total of 93 different secretaries and learned that after working for her, these secretaries formed their own support group). Murphy almost left *F.Y.I.* when the rival Wolf network offered her an efficient secretary named Barbara (Patti Yasutake).

Charles Kimbrough, Candice Bergen, Joe Regalbuto, Faith Ford, and Grant Shaud. *CBS/Photofest. ©CBS*

Kelly Green was the network's attempt to do a comical version of *F.Y.I.* with Morgan Fairchild as Julia St. Martin playing Murphy clone Kelly Green. A children's version was attempted called *F.Y.I. for Kids* with Mayim Bialik (as Natalie Moore, a mini-Murphy), Laura Mooney (as Tracy Knight, a mini-Corky), Mark-Paul Gosselaar (as Wes Jordan, a mini-Jim), and Troy Slaten (as Hank Caldwell, a mini-Frank).

Murphy, Corky, Jim, and Miles competed against Yale University on the game show *Collegiate Q&A* but lost (110 to 155); their consolation prizes were Scuffy Shoe Shine kits, Rice-a-Roni, and dinner at the Black Angus Restaurant. In 1991, the network was purchased by American Industrial, a company that manufactures appliances (like talking coffeemakers).

MURPHY BROWN

Parents: Bill Brown (Darren McGavin), publisher of the *Chicago Voice*, and Avery Brown (Colleen Dewhurst). After divorcing Avery, Bill married Karen Brown (Susan Wheeler).

Birthday: May 1948 (also mentioned as November 26, 1948).

Address: Cambridge Place, Washington, D.C.

Nicknames: Called "Susie Q" by her father, "Stinky" by her friends for playing practical jokes on them, and "Slugger" by Jim Dial.

Childhood Pet Dog: Butterscotch.

Education: Penn State College (majoring in journalism). Her eleventh-grade high school teacher, Ken Hamilton (William Schallert), inspired her to become a journalist (he later began the Murphy Brown School of Journalism); she was also editor of the school newspaper.

Hero: Newsman Howard K. Smith. Murphy submitted a videotape audition to him. Six weeks later, he responded, "You stink, but you have a nice tush."

Occupation: Journalist and TV news anchor. She worked previously as a foreign correspondent, and on August 16, 1977, she was hired by *F.Y.I.* (beating out newswoman Linda Ellerbee for the part). She also had her own business, the Murphy Brown School of Broadcasting, and was offered a role in the feature film *Deadline* (but was fired for rewriting the script).

Awards: The Robert F. Kennedy Journalism Award (for her story "No Place to Call Home"), an Emmy (best newscaster), and eight Humboldt News Story Awards.

Magazine Covers: Time, TV Guide, Esquire, and *Harper's Bazaar.* She was the subject of the *National Enquirer* story "Murphy Brown Having Big Foot's Baby" and was lampooned as "Mouthy Brown" in newspaper comics.

Character: A reputation for getting even with anyone who crosses her. She is easily exasperated, has a tendency to yell a lot, and has a caring side: "I once fed the cat next door." It is said Murphy could never care for a pet, but she claims, "I got a Chia Pet to grow." She goes through number 2 pencils quickly and has "only a 27-inch TV at home," and guests interviewed by Murphy claim, "It was like sticking my face in a buzz saw." Murphy has been banned from the White House (for running over President George Bush with her motorcycle). For her forty-second birthday in 1990, Murphy's coworkers, Corky, Miles, and Jim, gave her a home blood pressure kit, while Frank gave her something she never had: a sister (actress Christine Ebersole was hired to play Murphy's sister, Maddie Brown, for a day).

Car: A white Porsche (license plate 189 347, later MURPHY).

Favorite Flower: Sterling Roses.

Favorite Song: "Respect" by Aretha Franklin.

Child: Avery (named after her mother but first called "Baby Brown," "Winston Churchill Brown," "Woodward and Bernstein Brown," "Jacques Cousteau Brown," and "Adlai Stevenson Brown").

Avery's Father: Jake Lowenstein (Robin Thomas). They met at the 1968 Democratic National Convention and fell in love during a demonstration. They were arrested and married by the judge who heard their case (on August 28); their wedding dinner consisted of two corn dogs and a candied apple; five days later, they divorced. Jake reentered Murphy's life in 1990, and after a brief affair, Murphy became pregnant. Murphy chose to raise the baby alone (he was born on May 18, 1992, at 5:32 a.m. and weighed 9 pounds, 7 ounces; Murphy was in labor for 39 hours).

Replacement: Hillary Wheaton (Kate Mulgrew) anchored *F.Y.I.* during Murphy's maternity leave.

Flashbacks: Murphy as a girl (Meghann Haldeman).

CORKY LYNN SHERWOOD

Parents: Bootsie (Alice Hirson) and Edward Sherwood (Bryan Clark).

Sisters: Cookie Sherwood (Courtney Gebhart) and Kiki Sherwood (Sarah Abrell).

Place of Birth: Louisiana (where her family operated a farm).

Education: Eastern Louisiana University.

Occupation: F.Y.I. news team reporter. She represented Missouri in the Junior Miss Pageant when she was 18 and a year later was crowned Miss America. She also worked as a model ("The Check Girl") for the First Bank of New Orleans.

Awards: The 1989 Humboldt Award (for her story "A Woman's Touch at West Point," which broke Murphy's eight-year winning streak). Her typical stories, however, are fluff, such as "Woody Woodpecker's 50th Anniversary," an interview with the San Diego Chicken, and First Lady Nancy Reagan performing stomach exercises on TV.

First F.Y.I. Special: Corky's Place (wherein she interviewed actors Gary Collins and Mary Ann Mobley; cookie queen Mrs. Fields and Murphy Brown). Corky is also the cheerleader for the *F.Y.I.* football team, the Bulletins, and appeared on the CBS-TV series *Circus of the Stars* (performing a trapeze act with actor Robert Urich).

Ability: Can recite all the books of the Bible by heart.

Bra Size: 34B. She has blonde hair.

Hobby: Collecting First Lady Dolls.

Pet Cat: Mr. Fluffy.

Phone Number: 555-7261.

Trait: Has a difficult time saying no to people.

Husband: Will Forrest (Scott Bryce). They married in 1989 and divorced a year later due to their incompatibility; she was known as Corky Sherwood-Forrest. Will proposed to Corky at the Air and Space Museum and gave her a moon rock landing engagement ring. Will, a struggling writer, penned the book *The Dutch Boy*.

FRANK FONTANA

Parents: Dominic (Barney Martin) and Rose Fontana (Rose Marie).

Sisters: Pat Fontana (Gracie Moore); Shanelle Workman and Brittany Murphy played his unnamed sisters.

Childhood Pet Dog: Cocoa.

Occupation: F.Y.I. investigative reporter. He joined *F.Y.I.* in 1977 and previously worked as a reporter for the *New York Times*. He and Murphy also cohosted the premiere of the network's *Overnight News* program.

Home: Apartment 304 in an unnamed building.

Education: The Bishop Fallon High School for Boys.

Favorite Movie: The Maltese Falcon.

Character: Babied as a child and fears sleeping with his closet door open as a result of watching the film *Poltergeist*. He wrote a four-and-a-half-hour play called *Life Changed* and mentions having been in therapy for "13 or 14 years." In *TV Guide* listings for the show, his name is misspelled as "Fred Fontana."

Award: The Humboldt News Award (for his story "A Death in Dade County").

Relatives: Uncle, Sal (Richard Zavaglia).

Flashbacks: Frank as a boy (Sean Baca).

JAMES "JIM" DIAL

Occupation: F.Y.I.'s senior anchor. He has been with CBS News for 25 years. In 1956, he was the only news correspondent to get an interview with John F. Kennedy when he lost the vice-presidential nomination. If Hubert Humphrey had won the presidential race in 1968, Jim would have become his press secretary. It is also mentioned that Jim was a struggling news reporter for Channel 9 in Chicago who doubled as the host of the kiddie show "Poop Deck Pete and Cartoons Ahoy."

Address: 3134 South Bedford Drive.

Character: Very distinguished. He wears expensive Italian suits and has been called "America's Most Trusted Newsman." He has a blue and pink coffee mug shaped like a fish; before each broadcast, he orders fried rice from Wo Pong's Chinese restaurant and taps his knee three times for good luck. His proudest moment occurred when he interviewed Gandhi (but, as Jim says, "It got killed in the ratings. It was opposite an episode of *The Facts of Life* in which Tootie got her first bra"). He is also part owner of a gay bar called The Anchorman.

Most Embarrassing Moments: Laughing uncontrollably on live, national TV when reporting that the president had been stung by a wasp; interviewing the Queen of England with his fly open.

Most Famous For: The Dial family apple prune turkey stuffing.

Religion: Presbyterian.

Favorite Dinner: Lamb chops, mashed potatoes, and mint jelly.

Hobby: Tackling the *New York Times* crossword puzzle.

Wife: Doris (Janet Carroll). They have been married for 30 years and honeymooned at historic Williamsburg; Doris's maiden name is O'Rourke.

Pet Dog: First called Victor, then Trixie, and finally Trixter.

Club Affiliation: He and Murphy are members of the Dunfriars Club (for distinguished newspeople).

Quirk: Jim mentions that he never had a dream (until 1992, when he mentioned having one about terrible service at Heck's Shoe Store).

MILES SILVERBERG

Mother: Unnamed (Eva Chainey).

Age: 27.

Childhood Pet: Whitey (a hamster).

Occupation: The executive producer of *F.Y.I.* and the news show *The New Wave.*

Education: The Little Bo Peep Prep School; Harvard University, Class of 1984 (where he was known as "Miles Silverbrain" and acquired a master's degree in business).

Favorite "Drink": Mylanta (for all the aggravation Murphy causes him). He claims he is a good candidate for a heart attack and hears Murphy's voice in his sleep ("They should pipe it into cornfields to scare the crows away").

Car License Plate: 400 928 (later 452 689J).

Wife: Corky Sherwood (they married in 1996 "on a spur-of-the-moment thing" after Corky divorced Will Forrest).

Additional Duties: Getting "the good doughnuts" each morning for the staff at Marino's Bakery.

Replacement: Kay Carter-Shipley (Lily Tomlin) became the producer of *F.Y.I.* when Miles quit to oversee CBS News operations in New York City. Kay has a dog named Sparky and previously hosted the game show *Celebrity Face-Off 2000.*

Relatives: Brother, Josh Silverberg (Jon Tenney).

Flashbacks: Miles as a child (Jason Marsden).

OTHER CHARACTERS

Eldin Stanislaus Bernecky is Murphy's around-the-clock house painter (he has a very difficult time matching colors with Murphy's continually changing moods). He normally paints murals, uses Murphy's expensive panty hose to strain paint, buys his supplies at Ed's Paints, and created a mural of the Iran-Contra hearings on Murphy's bathroom ceiling. He has an apostles watch (each of the 12 are represented by an hour) and became Avery's nanny when Murphy could not find someone suitable to care for him. He became rich (sold a mural for $1.2 million) and left in 1994 to pursue his dream of studying art in Spain with Diego Garcia, a famous artist.

Phil (no last name given) is the owner of the local watering hole, Phil's Bar and Grill (established in 1919 and located at 1195 15th Street, although the street number 406 appears on the front door). Phil donated the swinging door to the men's room, which had signatures of various vice presidents, to the Smithsonian Institution. A Phil Burger and Fries is Murphy's favorite meal to order. Jerry Corley played Phil's unnamed nephew.

Newhart
(CBS, 1982–1990)

Cast: Bob Newhart (Dick Loudon), Mary Frann (Joanna Loudon), Julia Duffy (Stephanie Vanderkellen), Tom Poston (George Utley), Peter Scolari (Michael Harris), William Sanderson (Larry), Tony Papenfuss (Darryl One), John Volstad (Darryl Two).

Basis: A history buff and informational book author (Dick Loudon) and his wife (Joanna) attempt to run a quaint inn in Vermont.

RICHARD "DICK" LOUDON

Father: Bill Loudon (Bob Elliott).

Place of Birth: Allentown, Pennsylvania (he mentions, "I'm originally from New York" in another episode).

Occupation: Operator of the Stratford Inn at 28 Westbrook Road in River City, Vermont (off Route 22; rooms are $25 a day or $45 a day with a bath). It was built in 1774 by Nathan Potter, but this is contradicted when Dick and Joanna learn that the body of Sarah Newton, born in 1660 and hanged as a witch in 1692, is buried in the inn's basement (southwest corner) when she was refused a church burial. It is also revealed that the flounder is the town fish, the flying squirrel is the town's bird, and the key to the city will not open anything but will start Willie Frye's tractor.

Education: Cunningham Elementary School; Penn State College (played drums as "Slats Loudon" in a band called the Jazz Tones).

Childhood: Had a goldfish he named after actress Ethel Merman; attended Camp Cowapoka; experienced his first disappointment when he went to the circus eager to see the tigers but learned they were taken away after eating their trainer.

Favorite TV Series: Reruns of *The Bob Newhart Show.*

Favorite Sport: Skin diving (not really explained why).

Peter Scolari, Julia Duffy, Tom Poston, Bob Newhart, and Mary Frann. *CBS/ Photofest. ©CBS*

Idol: NBC newsman Edwin Newman.

Published Books: How to Build Plywood Furniture Anyone Would Be Proud Of, Pillow Talk (how to make pillows), *How to Make Your Dream Bathroom, How to Fly Fish, Installation and Care of Your Low Maintenance Lawn Sprinkler, A Hundred and One Uses for Garden Hoses, How to Build a Media Room, You Too Can Carve* (his best-selling book), *Know Your Harley* (motorcycle), *How to Panel in Hard-to-Reach Places, The Joy of Tubing, How to Make a Patio Cover,* and *How to Write How-To Books* (his thirty-fifth book). Bob also writes travel books; those mentioned are *Amazing Arkansas* and *Captivating Kansas.*

Novel: Murder at the Stratley (a takeoff of the Stratford Inn).

TV Show: Host of the interview program *Vermont Today* on WPIV, Channel 8 (when guests cancel, the psychic "The Unbelievable Jerry" steps in). Dick also hosted the kids show *Pirate Pete* (when the host became ill) and was co-host of *Vermont Tonight*, hosted by insult comic Don Prince (Don Rickles).

Shoe Size: 8½ DDD.

Catchphrase: "Rats" (which he says when something goes wrong).

Most Devastating Act: Burning down the French restaurant Maison Hubert (carelessly tossing a cigarette in the men's room wastebasket).

JOANNA LOUDON

Mother: Florence McKenna (Peggy McCay).

Place of Birth: Gainsville, Ohio.

Maiden Name: Joanna McKenna.

The Meeting: Joanna, a student at New York University and a part-time secretary at an unnamed ad agency in Manhattan, met Bob, an ad executive, when she was first hired. A Memorial Day picnic was their first date, and after marrying, Joanna quit college to work full-time when Bob pursued his writing career. Bob had dreamed of owning and restoring a historic inn, and when the Stratford became available, he purchased it (with a $2,000 down payment). At this time, they lived in a Manhattan apartment, and Joanna was on six committees to help raise money for disease-themed charities.

Wedding Anniversary Gift: Dick gives Joanna a yellow scarf (not a sweater, as she normally wears). They are first said to be married 16 years (1982), then 15 years (1986).

Occupation: Real estate broker ("Joanna Loudon, Real Estate"; she originally applied for but turned down an office job with the Herzoff Travel Agency). She is also a member of the Community Theater and starred in *The Girl from Manhattan*, a play written by Dick and reflecting how he and Joanna met.

TV Show: Host of *Your House Is My House* (later called *Hot Houses* to capitalize on Joanna's gorgeous looks).

Record: Rented the video *60 Days to a Tighter Tummy* more than anyone else.

Relatives: Aunt, Louise (Nancy Walker).

GEORGE UTLEY

Place of Birth: Vermont. He lives in an upstairs room at the inn.

Occupation: Dick's handyman. He has been working at the inn for 30 years and took over the position from his father (who made the inn's front-door welcome mat). Being a handyman is all he knows how to do. He tried becoming a salesman at the Auto Barn but was unable to do something different.

Secret Childhood Shame: To join the Vermont Hooligans gang, George had to find a car and "turn up the radio real loud." He did, but the car was in gear and rolled into a swamp. George was given the street name "Pliers" when he joined.

Typical Dress: A plaid shirt with overalls and a red baseball-like cap.

Lodge: The Beaver Lodge (the Memorial Day weekend feast is a spaghetti and tomato sauce sit-down dinner).

Education: Class of 1947 in an unnamed high school (a member of the welding club; he tried to join the glee club but couldn't sing and was made a listener).

Favorite Hammer: Old Blue.

Favorite Real 1940s Radio Program: The Goldbergs.

Favorite TV Series: Barnaby Jones (real) and *It's Always Moisha* (a mythical series about a nasty deli owner starring Don Rickles).

Favorite Movie: It's a Mad, Mad, Mad, Mad World (watches when he is upset).

Hobby: Bird watching (at Johnny Kaye Lake).

Creator: Invented the board game "Handyman: The Feel Good Game."

Good-Luck Charm: A penny (which he keeps in his shoe or sock).

Quirk: He must be the race car when he plays the game of "Monopoly."

Relatives: Aunt, Bess (Ann Guilbert); cousin, Eugene Wiley (Derek McGrath).

Flashbacks: George as a boy (Jason Marin); George's father (Tom Poston).

STEPHANIE VANDERKELLEN

Parents: Arthur (Richard Roat, then Jose Ferrer) and Mary Vanderkellen (Priscilla Morrill).

Place of Birth: Mentioned as Newport, Rhode Island, then Vermont.

Occupation: Maid at the Stratford Inn (where she lives in an upstairs room). Following her divorce after a two-day marriage to a man (Carl) she felt was not right for her, Stephanie felt she needed to start a new life and replaced her sister Leslie Vanderkellen (Jennifer Holmes) as the inn's maid; Leslie left to complete her education at Oxford University in England (she previously mentioned she was working part-time at the inn while attending Dartmouth University [seeking a degree in Renaissance theology] and training to become a member of the Olympic ski team).

Fear: Growing old and losing her "beautiful and dazzling looks."

Car License Plate: CUPCAKE.

Talent: "Avoiding work better than anyone else."

Nail Polish Shade: Mystic Lilac.

Character: Very demanding and moody and looks down on people of lesser social standing. She pouts when she doesn't get her way and has to always be in fashion (purchases her clothes at Peck's Department Store).

TV Series: Stephanie played twins Jody and Judy Bumper on the sitcom *Seein' Double* (Dick Loudon played her father, Henry Bumper, and it was written, produced, and directed by Michael Harris). She was Dick's cohost on

Channel 8's *Home Shopping with Dick and Stephanie* and temporary leader of the Ranger Girls scout troop.

Worst Day of Her Life: Feeling inferior when a couple, cuter than she and Michael, moved into the community.

MICHAEL HARRIS

Parents: Tad (Henry Gibson) and Lily Harris (Ruth Manning). Tad, an actor who works under the name Tad Barrows, deserted the family when Michael was a toddler. Michael has a birthmark in the shape of a mandolin on his left butt cheek.

Place of Birth: Vermont.

Girlfriend: Stephanie Vanderkellen.

Occupation: Executive at WPIV-TV, Channel 8, then, after being fired for insulting the boss's daughter, a salesman at Circus of Shoes, produce manager at Menke's Market, a street mime, and a singer at the Gun Powder Room of the Drummond Family Restaurant on Route 14. He became a resident of the Pine Valley Psychiatric Hospital (when his world tumbled down around him) and with Stephanie sought counseling (as Chuck and Dawn) when their relationship appeared to be ending. He eventually regained his job at Channel 8.

Address: Apartment 9B (in it is a shrine to Stephanie called "Cupcake Corner").

Nicknames for Stephanie: "Gumdrop," "Cupcake," and "Muffin."

Holiday: Michael's relentless efforts to shower Stephanie with gifts led him to create "Cupcake Day" (between Valentine's Day and Easter). In 1989, Stephanie gives birth to a girl they name Baby Stephanie (played in a flash-forward [at age five] by Candy Hutson).

Childhood: Michael worked on TV as "Little Mikey," the singing assistant on *Captain Cookie's Clubhouse* during the 1964–1965 season.

LARRY, DARRYL, AND DARRYL

Relationship: Unkempt friends of Dick and Joanna. They are brothers, but only Larry speaks. According to Larry, his brothers never speak because they have nothing to say (Larry also mentions that one of the Darryls accidentally sat on a porcupine "and he ain't never talked since"). The Darryls were numbered as such to avoid confusion when they were growing up. While Larry is an expert on wine and enjoys crawling under houses, Darryl Two has an invisible friend named Ronald.

Occupation: Owners of the Minuteman Café on Westbrook Road. They purchased it from Kirk Devane (Steven Kampmann) and will take any unpleasant job for money—like cleaning drainage ditches. Larry mentions they have two other businesses: "Anything for a Buck" and "Elegant Mouse, Rat, and Weasel Skins for the Discriminating Buyers Who Are Tired of Wearing Feathers."

Quirks: The brothers enjoy whittling; Larry places a quarter in his ear for good luck; Darryl One has a talent for catching mice.

Education: Larry attended the Mount Pillared Technical School; Darryl One was enrolled at Oxford University; Darryl Two majored in royalty at Cambridge University under a rowing scholarship.

Character: Larry talks for his brothers. When he enters a scene, it's "Hello. My name is Larry. This is my brother Darryl, and this is my other brother Darryl." If Larry is alone, he says, "Hi, I'm Larry, party of one." The brothers just arrived in town in 1984, purchased their café, and have kept everything about themselves a secret, even their last name. Larry did reveal that the brothers are reeling over the fact that England is going on the metric system and that for fun they often play with mops and look forward to their "Daily Naked Hour." At one point, they were the producers of *The Carol Burnett Show* and befriended show costar Tim Conway (who now joins them for their weekly Wednesday night poker game).

Family Shame: Larry, thought to be the oldest brother, was actually born second (birth certificates indicate that Darryl One, delivered by a midwife at the same time she was delivering a heifer, is the oldest).

Criminal Activity: Teasing chickens and taunting sheep. When arrested, their bail is set at $85 each, or all three for $200.

"THE LAST NEWHART"

It is 1995, and everyone but Dick and Joanna has moved on. Mr. Takadachi (Gedde Watanabe) purchased the properties (at $1 million each) surrounding the inn with a plan to build the 5,000-room Takadachi Hotel and Golf Course. The Stratford Inn is now on the fourteenth fairway of a golf course and has a Japanese motif. Stephanie and Michael have moved to Switzerland to build "Stefi Land," George plans to build "Utley Land" (an amusement park for handymen), and Larry and the Darryls have moved to Chicago to live with an uncle. Larry is now married to Rhonda (Christine Mellot); Darryl One has wed Sada (Lisa Kudrow), and Darryl Two is married to Zora (Nada Despotovich).

Dick and Joanna are hosting a reunion of the "old gang" when the Darryls speak for the first time (yelling "Quiet!" to their arguing wives). Dick is standing in the doorway when a stray golf ball hits him in the head. The screen dissolves to black. A figure is seen in bed and switches on the light. We see that it is not Dick Loudon but Dr. Bob Hartley (from *The Bob Newhart Show*). His wife Emily (Suzanne Pleshette) from that show asks, "What's wrong?" Bob explains he had a horrible nightmare wherein he was married to a beautiful blonde (the owner of an inn), had an heiress for a maid, and was friends with three strange brothers. Apparently, the eight years of *Newhart* were but the one night dream of Dr. Bob Hartley.

Night Court
(NBC, 1984–1992)

Cast: Harry Anderson (Harry T. Stone), Markie Post (Christine Sullivan), Richard Moll (Bull Shannon), John Larroquette (Dan Fielding), Charles Robinson (Mac Robinson), Marsha Warfield (Roz Russell).

Basis: Life in a Manhattan night court as seen through the cases of Harold T. Stone, an arraignment judge at the Manhattan Criminal Courts Building (also called the Municipal Court House) in New York City. Harry's sessions are held on the eighteenth floor in room 808 (also seen as 1808).

HAROLD T. "HARRY" STONE

Place of Birth: Chesapeake, Ohio.

Education: Chesapeake State College (majored in law).

Occupation: Lawyer, then judge (although after graduating from college, he attempted to break into show business as a magician).

Job Acquisition: After serving as a New York defense lawyer, Harry's name was put on a list of 1,000 perspective judges for the night court system. The mayor called each name on the list, but nobody was home—except for Harry. ("It was a Sunday. I was home and I got the job.") He was 34 at the time.

Trait: Known for his "$55 fine and time served" sentences. He also processes 12 percent fewer cases than other judges due to his long lectures to defendants.

Idol: Singer Mel Torme. Harry has his complete record collection and will marry the first girl who is impressed by that. A framed picture of Mel sits on his desk; a picture of his favorite actress, Jean Harlow, can be seen on the wall. Harry's inability to meet Mel under normal circumstances is a recurring gimmick of the show.

Hobbies: Genetics and magic (he idolizes magician Harry Houdini).

Sport: Bowling (uses the Bowl-a-Lane Alleys).

Favorite TV Show as a Kid: Magic Time.

Favorite Breakfast Cereal: Zipp Bits.

Favorite Drinks: Cherry Kool-Aid and Fresca soda.

Favorite Candy: Chocolate cigarettes.

Pet Rabbit: Cecil (as a kid, he had a dog named Oliver and a teddy bear, Jamboree).

Lucky Charm: A Mercury head dime.

Teaching: Harry conducts law classes at the Ed Koch Community College (Koch is a former mayor of New York; a pigeon caught in the air-conditioning vent is the school's mascot). He is also the faculty adviser for the school newspaper, *Harpoon.*

Crime: When Harry was a teenager, he stole a 1964 Cadillac convertible for a joy ride. His foot slipped off the gas pedal and "knocked over" a liquor store when the car crashed. He spent two nights in jail and two weeks in a reformatory as a result.

Honor: Voted "Most Fascinating Judge in New York City" by the Empire Magicians Society and "Man of the Month" by the Society of Goodfellows.

TV Role: The adult judge on *The Littlest Lawyer* (about a kid attorney).

Relatives: Stepfather, Buddy (John Astin). Buddy, now married to Amanda (Karen Morrow), spent time in a mental hospital (where he devised 10,000 ways, excluding building a raft out of bamboo, to get the castaways off *Gilligan's Island*). Harry's unnamed mother abandoned the family when Harry was five years old.

CHRISTINE SULLIVAN

Position: Legal aid attorney.

Place of Birth: North Tonawanda (near Buffalo, New York; she had a dog named Puddles and dreamed of becoming an ice skater, entering the Olympics, and winning a gold medal for America; the ice stopped her: "It's slippery on that stuff").

Education: Buffalo State College (majoring in psychology; she is now an expert on depression). She entered the Greater Miss Buffalo Beauty Pageant of 1978 but lost for taking a stand on women's rights. Christine mentioned that she gave up a chance to become the Buffalo Starch Queen and that her father called her "Peaches."

Measurements: 37-23-35.

Trait: Very nervous and despises people who treat her "differently because I have breasts." She is beautiful, always fashionably dressed, but also easily exasperated and often remarks, "I should have worn my underwire bra" (as "I tend to jiggle when I get upset").

Address: While exact addresses are not given, she lived in the following apartments: 1611-E, 616, and 7-C.

Club Membership: Ha Ha ("Happy Alone, Happy Adults"; their slogan is "Happy to Be Happy").

Car: While not shown, it has "Happy Face" hubcaps.

Clients: "The most artistic people I get as clients are hookers with makeup skills." Christine lost the first case she had: a man who dismantled a record store with his hands. She broke out in tears, hyperventilated, and had to be dragged out of the courtroom.

Life Changer: A one-night stand with undercover cop Tony Juliano (Ray Abruzzo) led to Christine becoming pregnant in 1990 (she gave birth to Charles Otis; "The Song of the Humpback Whale" was her birth song). When Christine returned from maternity leave, she handed out videos called *Charles Otis Juliano—The Movie.*

Artistic Inspiration: Artist Ian McKee (Bill Calvert) painted a naked mural of Christine on a warehouse door that he called *The Naked Body of Justice.*

Book: Under the pen name Mother Sullivan, Christine wrote the children's book *Mommy's World.*

Final Episode: Christine runs for congresswoman of the Thirteenth District, is elected, and moves to Washington, D.C., to begin a new career.

DAN FIELDING

Parents: "Daddy" Bob (John McIntire) and Musette Elmore (Jeanette Nolan).

Sister: Donna Elmore (Susan Diol), vice president of Farmer Frank Meats, Inc.

Real Name: Reinhold Fielding Elmore (he assumed the name of Dan Fielding when he started school).

Place of Birth: A farm in Paris, Louisiana (founded by his great grandfather). His parents were rural, and he lived with pigs in his room; he was six years old before he realized he wasn't related to them. As a child, he thought he had a pet turtle named Scruffy (it was actually a potato painted by his father to resemble a turtle).

Occupation: Prosecuting attorney. As a teenager during the summer of 1967, he worked as a lifeguard at the Lone Star Beach Club in Galveston, Texas.

Address: An apartment on Hauser Street and Third Avenue.

Mercedes License Plate: HOT TO TROT (he considers himself a ladies' man and calls the car "The Dan Mobile").

Favorite Actress: Annette Funicello (he claims to have "an Annette inflatable collector doll on back order").

Military Service: Army Reserve.

Stock Holdings: The Fletko Corporation (famous for tearing down landmarks).

Executor: Dan oversees the Phil Foundation, a charity that supports needy causes (when a bum named Phil Alfonse Sanders [Will Utay] was killed by a falling piano, it was discovered he was rich and had willed Dan [for whom he worked as a flunky] $8 million to use for charity).

TV Program: Host of *In Your Face* (a show that degrades people).

Favorite Club: The Sticky Wickey.

Contest: When Christine became pregnant, Dan started the "Guess the Size of Her Boobs" contest on TV (where he referred to her breasts as "Puppies").

Dream: Working for the prestigious law firm of Taylor, Woods and Johnson.

Nickname: Called "The Prince of Passion" by girls.

Final Episode: Quit his job to pursue his dream girl, Christine, to Washington.

BULL SHANNON

Mother: Henrietta "Hank" Shannon (Paddi Edwards).

Place of Birth: Manhattan.

Position: Harry's bailiff. He first worked as an usher at the Majestic Theater, then had a short career as a wrestler called "Bull, the Battling Bailiff."

Full Name: Aristotle Nostradamus Shannon (his mother named him "Bull" when she found out she was pregnant).

IQ: 181 (although high, his friends think "I'm dumber than dirt").

Height: 6 feet, 8½ inches tall. He weighs 200 pounds.

Salary: $320 a week.

Ritual: Uses lacquer thinner to polish his bald head (in the pilot episode, Bull had hair).

Volunteer: The Volunteer Father Organization (the first child he "adopted" was Andy [Pamela Segall], who he thought was a boy; Andy [real name Stella] pretended to be a boy so the organization would accept her, as they would not assign fathers to girls).

Wife: Wanda (Cathy Appleby), who Bull married in 1991 on the courthouse roof. Bull wore his mother's wedding dress (which she made into a jacket), and Harry presided.

Address: Only given as Apartment 7 (there is a large "B" on his front door; he has a concrete sofa—"durable, practical and easy to patch" that he made himself). The apartment, next to a subway line, shakes when a train passes.

Christine Comment: Because she is kind, he calls her "a lily pad in a pond of sludge." Bull is also devoted to Harry—"I'd swallow molten lava for that man. Fortunately he never asked me." He says people mistake his humor for a rare pituitary disease, has a hand puppet called Bull Puppet, and still believes in Santa Claus. He shows people he is smart by picking a strange word from a dictionary and using it in conversation.

Favorite TV Show: The Smurfs.

Favorite Cereal: Frosted Neon Nuggets. He entered its contest ("Little Tikes Golly-Gee-O-Rama") and won the mystery prize, the Shatner Turbo 2000 Wimberly Wig.

Pet Python: Bertha (later called Harvey).

Author: Wrote the children's book *Bully the Dragon* (but it frightened kids), then *The Azzari Sisters: An Adventure in Fun, The Snake Pit of Chuckie's Mind,* and *Bull on Bull* (which was rejected by 426 publishers; he used the vanity press Random Author to publish it and bought enough copies at $11 per copy to make it a best seller).

Quirk: Talks to the early man exhibit at the Museum of Natural History when he becomes depressed.

Relatives: Cousin, Ralph Shannon (Gordon Clapp), a crooked lawyer.

Final Episode: Bull is taken to the planet Jupiter by two aliens to become somebody—"The man who can reach the items on our top shelves."

MAC ROBINSON

Father: Clarence Robinson (Charles Lampkin).

Position: Court clerk. In his youth, he was a singer with a group, the Starlights, "before they became famous."

Wife: Quon Le Dac (Denice Kumagai), who works as a checker at the Vegetable Mart.

Meeting: While serving with the army in Vietnam, Mac helped Quon Le's family overcome the ravages of a bombing. Quon Le, 12 at the time, fell in love with him. In 1985, when the new regime took over, Quon Le left Vietnam and came to New York to find Mac. Mac married her in an attempt to keep her in the United States. They had planned to annul the marriage but did not when they found they loved each other.

Hobby: Filmmaking. He taped 60 hours of Bull's wedding and turned it into a movie he called *Connubial Fusion*. He chose to study film at City College as the series ended.

Relatives: Quo Le's father, Ho Dac (Keye Luke).

ROSALIND "ROZ" RUSSELL

Position: Bailiff. She previously worked as a stewardess for Paramus Airlines (where, dealing with annoying passengers, she found her goal in life "was to kick butt").

Salary: $410 a week.

Volunteer: Works for Toys for Toddlers at the Canal Street Youth Center.

Dislike: Having her picture taken (people say she looks like comedian Slappy White).

Ex-Husband: Eugene Westfall (Roger E. Mosley). They divorced after six weeks of marriage (he was a member of a band, the Expectations).

Relatives: Aunt, Ruth (Della Reese); unseen was Roz's Uncle Lionel.

OTHER CHARACTERS

Lana Wagner (Karen Austin) was the original court clerk (she was engaged to the never-seen Emerson). She was on the dean's list at college (a top student) and edited the school's poetry magazine. She was replaced by Charli Tracy (D.D. Howard); Mac Robinson then replaced Charli.

Sheila Gardner (Gail Strickland) was the original public defender; she was replaced by Liz Williams (Paula Kelly), who in turn was replaced by Wilhelmina "Billie" Young (Ellen Foley). Mary (Deborah Harmon) replaced Billie, and Christine Sullivan replaced Mary as the legal aid attorney.

Selma Hacker (Selma Diamond) and Florence Kleiner (Florence Halop) were the female bailiffs before Roz. Selma was a chain smoker and hadn't missed a day of work in 27 years. Florence had the maiden name of Nightingale "and went through hell in grade school."

Perfect Strangers
(ABC, 1986–1992)

Cast: Bronson Pinchot (Balki Bartokomous), Mark Linn-Baker (Larry Appleton), Melanie Wilson (Jennifer Lyons), Rebeca Arthur (Mary Anne Spencer).
Basis: Distant cousins attempt to live together when the American-born Larry and the foreign-born Balki discover they are long-lost relatives.

OVERALL SERIES INFORMATION

Balki, a sheepherder from the small Mediterranean Island of Mypos and his American cousin Larry (who is one-sixty-fourth Myposian) live in Chicago, Illinois, at the Caldwell Hotel, Apartment 203 (also seen as Apartment E) at 627 Lincoln Boulevard. They first work for Donald "Twink" Twinkacetti (Ernie Sabella), the gruff owner of the Ritz Discount Store (they are also members of the Ritz Discount Royals softball team). Donald; his wife, Edwina (Belita Moreno); and their children, Donnie (Matthew Licht) and Marie (Erica Gayle), live at 2831 Garfield Street.

Larry and Balki next work for the *Chicago Bulletin* (Larry as the city editor's assistant, Balki as a mailroom clerk). Apartment 209 at 711 Caldwell Avenue is their address, and they are members of the newspaper's Strike Force bowling team. Belita Moreno is now Lydia Markham, a columnist (of "Dear Lydia") and host of the TV series *Lydia Live*.

Sheepherding is the number one occupation on Mypos, and the national debt is $635; a cow's picture graces Myposian money. It is when Balki discovers he has an American cousin that he sets out to find him and become a part of his life.

BALKI BARTOKOMOUS

Mother: Not named (Bronson Pinchot).
Cousin: Bartok (Bronson Pinchot).
Nickname for Larry: "Cousin Larry."

Phone Number (1992): 555-9876.

Favorite Foods: Eel wrapped in grape leaves; sheepherder's bread with a side dish of Ding Ding Mac-Mood (pig snout). He eats yak links for breakfast.

Reputation: The best baker in Mypos and famous for cream puffs (although they must be slow baked; if not, "the bib in the baca goes boom" [explodes]).

Favorite Houseplant: Marge (a Popadaluodipu plant that grows only on Mount Mypos and can cure the common cold [but it also grows mustaches on women, and the cold returns in two weeks after the effects wear off]).

Education: The Mypos School; Chicago Community College (taking classes in American history; ran for student body president with the slogan "Pro Sheep, Anti Wolf").

Favorite TV Show: Uncle Shaggy's Doghouse.

Favorite Singer: Wayne Newton.

Bath Wash: Mr. Ducky's Bubble Bath.

Pets: Steve and Eydie (pigeons named after singers Steve Lawrence and Eydie Gorme); Yorgi (parrot named after his pet goat on Mypos). He also adopted a stray dog he called Super Dave. As a child, Balki had a 300-pound pet turtle (Bibby), a dog (Koos Koos), and a horse (Trodsky). To remind him of his childhood, he rides Blue Thunder, the coin-operated horse at the Shop and Save supermarket.

Shoes: Balki has named his favorite pair Phil and Andy.

Artistic Ability: Draws the comic strip "Dimitri's World" for the newspaper (about a cuddly little sheep). He has a stuffed sheep named Dimitri.

Greatest Fear: The Gabuggies, the Myposian Fib Faeries. If he ever lies, he believes Eva, Zsa Zsa, and Magda, the agents of their god, Vertosh, will punish him.

Volunteer Work: Candy striper at Chicago General Hospital (where he won the "Bed Changer of the Month" award).

Stardom: Balki's song "Balki B" was produced by Knight Records, and Balki performed as "Fresh Young Balki."

Girlfriend: Mary Anne Spencer (they married on April 18, 1992).

LAWRENCE "LARRY" APPLETON

Father: Not named (James Noble).

Siblings: Brother, Billy Appleton (Ted McGinley); sister, Elaine Appleton (Sue Ball).

Grandfather: Buzz Appleton (John Anderson).

Place of Birth: Madison, Wisconsin.

Childhood Pet Dog: Spot.

Education: Madison High School (he asked 12 girls to the senior prom; 13 girls turned him down; one said, "Don't even think of asking me"); Chicago University (majored in journalism).

Quirk: Gargles to the song "Moon River."

Catchphrase: "Oh My Lord" (says it when something goes wrong).

TV Appearance: He and Balki attempted to win money on *Risk It All* (and lost).

Investments: A racehorse called Larry's Fortune and virtually worthless stock in Unicorn, Inc., the company that makes Balki's favorite cereal, Raisin Puffs.

Girlfriend: Jennifer Lyons. They married on September 27, 1991, and moved into a home on Elm Street. When the expenses became overwhelming, Balki and Mary Anne become their boarders. Prior to the marriage, Balki called Jennifer "Future Cousin Jennifer."

OTHER CHARACTERS

Jennifer and Mary Anne: Friends since they were eight years old. Both are stewardesses for an unnamed airline. Jennifer feels that living with Mary Anne is like living with a Barbie doll (too neat and perfect); Jennifer feels that Mary Anne is untidy and hates it when she hogs the bathroom ("It takes her two hours to put on her makeup"). Jennifer was born in April in Iowa, where her parents owned a corn-canning business. Mary Anne was "Little Miss Gingivitis" in her sixth-grade hygiene play. Marla Adams played Jennifer's mother, Kathleen Lyons; Robert King was Jennifer's father, Mr. Lyons.

Note: In the unaired pilot version, Louie Anderson played Cousin Larry.

Quantum Leap
(NBC, 1989–1993)

Cast: Scott Bakula (Sam Beckett), Dean Stockwell (Al Calavicci), Deborah Pratt (voice of Ziggy).

Basis: A scientist (Sam Beckett) travels through time, leaping into the bodies of people he does not know, to help them correct a mistake they made and set history straight.

SAMUEL "SAM" BECKETT

Parents: John (Scott Bakula) and Thelma Beckett (Caroline Kava).

Siblings: Tom Beckett (David Newsom) and Katherine Beckett (Olivia Burnette).

Birthday: August 8, 1953 (born at 12:30 p.m.); Sam mentions 1955 in another episode.

Place of Birth: A dairy farm in Elkridge, Indiana.

Social Security Number: 563-86-9801.

Education: Elkridge High School and the Massachusetts Institute of Technology (MIT) (entered at the age of 15). He has doctorates in medicine, quantum physics, music, and ancient languages. He can speak German, and his writings on science earned him a Nobel Peace Prize; he has been dubbed "The Next Einstein" by *Time* magazine for his theories on time travel.

Height: 6 feet tall. He weighs 175 pounds.

Wife: Dr. Donna Eleese (Teri Hatcher).

Current Address: PO Box 555, Stallions Springs, New Mexico 87501.

Driver's License Number: 5738457 (expires in 1998).

Idol: Albert Einstein.

Occupation: Quantum physicist.

The Experiment: Quantum Leap, a $43 billion time-traveling government project located in a secret lab 30 miles outside of Destiny County, New Mexico.

The Reason: "To make the world a better place; to make right what was once wrong."

The Test: Threats of the government ending its $2.4 billion in funding forces Sam to become his own test subject to prove that Quantum Leap works. A malfunction within the acceleration chamber traps Sam in time, and he cannot be retrieved until the computer, which he calls "Ziggy," can be fixed. Sam now travels in time but only within 30 years of his own lifetime. For reasons that are unknown, Sam "leaps" into the bodies of people he does not know to help them correct a mistake. The viewer sees Sam as himself, but people see him as the person he has become; dogs, some children, and mentally impaired people can also see Sam as he really is. The people Sam becomes are transferred to Ziggy's Waiting Room until Sam completes his mission and they can be returned to their lives.

The Problem: In 1966, Sam encounters Alia (Renee Coleman), a futuristic time traveler, and her hologram, Dr. Zoey Malvison (Carolyn Seymour); her assignments are controlled by an artificial intelligence (Lothos). Alia is evil and Sam's direct opposite; her missions are to destroy people, not save them (as Sam does). Sam cannot kill her, as it would mean destroying himself. Sam believes he is trapped in time to stop Alia, while Alia believes she has to stop Sam from changing the fates she creates.

Final Episode: "Mirror Image, August 8, 1953." Sam leaps into himself but never returns home.

Fear: Heights (after seeing a *Tarzan* movie as a child, Sam rigged a homemade vine from the barn roof, attempted to swing, but failed, hence his fear).

Catchphrase: "Oh, boy!" (said when he involuntarily leaps).

Flashbacks: Sam as a boy (Adam Logan).

AL CALAVICCI

Occupation: Quantum Leap Project Observer (called "The Observer").

Ability: Appears to Sam as a hologram via a handheld miniature (and slightly defective) version of Ziggy. Al supplies Sam with information about the person whose life he assumes.

Birthday: June 15, 1945 (but when Sam leaps into 1957, Al is 23 years old, making his birth year 1934).

Background: Al grew up in an orphanage (where his only "pet" was a roach named Kevin; Al mentions being eight years old at this time in 1942). He ran away from the orphanage to join the circus and later enlisted in the navy (he became an ensign in 1957 and was called "Bingo" by his buddies; he retired as an admiral). Al was married to Beth (Susan Diol), the only girl he ever loved. While serving in Vietnam, Al was reported as missing in action and presumed dead. In 1973, he was found alive and learned that Beth had remarried; he kept his "death" a secret and never returned to her.

Habit: Smoking a good cigar.

Social Security Number: 563-86-9801.

Ferrari Cars: A 1981 Berlinetta convertible; a 1987 Testarossa.

Education: Al mentions having attended MIT.

Remington Steele
(NBC, 1982–1986)

Cast: Stephanie Zimbalist (Laura Holt), Pierce Brosnan (Remington Steele).
Basis: A man who does not actually exist (Remington Steele) joins forces with private detective Laura Holt to solve crimes.

OVERALL SERIES INFORMATION
Feeling that a female-owned detective agency is not appealing to clients, Laura Holt changes Laura Holt Investigations to Remington Steele Investigations. By taking the first name of a typewriter and the last name of her favorite football team, business is suddenly booming. To explain Remington's absence, Laura tells clients, "Mr. Steele never involves himself in a case; he functions best in an advisory capacity." If a client insists on seeing Mr. Steele, Laura passes on a case.

All is progressing well until an assignment to safeguard the Royal Lavallette diamonds unites Laura with a sophisticated jewel thief (unnamed) out to steal them. The thief is the picture of the man Laura envisioned as Remington Steele. When Laura sees that the thief is in danger of being captured, she saves him by telling authorities he is her partner, Remington Steele. Remington, being the con man he is, convinces Laura to let him continue assuming the name as her partner in the agency. Laura agrees but under the condition "I do the work; you take the bows."

Remington Steele Investigations is located in suite 1157 of a building at 606 West Beverly Boulevard in Los Angeles; its phone numbers are 555-9450, 555-3535, and 555-9548. Canary yellow memo pads are used in the office. Laura believes that Remington solves cases quite by chance and constantly complains about the amount of money he spends on a case. The comic strip "Blaster" used images of Remington and Laura as "Dashing Dave" and "Doll Face."

Pierce Brosnan and Stephanie Zimbalist. *NBC/Photofest.* ©*NBC*

REMINGTON STEELE

Real Name: Never revealed; referred to as "The Mysterious Remington Steele."
Place of Birth: Ireland on September 6, 1952.
Background: Apparently an orphan, as he grew up on the streets and was taught
   the fine art of crime by master con artist Daniel Chalmers (Efrem Zimbalist

Jr.), who was actually his father (but suffered a heart attack before he could tell Remington his real name). Before relocating to America to pursue a career as a thief, Remington became a professional boxer called "The Kilkearney Kid."

Address: 1594 Rossmore Street (also given as 5594 Rossmore), Apartment 5A, in Los Angeles.

Cars: 1936 Auburn (plate R STEELE); Mercedes (plate IDR 0373).

Favorite TV Series: The Honeymooners.

Quirk: Associates motion pictures with real life and solves crimes based on their plots. He claims that old movies are for therapeutic value, as they relax him. His living room wall displays posters from *Casablanca, Hotel Imperial, Notorious,* and *The Thin Man.*

Passport: Remington has five passports from five different countries with five different aliases. In addition to Remington Steele, all are characters played by his favorite actor, Humphrey Bogart: Michael O'Leary (Ireland; from the 1939 film *Dark Victory*), Paul Fabrini (Italy; from the 1940 film *They Drive by Night*), Douglas Quintain (England; from *Stand-In,* 1937), John Morrill (France; from the 1940 film *Virginia City*), and Richard Blaine (Australia; from *Casablanca,* 1942).

Book: In the episode "Etched in Steele," Remington is seen negotiating a deal with Forsythe House Publishers for a book called *Remington Steele's Ten Most Famous Cases* (it is not disclosed whether the deal was made or the book even written).

Recognition: Voted one of the five most eligible bachelors by *Upbeat* magazine.

Ex-Lover: Felicia (Cassandra Harris; Pierce Brosnan's first wife).

LAURA HOLT

Birthday: January 28, 1956.

Mother: Abigail Holt (Beverly Garland).

Sister: Frances Piper (Maryedith Burrell). She is married to Donald Piper (Michael Durrell).

Address: 800 10th Street, Apartment 3A, in a building owned by the Commercial Management Corporation.

Pet Cat: Nero.

Education: Stanford University (majored in criminology and was a member of the glee club). She shared a fourth-floor dorm with three girls, and they were known as "The Four East." After graduating, Laura became an apprentice detective at the Havenhurst Detective Agency. She later quit to start her own agency.

Home Phone Number: 555-6235.

Mobile Phone Number: T-7328.

Car License Plate: JEL 1525 (later 1EY 9463).

Childhood: Nicknamed "Binky"; *Atomic Man* was her favorite TV show; showed an unusual fascination in crime for a young girl.

Favorite Radio Station: KROT (her clock radio alarm rings at 6 a.m.).

Family Oddity: The Holt Curse (a craving for chocolate).

Quirk: Never carries a gun ("I never found the need to use one"). The reading glasses Laura is seen wearing date back to her college days when she bought them to impress her calculus professor ("To make me look brainy").

Ability: Practical but intuitive, logical and brilliant. No matter how bleak the situation (case), she never loses her sense of humor.

OTHER CHARACTERS

Murphy Michaels (James Read) assisted Laura in first-season episodes, and Bernice Foxx (Janet DeMay), whom Remington called "Miss Wolf," was their receptionist. Mildred Krebs (Doris Roberts) replaced both characters as an IRS auditor who found excitement as a secretary and sleuth (Murphy was said to have left to open his own detective agency in Colorado and Bernice to have run off with a saxophone player). Mildred is a member of the Dragon Ladies bowling team and has an uncontrollable urge to attend séances. She calls Remington "Mr. Steele" (and upsets him when she doesn't have his coffee and morning paper on his desk by 9 a.m.) and Laura "Miss Holt." Mildred's last name is seen in the closing credits as "Krebs" but in episodes as "Krebbs." Albert Macklin played her nephew Bernard.

Roseanne
(ABC, 1988–1997)

Cast: Roseanne (Roseanne Conner); John Goodman (Dan Conner); Alicia Goranson, then Sarah Chalke (Becky Conner); Sara Gilbert (Darlene Conner); Michael Fishman (D.J. Conner); Laurie Metcalf (Jackie Harris).

Basis: Life with a dysfunctional American family (parents Roseanne and Dan) and their children (Darlene, Becky, and D.J.) living in Lanford, Illinois. In 1995, Roseanne, now in her forties gives birth to a son she and Dan name Jerry Garcia Conner (homage to Jerry Garcia of the Grateful Dead; played by Morgan and Cole Roberts).

ROSEANNE CONNER

Parents: Al (John Randolph) and Beverly Lorraine Harris (Estelle Parsons). Beverly has a half sister named Sonya and divorced Al when she discovered he had a mistress. In 1996, she was revealed to be a lesbian. Joyce DeVine

Roseanne Barr, Michael Fishman, John Goodman, Alicia Goranson, and Sara Gilbert. *ABC/Photofest. ©ABC*

(Ruta Lee), a lounge singer at the Lanford Holiday Inn known as Joyce, the Rotating Voice, was her lover.

Maiden Name: Roseanne Harris.

Nicknames: "Big Red," "The Big R," "Rosilla," "Ro," and "Elsie."

Address: 714 Delaware Street.

Education: Lanford High School (where she dreamed of becoming a writer and penning "the great American novel").

Occupation: Housewife; assembly line worker at Wellman Plastics; order taker at Divine Chicken; bartender at the Lobo Lounge; cleanup lady at Art's Beauty Parlor; waitress at Rodbell's Luncheonette in the Lanford Mall; telephone solicitor for *Discount House Magazine*; partner in the Lanford Lunchbox; product sample girl (pushing cheese in a can at the Buy & Bag Supermarket); TV commentator ("Roseanne Reports from the Heartland") on WERG-TV, Channel 4, in Chicago.

Grocery Shopping: Buy & Bag Supermarket.

Most Dislikes: The kids leaving jelly in the peanut butter jar.

Relatives: Grandmother, Mary Harris (Shelley Winters), called "Nana Mary."

DANIEL "DAN" CONNER

Parents: Ed (Ned Beatty), a traveling salesman, and Audrey Conner (Ann Wedgeworth, then Debbie Reynolds). Audrey died in a mental institution; Ed then married Crystal Anderson (Natalie West), whose prior husband, Sonny, died a year after their marriage. Crystal, half Ed's age, had two children with Ed: Little Ed and Angela. It was said that Dan was born in January, then in November.

Education: Lanford High School (a member of the school's football team). He was called "Yor" when he rode his motorcycle.

First Date: The A&W drive-in. On their second date, at the Blue Swan Café off Highway 72 (where Roseanne had a New York steak and Dan a shrimp cocktail), Dan proposed to her. Their make-out spot was Lanford Leap.

Occupation: Originally the owner of the 4 Aces Construction Company, then owner of Lanford Custom Cycles (repairing and selling motorcycles); "The guy who fixes trucks at the Lanford Garage"; a job in construction installing drywall at the local prison.

Truck License Plate: 846 759C.

Family Sedan License Plate: 846 779.

Favorite Drink: Beer.

Favorite Girlie Magazine: Girls, Girls, Girls.

Favorite Dessert: Chocolate cake.

Famous For: His chocolate chip milkshake.

Most Dislikes: The kids leaving toast crumbs in the butter.

Tattoo: The name "Rose" is seen on his arm.

Shoe Size: First mentioned as size 13D, then size 11.

REBECCA "BECKY" CONNER

Birthday: March 15, 1975 (the eldest child, 14 when the series begins). Four years later (1992), she is said to be 17; five years later (1993), she is 16.

Education: Lanford High School.

Character: Sweet, feminine, and pretty. She is fashion conscious and loves shopping for clothes at the mall. She is closer to her mother than to her father.

Favorite Color: Red.

Favorite Food: Dannon yogurt.

Pet Hamsters: Pebbles and Bamm Bamm (after *The Flintstones* TV series).

Allowance: $10 a week.

Occupation: Student (her first job was cashier at the Buy & Bag Supermarket).

First Ticket: Parking her car in a handicap zone ($50 fine).

Changes: Becky became more aggressive and independent and constantly defied parental authority. She married Mark Healy (Glenn Quinn), Dan's motorcycle shop mechanic (rides a British Triumph motorcycle), and moved to Minneapolis (where she worked as a waitress at the Bunz Restaurant). They moved back home and into the Lanford Trailer Park when money became tight. Mark, working as Hans the Hare (mascot) at the Edelweiss Garden Amusement Park, is interested in art and cooking (Ragu tomato sauce on bread is his specialty). Becky, hoping to better herself, enrolls in the University of Illinois to become a nurse.

DARLENE CONNER

Birthday: May 17, 1977 (the middle child).

Education: South Elementary School; Lanford Junior High School; Lanford High School.

Character: A tomboy and nasty. She loves sports, helping her father with repairs around the house (especially working with drywall), and is closer to her father than her mother.

Allowance: $5 a week.

Favorite Breakfast: Fruit Rings and Frank 'n' Berries cereal. Although she is not opposed to eating meat, she is later depicted as a vegetarian.

Changes: Lost her tomboy interests to become a moody 14-year-old girl who lived in her own dream world. She experimented with drugs and found romance with David Healy (Johnny Galecki), Mark's younger brother (originally called Kevin). He works as a busboy at Pizza World and married Darlene when she became pregnant (they name their daughter Harris Conner Healy). Lisa Healy (Clara Bryant) and Nicki Healy (Sarah Freeman) are David's sisters. At one point, Darlene and David attempted to write graphic novels (David illustrating and Darlene writing).

DAVID JACOB "D.J." CONNER

Birthday: November 4, 1981 (the youngest child).

Education: South Elementary School; James Madison Elementary School.

Hobby: Collecting doll heads (from Barbie, G.I. Joe, and Cher dolls) in one box and their body parts in another box—both of which he hides under his bed.

Quirk: Bad habit of getting his head stuck in drawers (as Roseanne says, "He has a knack for it"; she "unsticks" him by putting oil on his head). Sal Barone was D.J. in the pilot.

Pet Goldfish: Fluffy.

Occupation: Student (later works as a waiter at the Lanford Lunchbox).

Dream: Become a documentary filmmaker (makes his own movies by placing a video camera around the house to see what he gets); he rents movies from Lanford Video and wanted (but was not permitted) to tape Jerry Garcia's birth.

Girlfriend: Heather (Heather Matarazzo), a fellow film enthusiast (they both enjoy foreign films).

Favorite Movie: Return of the Jedi.

Role Model: Eddie Munster (from *The Munsters*), according to Roseanne.

JACKIE HARRIS

Relationship: Roseanne's younger sister by three years.

Real Name: Marjorie Harris. As a baby, Roseanne could not pronounce "Marjorie" and called her "My Jackie." "Jackie" stuck and replaced "Marjorie."

Address: Apartment A, then a house with the street number 465.

Education: Lanford High School.

Occupation: Assembly line worker at Wellman Plastics; Lanford Police Department Officer (trained in Springfield; quit when she injured herself falling down stairs while tackling a pervert); actress at the Lanford Theater Company (starred in a production of *Cyrano de Bergerac*); perfume "bottle squirter" at the makeup counter in the Lanford Mall; Buy & Bag Supermarket product sample girl (offering samples of soy sausage); big-rig truck driver; partner with Roseanne in the Lunch Box.

Favorite Bar: The Lobo Lounge.

Childhood: A doll named Mrs. Tuttle; attended Wild Oaks summer camp with Roseanne.

Ex-Husband: Fred Oakland (Michael O'Keefe), Dan's mechanic.

OTHER CHARACTERS

Nancy Bartlett Thomas (Sandra Bernhard) is part owner of the Lanford Lunch Box and Jackie's lesbian friend (came out as gay after her husband, Arnold "Arnie" Shemp Thomas [Tom Arnold], left her). Marla (Morgan Fairchild) and Sharon (Mariel Hemingway) were Nancy's lovers. They frequented the gay bar Lips; Marla worked as a salesgirl in the cosmetics department at Rodbell's

Department Store. Nancy believes she was abducted by aliens ("For one month after I would play championship chess; then it disappeared").

Leon Carp (Martin Mull) and his significant other, Scott (Fred Willard), are Roseanne's gay friends. Leon was a partner with Roseanne in the Lunch Box (previously her boss at Rodbell's Luncheonette); Scott is a probate lawyer. They were the 1995 canasta champions of Fire Island (in New York). Leon, a Republican, is a fan of Liza Minnelli and Broadway musicals.

FINAL EPISODE

Roseanne is seen at her writing desk. In a voice-over, it is learned that she is compiling her memories and that all that was seen never actually happened. Dan had died a year before this moment; Jackie, not Beverly, was actually a lesbian. She felt that Becky should have been named Darlene and would have been better with David and that Darlene, who should have been named Becky, would have had a better marriage with Mark. But most of all, Roseanne was achieving her dream. While it may not be "the great American novel," it is her dream book and has been written for all of us to see.

Saved by the Bell
(NBC, 1989–1993)

Cast: Tiffani-Amber Thiessen (Kelly Kapowski), Mark-Paul Gosselaar (Zach Morris), Elizabeth Berkley (Jesse Spano), Lark Voorhies (Lisa Turtle), Mario Lopez (A.C. Slater), Dustin Diamond (Screech Powers), Leanna Creel (Tori Scott), Dennis Haskins (Principal Richard Belding).
Basis: Comical incidents that befall Kelly, Jesse, Lisa, Zach, Slater and Screech, students at fictional Bayside High School in Palisades, California.

KELLY KAPOWSKI
Father: Frank Kapowski (John Mansfield).
Siblings: Sister, Nikki Kapowski (Laura Mooney); brother, Kyle Kapowski (Mark Neal).
Address: 3175 Fairfax Drive.
Phone Number: 555-4314.
Trait: The most beautiful girl at Bayside, although she admits she is not perfect (she wears a retainer at night).
Pet German Shepherd: Freddie.
Career Ambition: Actress or housewife (she later chooses medicine).
Activities: Captain of the girls' volleyball, softball, and swimming teams; also head cheerleader for the Bayside football team, the Tigers.
School Title: Homecoming Queen.
Show Host: Kelly Desire, a program of romantic music on the school station, Tiger Radio (KKTY, 98.6 FM).
Beauty Contest: The Miss Bayside Beauty Pageant (where she sang the song "Blue Moon" off-key).
Business: Buddy Bands, friendship bracelets that sell for $3.95 (formed with Jesse and Slater).

Calendar Girl: "Miss November" in the Girls of Bayside High Swimsuit Calendar.

Magazine: "The All-American Girl" in a *Teen Fashion* magazine photo spread.

Band: Lead singer (no longer off-key) in Hot Sundae (later The Zack Attack).

After-School Job: Waitress at The Max, the fast-food hangout (owned by Max, played by Ed Alonzo).

1991 Summer Job: Lifeguard at the Malibu Sands Beach Club.

SAT Score: 1,100.

College Choice: Palisades Community College. However, in the spin-off series *Saved by the Bell: The College Years* (1993–1994), Kelly is seen as a freshman at California State University (where she resides in room 218A and is a member of the Pi Psi sorority). She is studying to become a doctor and works at the Student Health Center.

Relatives: Grandfather, Harry Bannister (Dean Jones), the owner of the Hawaiian Hideaway Hotel in Hawaii.

JESSICA "JESSE" MYRTLE SPANO

Parents: Father, David Spano (George McDaniel); stepmother, Leslie Spano (Barbara Brighton).

Stepbrother: Eric Tramer (Joshua Hoffman).

Address: 1164 Martine Place.

Telephone Number: 555-0635.

Attributes: Pretty and very smart and strives for perfect grades (member of the Honors Society). She is sensitive to the fact that she is tall (5 feet, 10 inches) and is a talented dancer and singer.

Dislikes: Boys asking her out only because she is pretty; being called "Babe" or "Chick." She defends women's rights and will stand up for what she believes in.

Award: Her ability to speak French earned her the prestigious French Award.

Radio Host: Jesse Spano with the News on Tiger Radio.

Beauty Contest: The Miss Bayside Beauty Pageant (recited a poem in the talent competition).

Calendar Girl: "Miss July" in the Girls of Bayside High Swimsuit Calendar.

Magazine: "The Studious but Fashionable Girl" in *Teen Fashion* magazine.

Band: Singer in Zach's band, Hot Sundae.

High School Play: Snow White and the Seven Dorks. A hip-hop version of *Snow White* with Jesse as Snow White, Kelly as the Wicked Queen, Lisa as the Magic Mirror, Zach as Prince Charming, and Slater and Screech as dorks.

SAT Score: 1,205.

College Choice: Columbia University.

1991 Summer Job: Receptionist at the Malibu Sands Beach Club. She also
worked as a waitress at The Max.

LISA MARIE TURTLE
Parents: Judy (Susan Beaubian) and David Turtle (Henry Brown), both doctors.
In the episode "The Gift," Zach addresses David as "Mr. Turtlelay."
Address: 101 Melrose.
Phone Number: 555-9009.
Attributes: "I'm beautiful, charming, and always in fashion." She was the first
one in her group to get a credit card.
Hobby: Shopping ("Lisa is my name, shopping is my game").
Ability: "I can guess the contents of a gift before I open it."
School Title: Homecoming Queen.
Show Host: Lisa, the Galloping Gossip on Tiger Radio (she loves to hear and
spread gossip); "Princess" on *The Teen Hot Line.*
Beauty Pageant: The Miss Bayside Beauty Pageant (played the violin in the tal-
ent portion).
Calendar Girl: "Miss October" in the Girls of Bayside High Swimsuit Calendar.
Magazine: "The It's Happening Now Girl" in *Teen Fashion* magazine.
Band: Hot Sundae (singer); the Zach Attack (singer/guitarist); the Five Aces
(singer).
Locker Number: First 118, then 149.
After-School Job: Waitress at The Max.
1991 Summer "Job": Member of the Malibu Beach Sands Club (owned by Leon
Carosi [Ernie Sabella]; his daughter, Stacey [Leah Remini], assisted him as
the manager of the summer help; Leon called her "Honey Bunny," and she
called him "Papa Bear").
Allergy: In the episode "The Mamas and the Papas," it is seen that she is allergic
to Screech.
SAT Score: 1,140.
College Choice: The Fashion Institute of Technology in New York City.

ZACHARY "ZACH" MORRIS
Parents: Melanie (Melody Rogers) and Derek Morris (John Sanderford).
Address: 9760 Waverly Place.
Phone Number: 555-4432.
Talent: Natural-born con artist and schemer.
Home Away from Home: Detention.
Show Host: The disc jockey "Wolfman Zach" on Tiger Radio; "Nitro Man" on
The Teen Hot Line (phone number: 1-900 Crushed).
Band: Hot Sundae; the Zach Attack; the Five Aces (sings and plays bass guitar).

Girlfriend: Kelly Kapowski (an on-and-off relationship throughout the series).
Locker Number: 269.
Pet Turtle: Myrtle.
Business: He and Lisa formed friendship bracelets that they sold to students.
Sport: Member of the track team.
1991 Summer Job: Social director at the Malibu Sands Beach Club. His relationship with Kelly vanished when he pursued Stacey (Leah Remini) at the club.
SAT Score: 1,502.
College Choice: Yale University. However, in the spin-off series *Saved by the Bell: The College Years,* Zach is a freshman at California State University. He lives in dorm room 218B, is a member of the Sigma Alpha fraternity, and is majoring in finance.

SAMUEL "SCREECH" POWERS
Mother: Roberta Powers (Ruth Buzzi), an Elvis Presley fanatic.
Address: 88 Edgemont Road.
Phone Number: 555-5655.
Pets: Hound Dog (dog); Ted (spider); Oscar (lizard); Spin and Marty (white mice); Herbert (roach); Arnold (mouse).
Homemade Robot: Kevin.
Trait: A nerd but willing to give of himself to help others.
Contest Win: Fifth runner-up in an ALF (TV series) look-alike contest.
Shoe Size: 11.
School Activity: A member of the photography, science, chess, and glue clubs (as he says about the glue club, "Believe me, it's not as glamorous as it sounds").
Invention: Zit-Off, a blemish cream he developed after his first pimple (Murray) appeared; the cream, however, leaves a purple blemish after it is used.
Moneymaking Venture: Screech's Secret Sauce (a spaghetti sauce recipe that sold for $3 a bottle; his slogan: "The Sauce You Gotta Have, but the Secret, She's-a-Mine").
Girlfriend: Although Screech pines for Lisa (which unnerves her; he does have a "collection" of 16 of her broken finger nails), he fell for Violet Bickerstaff (Tori Spelling), a nerdy girl with a beautiful singing voice.
Locker Combination: 10-22-42.
Show Host: *Screech's Mystery Theater* on Tiger Radio. He is also "Ant Man" on *The Teen Hot Line.*
1991 Summer Job: Waiter at the Malibu Sands Beach Club.
Beauty Pageant: Contestant in the Miss Bayside Beauty Pageant (Zach entered him as a joke; he did a magic act and won the title; as Lisa said, "I can't believe it. I lost to a teenage mutant ninja geek").
SAT Score: 1,200.

College Choice: The final episode shows Screech being accepted into Clemson, Emerson, Princeton, and the Barbizon School of Modeling, but he had not made a decision. In the spin-off *Saved by the Bell: The College Years*, Screech is attending California State University. He shares dorm room 218B with Zach and Slater and is a member of the Sigma Alpha fraternity. After graduating, Screech becomes the college-trained administrative assistant to Bayside's principal, Mr. Belding.

ALBERT CLIFFORD "A.C." SLATER

Father: Major Martin Slater (Gerald Castillo).

Sister: J.B. Slater (Rana Haugen).

Address: Presently at the Palisades Army Base, as his father is in the military and constantly being transferred (he has been in 14 different schools in three years).

Trait: "The school hunk" (captain of the wrestling, track, and football teams).

Pet Chameleon: Artie.

Car License Plate: END 838.

Girlfriend: Originally Kelly (and Zach's rival) until he fell for Jesse (she called him "Bubba"; he called her "Mama").

Band: Played drums in the Zach Attack and the Five Aces.

1991 Summer Job: Lifeguard at the Malibu Sands Beach Club.

SAT Score: 1,050.

College Choice: Iowa State (for which he won a wrestling scholarship; prior to this, he was offered a football scholarship to Sainsbury University). In the spin-off *Saved by the Bell: The College Years*, Slater is a freshman at California State University. He shares dorm room 218B with Zach and Screech and is a member of the Sigma Alpha fraternity. He works as a waiter at the Falcon's Nest, the student union cafeteria.

OTHER CHARACTERS

Richard Belding is Bayside's principal, a man who is constantly plagued by Zach's antics (he calls him "My Zach Ache"). Richard served with the 55th National Guard in Indianapolis and was the 1963 Chubby Checker Twist-Off champion. He mentions that he was a student at Bayside, and on Tiger Radio, he was a deejay called "The Big Bopper." As a kid, he had two parakeets (Sonny and Cher) and two goldfish (Flipper and Jaws). He is best known for saying, "Hay, hay, hay, what's going on here" to students. Louan Gideon played his wife, Becky; Edward Blatchford was his brother, Rod Belding; and Jodi Peterson played his niece, Penny Belding.

Tori Scott is best described as an interim student, as she was the replacement for Kelly and Jesse when they were dropped without explanation at the start of the 1992 season. She had Kelly's beauty and Jesse's liberalism but also her own personality—a biker girl who appeared to be tougher than she really was. In the program's final episode, Tori suddenly vanishes (like she was never there) when Kelly and Jesse suddenly reappear to attend their graduation.

ORIGINS

The series began as the NBC 1987 pilot film *Good Morning, Miss Bliss.* Here, Hayley Mills was the featured sixth-grade teacher, Carrie Bliss. Oliver Clark as Gerald Belding was the principal (of an unnamed grammar school), and the students were Wendy (Samantha Mills), Bobby (Jaleel White), and George (Matt Shakman).

The Disney Channel reworked the pilot in 1988 with the same title but a revised cast: Hayley Mills was still Carrie Bliss but now an eighth-grade teacher at J.F.K. Junior High School in Indiana. The students were Lisa Turtle (Lark Voorhies), Zach Morris (Mark-Paul Gosselaar), Screech Powers (Dustin Diamond), Nicole Coleman (Heather Hopper), and Mickey (Max Battimo). Dennis Haskins was now the principal as Richard Belding, the Cosmos was the after-school hangout, and Robert Pine played Zach's father as Peter Morris. These episodes are retitled *Saved by the Bell* and seen in syndication with Zach appearing in a new opening segment to tell viewers that this episode "is from our junior high days."

Note: The series concludes in the 1994 TV movie *Saved by the Bell: Wedding in Las Vegas* when Kelly and Zach wed.

Scarecrow and Mrs. King
(CBS, 1983–1987)

Cast: Bruce Boxleitner (Lee Stetson), Kate Jackson (Amanda King).
Basis: A U.S. government agent (Lee Stetson) teams with an ordinary housewife (Amanda King) to investigate matters of national security.

LEE STETSON

Occupation: Field investigative agent (later intelligence operative) for the Agency, a secretive government unit that uses the cover of International Federal Film (a company that actually makes films, such as *The Romance of Earthworms* and *The History of the Tractor*).
Place of Birth: Virginia. He was orphaned at the age of four and raised by a military uncle on a number of different army bases.

Education: Various military schools; this piqued his interest in serving his country. He joined the Agency in 1973 as a member of "The Oz Team" (working under the code name "Scarecrow"; other team members were "The Tin Man," "The Lion," and "The Wizard," all based on the 1939 film *The Wizard of Oz*). His expertise in the field led to his becoming one of the Agency's top operatives.

Undercover Name with Amanda: Lee Steadman (usually posing as Amanda's husband; he also calls himself Lee Simpson and Lee Stanton).

Address: An apartment at 46 Hamblin Drive in Washington, D.C. (he hides the spare key under the potted plant in the hallway).

Quirks: Combs his hair with a comb that is missing two teeth because "it's the right comb for my hair." Works out when he gets upset.

Skills: Karate, fencing, and judo.

Car: A classic 1953 Porsche 350 (plate 3NG 105; later 9S1407, then 7G4 928).

Favorite Eatery: Milo's Daffy Dog (enjoys chili dogs).

Favorite Bar: Ned's Washington Pub (later called Emilio's, then Monk's). Ned's was originally called Nedlinger's Pub.

Affiliation: The University Athletic Club.

Pets: Two unnamed Siamese fighting fish.

Dislike: Being called a spy; he prefers "intelligence operative."

Relatives: Uncle, Colonel Robert Clayton (Arlen Dean Snyder).

Flashbacks: Father, Major Stetson (Bruce Boxleitner); mother, Jennie (Wendie Malick).

AMANDA KING

Place of Birth: Virginia.

Marital Status: Divorced (one year when the series begins).

Children: Jamie (Greg Morton), age 10, and Philip (Paul Stout), age 8.

Address: 4247 Maplewood Drive, Arlington, Virginia.

Telephone Number: 555-3100.

Education: Arlington High School (a cheerleader); the University of Virginia (a degree in American literature with a minor in photojournalism; also a member of the Drama Club and played the Tigress in a play called *Wailing Walrus*).

Occupation: Housewife and operative for the Agency (first as a seasonal employee transcribing tapes, then assisting Lee on assignments as the perfect undercover agent—an ordinary housewife posing as an ordinary housewife). Amanda works on occasion as a reporter for the *Washington Blaze* newspaper and does volunteer work (as a "bedside bluebell") at Galilee Hospital; she also works on behalf of United Charities (usually as the refreshment director), heads Mothers for a Safe Environment, and manages the Bombers, her sons' Little League baseball team.

Undercover Name: Amanda Keene (usually posing as Lee's wife).

The Meeting: Lee, on assignment and being pursued by the enemy, runs into Amanda at a train station. Before she realizes what is happening, she becomes his accomplice, and together they plug a leak at the Agency.

Security Clearance: GS-7. After training at the Agency's spy school, Station One, she acquires a Grade 10 clearance (her office is in the building's Film Library).

Favorite Dinner: Meatloaf with succotash.

Allergies: Horses.

Quirk: Does her housework while watching exercise tapes.

Station Wagon License Plate: JRY 502 (she took lessons at Barney's Driving Instructor School).

Marriage: Amanda and Lee wed on February 13, 1987.

OTHER CHARACTERS

William "Billy" Melrose (Mel Stewart) is the Agency's field investigation unit chief (who authorized Amanda's induction into the unit, which was founded by Captain Harry V. Thornton [Howard Duff] in 1954). He attended law school but chose counterintelligence over becoming a New York attorney. In his youth, Billy was a jazz musician known as Billy Blue Note. His superior is referred to as "The Blue Leader."

Dorothea "Dotty" West (Beverly Garland) is Amanda's mother, who lives with her and helps care for the children. She was unaware at first that Amanda secretly worked for the Agency and accepts Amanda's excuses, such as "I'm going to the club" or "Baby sit" (for pets, plants, and fish) when she is needed by Lee. Before she discovered Amanda's secret, Dotty believed Amanda was "a transcriber for the company you work for" (never giving a name). Dotty likes to take apricot-cinnamon bubble baths, is a fan of 1940s big-band music, and has a collection of Duke Ellington and Glenn Miller records. She called Amanda "Panda" as a child, gives books as gifts, and prepares meals while watching *Colonial Cookery* on TV.

Francine Desmond (Martha Smith) is an agency operative with the clearance level Green 13. She uses the alias Francine Dutton on assignments, and when she becomes frightened, she overindulges in chocolate. Francine is an expert in hand-to-hand combat and small weapons. She will date only "rich men between the ages of 30 and 40" and once rejected the marriage proposal of a prince "because his country was too small." "Scarecrow's methods might be unorthodox," Francine says, "but he gets the job done." She was born on November 16, 1953; measures 36-23-35; and stands 5 feet, 6 inches tall.

Philip and Jamie King attend Calvin Elementary School (where Amanda is a member of the PTA). Each year, Amanda and her sons spend a weekend at Camp Ana Costa. Philip and Jamie enjoy eating out at the Quickie Chickie Snack Shack and are members of the Junior Trail Blazers scout troop (Amanda is their leader; she won second prize at their jamboree with her apple pie). When it rains, Jamie makes sure to step in every mud puddle on his way home from school.

The Simpsons
(Fox, 1989–)

Voice Cast: Dan Castellaneta (Homer J. Simpson), Julie Kavner (Marge Simpson), Nancy Cartwright (Bart Simpson), Yeardley Smith (Lisa Simpson).

Basis: Events in the lives of a never-aging family living in the town of Springfield: parents Homer and Marge and their children, Bart, Lisa, and Maggie. The characters first appeared in short animated segments on *The Tracey Ullman Show* in 1987.

HOMER J. SIMPSON

Year and Place of Birth: 1956 in Springfield. He is 34 years old and weighed 9 pounds, 6 ounces at birth. A crayon lodged in his brain is said to cause

Lisa, Marge, Maggie, Homer, and Bart. *Fox Network/Photofest. ©Fox Network*

his stupidity. There is a "G" on Homer's head that stands for the show's creator, Matt Groening.

Parents: Abraham and Mona Simpson. It is said that Mona abandoned Homer when he was seven years old.

Half Brother: Herbert Powell (voice of Danny DeVito).

Address: 742 Evergreen Terrace. Homer, Marge, and infant Bart previously lived in a tiny apartment on the town's Lower East Side. When Marge became pregnant with Lisa, they purchased their current home (financed by Lincoln Savings and Loan). Their prior choices were a houseboat, a home in the Rat's Nest section of town, and a home next to a hog fat recycling plant.

Phone Number: 555-5555.

Education: Springfield High School.

Occupation: Nuclear safety inspector at the Springfield Nuclear Power Plant (originally Sector 7G technical supervisor). He also had a snow plowing business ("Mr. Plow").

Favorite Bar: Moe's Tavern on Walnut Street (where Duff's beer is served).

Home-Brewed Moonshine: Homer mixed hard liquor with Krusty the Clown cough syrup, set it on fire, and created a drink called the Flaming Homer. When he was 17, he used a fake ID under the name Brian McGee to buy beer.

Favorite Food: Pork chops.

Blood Type: A-positive.

Favorite Snack: Doughnuts.

Favorite Sport: Baseball (he was "Dancin' Homer," the mascot for the Isotopes baseball team).

Nickname: Called "Homey" by Marge.

Association: Member of the B-Sharps barbershop quartet and the Stonecutters.

Character: Dedicated to his family but overweight, incompetent, bald, lazy, and addicted to beer. He attempted to design a car he called "The Homer" and will no longer read books (he read *How to Kill a Mockingbird* and never learned how to kill one). He can't fix or build things and enjoys calling the local radio station with fake traffic jam tips.

Catchphrase: D'Oh! (said when he does something stupid).

Pride and Joy: Knows all the words to the Oscar Mayer Wiener TV commercial ("I wish I were an Oscar Mayer wiener . . .").

Fear: Spiders.

MARJORIE "MARGE" JACQUELINE SIMPSON

Parents: Jacqueline and Clancy Bouvier.

Year and Place of Birth: 1956 (in Springfield). She is said to be 34 years old.

Maiden Name: Marjorie Bouvier.

Half Sisters: Patty and Selma (see below).

Shoe Size: 13AA.

Occupation: Housewife. She owned a pretzel business in her youth, worked as a police officer (patrolling Junk Town), and was "Hooty McBoobs" when Homer tried to launch her as a singer. Marge was the spokeswoman for the Oven Mitt and Global Shoe Horn Convention.

Dream: A 48D bust (she had implants, but they were removed when she developed back problems).

Hair: Blue (in a beehive style). She frequents Jake's Unisex Hair Salon and mentions that her natural hair color is gray (she has been dying it since high school).

Favorite TV Series: Search for the Sun.

Novel: Wrote *The Harpooned Heart* (about a whaling father and his family).

Education: Springfield High School (she hoped to become an artist but was discouraged by a teacher who said she had no talent; she painted only one picture, that of her idol Ringo Starr).

First Meeting: It was 1974 when Marge, a radical high school student (fighting for women's equal rights), was sent to room 106 of the Old Building for burning her bra. Here, she met Homer, sent to detention for smoking in the boys' bathroom. Homer was attracted to Marge, but she found him repulsive. After three weeks of hounding her, Marge's hate turned to love, and they married shortly after graduating. In another scenario, it was 1980 when Homer and Marge began dating. Homer, 24 years old, was working at the local fun center, and Marge, also 24, was a waitress at Burgers Burgers. After an affair in the castle on the miniature golf course, Marge became pregnant, and they married at Shotgun Pete's 24 Hour Chapel; it cost Homer $20 for the service. At this time, Homer and Marge moved in with her parents; another episode states Homer and Marge moved in with his parents. Their song was "You Light Up My Life."

Relaxation: A retreat called Rancho Relaxo.

Ability: To make her own Pepsi Cola soft drink ("It's a little tricky," she says).

Childhood Pet: Cinnamon (hamster).

BARTHOLOMEW "BART" SIMPSON

Age: 10 (the eldest child; said to have been born in the 1980s). He has eight baby teeth and 16 permanent teeth and a supposed evil twin named Hugo.

Hair Color: Yellow.

Education: Springfield Elementary School (in the fourth grade and spends more time in detention hall and the principal's office than he does in classes; 36-24-36 is his locker combination number). He is seen in the opening theme writing his punishments on the blackboard; these include "I Shall Not Torment the

Emotionally Frail," "I Shall Not Draw Naked Ladies in Class," and "I Did Not See Elvis."

Occupation: Student. He also worked as a doorman at the Springfield Burlesque House (Maison Derrière), bartender at Fat Tony's Social Club, Krusty the Klown's assistant, and newspaper delivery boy.

Blood Type: OO-negative.

Pets: Santa's Little Helper (dog); Froggie (frog); Stampy (elephant).

Video Game Addiction: "Slug Fest" (he is the undefeated champion).

Favorite Comic Book: Radioactive Man.

Favorite TV Show: Krusty the Clown.

Favorite Movies: Jaws and the *Star Wars* trilogy.

Favorite Sport: Skateboarding.

Favorite Board Games: "Hippo in the House," "The Game of Lent," and "Citizenship."

Allergic Reaction: He cannot eat anything with butterscotch.

Catchphrases: "My name is Bart Simpson, who the hell are you?," "Eat my shorts," and "Don't have a cow, man."

Club: The Hole in the Underwear Club ("No Girls Allowed").

Character: Mischievous, mean, and wisecracking, the kind of child every parent dreads having. He sits in the back of the school classroom "because the front is for geeks."

Childhood Doll: Mr. Honey Bunny.

LISA MARIE SIMPSON

Age: Eight (the middle child). She has seven spikes in her yellow hair (Bart has nine).

Education: Springfield Elementary School (in the second grade).

IQ: 159.

Favorite Magazines: Teen Dream, Teen Scene, and *Teen Steam.*

Musical Ability: Plays the saxophone (loves blues music).

Favorite Song: "The Broken Neck Blues."

Hero: Bleeding Gums Murphy, a well-known street sax player.

Favorite TV Show: The Itchy and Scratchy Show (a violent cat-and-mouse cartoon variation of *Tom and Jerry*).

Favorite Movie: The Little Mermaid.

Favorite Comic Book: Casper the Friendly Ghost.

Pet Cats: Snowball 1, Snowball II, Snowball III, and Coltrane.

Beauty Pageant: The Little Miss Springfield Pageant but quit when she learned that Laramie Cigarettes was the sponsor.

First Baby Word: "Bart." Lisa could also say "Mommy" and "David Hasselhoff" but not "Daddy"; she now refers to Homer as "Homer" (as does Bart).

Homer, in his infinite wisdom, wanted to name Lisa "Bartzina," but Marge objected.

Character: Well behaved, dedicated to improving the world, precociously intelligent, and a self-proclaimed Buddhist. She is a vegetarian and holds strong political beliefs (unlike children her own age, which makes her somewhat of a loner).

Doll: Lisa Lionheart.

Hobby: Reading.

Shoe Size: 4B.

OTHER CHARACTERS

Maggie Simpson is Homer and Marge's infant daughter. She simply observes life while she enjoys her pacifier. Her favorite bedtime story is "The Happy Little Elves," and in the opening theme, when Maggie is passed over a supermarket scanner, she costs $847.63. Maggie's first word (voice of Elizabeth Taylor) was "Daddy." The Lay-Z-Mom Baby Monitor is in her room.

Charles Montgomery Burns (Christopher Collins, then Harry Shearer), called Mr. Burns, is the 104-year-old unscrupulous owner of the Springfield Nuclear Power Plant and Homer's boss. He is assisted by Waylon Smithers (Harry Shearer), his adviser and secret admirer. He clings to Old World technology and is often oblivious of the dangers that face his workers. Burns is the wealthiest man in Springfield, and "Excellent" is his favorite expression. He is the child of Daphne and Colonel Clifford Burns; he has a son named Larry and a teddy bear named "Bo Bo."

Nedward "Ned" Flanders (Harry Shearer) is Homer's next-door neighbor. He is an Evangelical Christian (follows the Bible) and considered a pillar of the community. Ned, born in New York City, is a Republican and the son of beatnik parents (he was never disciplined and was enrolled in the University of Minnesota "Spank-a-logical" program, where he was spanked for eight months; when cured of his rebellious ways, he attended Oral Roberts University, a religious school). After graduating, he became a pharmaceutical salesman and moved to Springfield, where he opened The Leftorium (a store for left-handed people). Although in his sixties, he attributes his youthful look to "clean living, chewing food thoroughly, and a daily dose of vitamin church." Ned, currently a widower (was married to Maude) and the father of Rod and Todd Flanders, later marries Edna Krabapple.

Moe Szyslak (Hank Azaria) is the owner of Moe's Tavern (a bar that is rather unsavory with a depressing atmosphere and filth; he threatens patrons with a shotgun). Moe has anger issues and a violent temper, and his annual Christmas tradition is attempting suicide (the Suicide Hotline has blocked his calls). He has an infatuation with Marge Simpson (whom he calls "Midge"), and his history varies: the son a Yeti, the son of a snake handler, the son of a circus freak, and born in Indiana, then claiming to be half American and half Armenian. His claims include being one of the 1930s *Little Rascals* (fired for killing the original Alfalfa), a student at Swigmore University (majoring in bartending), an ex-convict, and a boxing coach (the constant punches to his face account for his somewhat ugly look; it is also said that as a child, Moe's face was stomped on by an elephant, thus causing his look). He changed his appearance through plastic surgery and acquired a role on the TV soap opera *It Never Ends* as Dr. Tad Winslow.

Millhouse Mussolini van Houten (Pamela Hayden) is Bart's friend and often the target of the school bullies (Dolph Starbeam, Nelson Muntz, and Kearney Zzyzwicz). He has a crush on Lisa, is very gullible, and is easily taken advantage of. His heritage includes Italian, Greek, Dutch, and Danish, and he is quite hazard prone (falling down a waterfall, being run over by a train, being hit in the head with a hockey puck, and being electrocuted). He is allergic to many things (the red swirls of candy canes, wheat, dairy products, honey, mistletoe, holly, and his own tears), and he hopes to just survive each day unscathed. He is the son of Kirk (works at The Cracker Factory) and Luann.

Apu Nahasapeemapetilon (Hank Azaria) is the Indian immigrant and owner of the Kwick-E-Mart, the local convenience store (best known for his catchphrase, "Thank you, come again"). He claims to be a naturalized citizen and has a degree in computer science (from Calcutta Technical Institute; he graduated first in his class of 7 million). He is now taking classes at the Springfield Heights Institute of Technology to earn a doctorate degree in science. It is said he purchased an illegal birth certificate from the Springfield mafia that lists Herb and Judy Nahasapeemapetilon as his U.S. parents so that he could remain in Springfield as a documented alien. Apu is married to Manjula and the father of eight children.

Barnard "Barney" Gumble (Dan Castellaneta) is the town drunk (Moe's Tavern is his second home) and Homer's best friend. He is the son of Arnie Gumble, a World War II veteran and a mother who served in the navy and now lives in Norway. He believes it was Homer introducing him to beer that set him on his current path, and he claims to have worked as helicopter pilot, an astronaut and a snowplow driver.

Krusty the Klown, alias Herschel Krustofski (Dan Castellaneta), is the star of the Channel 6 TV show *Krusty the Klown* (Bart has badge number 16302 in the Krusty the Klown fan club and has based his life on Krusty's teachings; his room is also filled with Krusty merchandise). Herschel, the son of Rabbi Hyman Krustofski, was born on the Lower East Side of Springfield. His mother, named Rachel, died when he was 13 years old. Herschel felt his goal in life was to make people laugh and chose to become a clown. Sideshow Bob, then Sideshow Mel, is his TV sidekick. He has a daughter named Sophie (from an affair he had while serving in the 1991 Gulf War) and feels depressed by the misery he suffers being a clown.

Patty and Selma Bouvier (Julie Kavner) are Marge's older twin sisters (distinguished by different hairstyles: Patty has a puffy perm and Selma textured hair that is parted in the middle and forms an "M"). They continually smoke, and the smoke and ashes have changed their hair (Patty was a blonde, Selma a redhead) to a bluish-gray color. Patty is a lesbian; Selma, older by two minutes, is seeking a husband. Patty and Selma have gravel voices, a morbid outlook on life, and an obsession with the TV series *MacGyver*, and they live together at the Spinster City apartment complex. Their dislike for Homer is so strong that they have a tombstone for him that serves as their coffee table (inscribed with "Homer J. Simpson. We Are Richer for Having Lost Him"). They have a voodoo doll, made in Homer's image, that they use to inflict pain on him and produced a billboard that urged voters to evict Homer from Springfield. It is revealed that when Marge was a child, Patty and Selma treated her like Cinderella (paying her to do their chores). Selma has a pet iguana named Jub Jub.

Seymour Skinner (Harry Shearer) is the principal of Springfield Elementary School who is fighting a losing battle (no resources and unruly students) to keep the school afloat. Principal Skinner, as he is called, was a Green Beret and served in Vietnam. He is a strict disciplinarian and is genuinely concerned for the welfare of his students but is hated by his boss, Superintendent Chalmers. He suffers from posttraumatic stress disorder due to his time as a prisoner of war (witnessed his squad being devoured by an elephant). It is later revealed that Seymour was born Armin Tamzarian in 1953 and grew up as an orphan in Capital City. During the Vietnam War, he served under Sergeant Seymour Skinner, a man he came to admire. When Seymour is reported as missing in action and presumed dead, Armin traveled to Springfield to inform Seymour's mother but was instead mistaken for Seymour by his mother. Armin assumed Seymour's identity and followed the path Armin would have taken—becoming a school principal.

Clarence "Clancy" Wiggum (Hank Azaria) is the incompetent chief of the Springfield Police Department. He was born in Ireland and raised in Springfield when his parents immigrated to the town in the 1940s. It is implied that Chief Wiggum is corrupt, and he often does not take emergency calls seriously. He is married to Sarah and is the father of Ralph (voice of Nancy Cartwright), Lisa's schoolmate.

St. Elsewhere
(NBC, 1982–1988)

Cast: Ed Flanders (Donald Westphall), William Daniels (Mark Craig), Norman Lloyd (Daniel Auschlander), Christina Pickles (Helen Rosenthal), David Birney (Ben Samuels), Ed Begley Jr. (Victor Ehrlich), David Morse (Jack Morrison).

Norman Lloyd, Ed Flanders, and William Daniels. *NBC/Photofest.* ©*NBC*

Basis: St. Eligius, a hospital named after the patron saint of artists and crafts-
men, was established in 1935 by Father Joseph McCabe of the Boston
Catholic Archdiocese (later taken over by a company called Ecumena). It
soon became a dumping ground for patients with no place else to go and
was nicknamed St. Elsewhere. Although called a teaching hospital, its ad-

ministrators believe it is a learning hospital, and incidents in the lives of its staff are depicted.

DR. DONALD WESTPHALL

Donald, born in 1930, is the director of medicine. He is also a liver and kidney specialist and began working at St. Eligius on April 14, 1955 (at age 25). It was in 1936, when Donald was six years old, that a house fire killed his family. He was raised by relatives and appeared to be headed for a life of crime until Father Joseph McCabe (Edward Herrmann) rescued him and helped him enter the medical profession.

Donald was married to Maureen (killed in a car accident in 1975) and is the father of Lizzie (Dana Short, then Melanie Gaffin) and Tommy (Chad Allen), an autistic child. The pressures of the job eventually led Donald to volunteer his services with the Peace Corps in the hope of finding a more rewarding life. His return to St. Eligius after serving in Africa made him more demanding, especially on interns (requiring that they increase their community service). The rejection of his idea to add a food bank to the hospital prompted Donald to hand his superior, Administrator John Gideon (Ronny Cox), his resignation papers with these words (and his pants down and butt exposed): "You can kiss my ass, pal" (from the episode "A Moon for the Misbegotten").

Joshua Harris played Donald at age six; Michael Sharrett, Donald as a teenager; and James Stephens, Donald as a young man (and intern).

DR. MARK CRAIG

Mark, born in 1927, is a brilliant cardiologist and a mentor to the hospital's interns. He began his internship at St. Eligius in 1951 under Dr. David Domedion (Dean Jagger, then Jackie Cooper) and felt his talents were being wasted, as he could not perform open-heart surgery. Mark left St. Eligius to practice at Boston General, feeling he could better use his skills. He was lured back to St. Eligius with a promise of a higher salary and state-of-the-art equipment.

The death of Eve Leighton (Marian Mercer) from complications following heart surgery left Mark with self-doubts but enabled him to create "The Craig 9000," an artificial heart that looked promising until it was implanted in a patient and failed to operate as expected. Mark is married to Ellen (Bonnie Bartlett) and the father of Steven (Scott Paulin), who died from a drug overdose. In a rather disturbing moment, Mark is seen holding Steven's heart in his hand following an autopsy to reflect on the good times they once shared. Mark leaves St. Eligius when Ellen (maiden name Harper) is offered a job as director of food services at a Cleveland hospital, and they relocate. Mark was often disturbed by all the gunshot and stabbing victims sent to the hospital and called St. Eligius "a slaughterhouse."

DR. DANIEL AUSCHLANDER

Daniel, the chief of hospital services, shares administrative duties with Mark and Craig. He is not as arrogant as Mark or as strict as Craig and is the most approachable of the staff for interns. Early in his career Daniel felt he was discriminated against due to his Jewish heritage; in 1981, he was diagnosed with liver cancer and given little chance for survival. He opted for radical chemotherapy treatments that after two years successfully put his cancer in remission. Although Daniel was married to Katherine (Jane Wyatt), a hospital volunteer he met in the 1940s (now head of the hospital's Women's Auxiliary), he had an affair with Margaret Ryan (Geraldine Fitzgerald), and the child she bore was given up for adoption (Daniel would see him as an adult [played by Lawrence Pressman], but each decided it would be best if they did not remain in contact). Although his cancer treatment was successful, Daniel succumbs to a stroke in the final episode.

NURSE HELEN ROSENTHAL

Helen, the senior head nurse, is burdened by understaffing, numerous trauma cases occurring at the same time, and an antiquated computer system. She has been divorced three times and is currently married to Ira Rosenthal (Alan Oppenheimer). They are the parents of Jeffrey, and Helen jeopardized her marriage when she had an affair with Richard Clarendon (Herb Edelman). In 1982, Helen was diagnosed with breast cancer and opted for a mastectomy to save her life. Following a nurse's strike in 1985, she chose to work in the emergency room and was replaced by Nurse Lucy Papandreo. Helen became the director of nurses in training in 1986 and shortly after became addicted to prescription pills (she recovered through treatment in the Chemical Dependency Unit of the hospital). It can be seen that Helen is the only nurse who was on a first-name basis with Daniel, Mark, and Craig.

DR. BENJAMIN "BEN" SAMUELS

Ben, a staff surgeon, is addicted to women. Although this does not interfere with his medical duties, it causes stress when he is diagnosed with gonorrhea and must contact the women he slept with (most of whom he cannot even remember). Ben's first marriage (to Cynthia) ended in divorce and tragedy. Fearing to live by herself, Cynthia purchased a gun and carelessly left it where Billy, their child, could find it. While playing with the gun, it discharged and killed him. Nancy Paxton (Dorothy Fielding), a doctor just returning to St. Eligius after serving in the Peace Corps, becomes Ben's next love interest, but their inability to each overcome their past marital difficulties ends the relationship. As the series ends, Ben becomes romantically involved with Annie Cavenero.

DR. VICTOR EHRLICH

Victor, distinguished by his basic wardrobe of aloha shirts and ties, was born in California and studied medicine at Berkeley. He was five years old when his parents, Lech (Steve Allen) and Olga Osoranski (Jayne Meadows), government undercover agents, were killed in a car accident; he was raised by his aunt, Charise (Louise Lasser), and took her last name.

Victor's belief that he was superior to other surgeons at St. Eligius earned him the nickname "Pig." Craig felt that Victor was gifted but despised his personality (something Victor sensed and, in retaliation, would pretend to be clumsy around him). Victor's neurotic tendencies led him to fall in love with Roberta Sloane (Jean Bruce Scott), an equally neurotic hospital candy striper. A marriage resulted, but after two weeks, it ended in divorce. The experience did mature Victor, and he later fell in love with and married Lucy Papandreo, but their child was lost through a miscarriage. Victor's first solo operation is also seen as tragic: he was held hostage by Barbara Lonnicker (Judith Light), a pregnant woman armed with a gun.

DR. JACK MORRISON

John Steinbeck Morrison, nicknamed "Boomer" and "Jack," is a compassionate surgeon whose inability to distance himself from his patients' cases made it difficult for him to treat them. His wife, Nina (Deborah White), died shortly after the birth of their son Peter; her heart was donated to save the life of one of Craig's patients. After a brief romance with Clancy Williams (Helen Hunt), John met and later married Joanne McFadden (Patricia Wettig). It was at this time, after completing his residency, that John and Joanna moved to his hometown of Seattle.

John faced disqualification as a physician when it was discovered he took a medical course in Mexico that did not meet U.S. standards and had to repeat the course to maintain his residency. He was also the victim of rape when, as part of his community service (Westphall's Outreach Program), he was assigned to a prison ward.

OTHER CHARACTERS

Dr. Hugh Beale (G.W. Bailey) is the hospital psychiatrist whose unorthodox methods raised eyebrows among the senior hospital staff. The character disappeared after the first season.

Dr. Robert Caldwell (Mark Harmon) is the plastic surgeon addicted to sex. He was first revealed to be having an affair with Joan Halloran, the hospital administrator, and his promiscuous ways led to him contracting HIV. He was stripped of his duties with patients and left St. Eligius in 1986 to work at an AIDS hospice in California; he succumbed to the disease shortly after.

Dr. Anne "Annie" Cavanero (Cynthia Sikes) is an obstetrician/gynecologist who just completed her residency training and is beginning practice at St. Eligius. She is a feminist and often criticized by some male doctors for her stand. Annie is struggling to maintain her independence, but her views prevent her from having a serious relationship with a man (she was at one point suspected of being a lesbian and having an affair with Christine Holtz [Caroline MacWilliams], a visiting doctor). Annie and Christine were revealed to be only friends, and Annie disappeared from the series without explanation.

Dr. Wayne Fiscus (Howie Mandel), preferring to wear a Boston Red Sox baseball jersey instead of his white hospital coat, exhibits clownish behavior but is a brilliant trauma surgeon and able to treat the worst emergency room cases. He enjoyed pulling pranks until a near-death experience after being shot changed him and he abandoned his childish ways (later becoming a mentor to the interns). Wayne, a ladies' man, was known to have had affairs with the female doctors and nurses.

Dr. Catherine "Cathy" Martin (Barbara Winnery) is a pathology resident with an addiction to sex (pursuing both male and female staff and residents). Her life changed dramatically when she was raped (twice) and dropped pathology to pursue psychiatry to help victims of rape.

Dr. Peter White (Terence Knox) is a brilliant diagnostic technician whose personal life often hindered his residency. He is separated from his wife, Myra (Karen Landry), and often relied on prescription pills to get through the day (which led to an addiction and a promiscuous sex life; he was charged with rape, and his residency from St. Eligius was terminated). He was eventually acquitted, and a lawsuit filed by Peter forced Dr. Westphall to reinstate him; he was now assigned to duties that kept him away from the hospital staff and patients. In an ironic twist, rapes continued at the hospital (the deeds of a copycat), and Peter lost his life when he was shot in the hospital morgue by Nurse Shirley Daniels (Ellen Bry), believing he was the rapist (Peter was then seen as a ghost in two dreamlike sequences).

Dr. Phillip Chandler (Denzel Washington) is an arrogant physician who was overconfident in his patients' diagnoses, which were what he said and nothing else. He grew up in a white Chicago suburb and remarked, being African American, that he was "too white for his black friends and too black to be accepted by his white friends." Phillip later became a chief resident but also realized that it was his father's desire for him to become a doctor, not his. After beginning a relationship with Dr. Roxanne Turner, he chose to end his medical career, and she and Phillip moved to her hometown in Mississippi to rebuild their lives. Phillip mentions that he had an older brother (Russ) who was killed during the Vietnam War.

Dr. Vijay Kochar (Kavi Raz) is a hospital anesthesiologist. He was born in India and often incurred the wrath of Dr. Craig, who insulted him with condescending remarks. It changed when he and Craig were stranded in a blizzard and Vijay saved Craig's feet when they became frostbitten.

Dr. Wendy Armstrong (Kim Miyori) bragged that she had the ability to eat whatever she wanted and never gain weight (suffering from bulimia) but was unable to connect with her patients or her colleagues. She was born in Tallahassee, Florida, and was an overachiever and frequently suffered from stress and depression. An attempted rape by Peter White, coupled with a misdiagnosis that caused a pregnant woman to miscarry, led Wendy to a drug overdose that took her life.

Dr. Jacqueline Wade (Sagan Lewis), born in Lewiston, Maine, was a surgical resident, addicted to sweets, and somewhat of a joker. She married Robert (never seen) when she was a teenager; even though he put her through medical school, he left her for another woman when her residency literally alienated them. Her mentor was Dr. Craig, and she later became a chief resident.

Shirley Daniels (Ellen Bry) is an emergency room nurse and responsible for shooting Dr. Peter White, a convicted rapist. She was arrested and charged with murder. She was terminated from St. Eligius but later filed a lawsuit to regain her position while on bail; however, she is eventually convicted and sent to Farmingdale State Prison.

Luther Hawkins (Eric Laneuville) began his career at St. Eligius as an orderly, then became a paramedic and finally an assistant physician student (taking courses at Northwestern University). He became bitter with age; he was a loner (his only known relative, his father, died in a demonstration against busing; his mother is mentioned as being a nurse at St. Eligius when he was born) and grew unhappy with his orderly job and life in general. He did find happiness when he married Penny Franks (Stacey Dash).

Dr. Elliott Axelrod (Stephen Furst) became interested in medicine during high school and first saw St. Eligius (where he later becomes a resident) when he was in medical school. Although he is a bit overweight and awkward, Elliott managed to prove his abilities, but a heart attack ended his life in 1986 (he joined the staff in 1983).

Lucille "Lucy" Papandreo (Jennifer Savidge) began her career as a ward nurse and was later promoted to head nurse. Lucy is headstrong and must have her own way when it comes to dealing with patients, often butting heads with other nurses, especially Helen Rosenthal. Despite her attitude (harsh to those who disagreed with her), she did find romance with Victor Ehrlich, and they married in 1986; her feud, however, with Helen continued throughout the series.

Dr. Roxanne Turner (Alfre Woodard) was an obstetrician/gynecologist who appeared after the disappearance of Annie Cavanero. Roxanne was born in a small Mississippi town, and although she enjoyed her job at St. Eligius, the death of her former hometown doctor changed her life. Although she had begun a relationship with Dr. Chandler, she was drawn to return home to take over the job as the community's physician; Chandler later joined her.

Mrs. Hufnagel (Florence Halop) was the elderly lady who could be considered a "serial patient" as well as the staff's most annoying patient. She was demanding and insulting, and nearly every resident felt uncomfortable treating her imagined illnesses. She was "killed off" when her hospital bed supposedly malfunctioned and she was crushed when it folded up on her (later revealed that a mistake on Dr. Craig's part caused the mishap).

Dr. Paulette Kiem (France Nuyen) was born in Vietnam and studied medicine in Baltimore. She lived in Maryland before joining St. Eligius (she now maintains a long-distance relationship with her husband, joining him only on weekends). She is a gifted surgeon and often treated unfairly by Dr. Craig (who has a seemingly racist attitude toward her). She eventually became the hospital's director of education.

Note: During the closing theme, the MTM production logo, a cat, is seen in a surgical cap and mask (in the final episode, the cat pulls his life support plug). The final episode reveals through a snow globe possessed by Dr. Westphall's autistic son, Tommy, that St. Elsewhere was just his imagination professing itself as he looked into the globe.

Star Trek: The Next Generation
(Syndicated, 1987–1994)

Cast: Patrick Stewart (Jean-Luc Picard), Gates McFadden (Beverly Crusher), Marina Sirtis (Deanna Troi), LeVar Burton (Geordi La Forge), Jonathan Frakes (William Riker), Denise Crosby (Natasha Yar), Brent Spiner (Data).

Basis: A spin-off from *Star Trek* (1966–1969) that continues the voyages of the starship *Enterprise* as it explores the unknown realms of the universe.

JEAN-LUC PICARD
Position: Captain (then commander) of the starship *Enterprise NCC 1701-E.*
Year and Place of Birth: July 13, 2305 (on Earth in France).
Parents: Maurice and Yvette Picard.
Childhood: Took piano lessons but quit when performing in public bothered him. His dream was to join Starfleet and command a spaceship. As his interest grew, he began building airships in bottles and wrote reports about starships. By the time he entered the fifth grade, he was able to read and understand the ancient Bajoren language. He was a star athlete, school president, and valedictorian of his graduating class.

Education: Starfleet Academy (2323–2327). He was the only student to win the Academy's marathon and graduated at the top of his class.

Commissions: Captain of the USS *Stargazer* (in 2332). Twenty years later, he commanded *Enterprise NCC 1701-D* (the first of the Galaxy class of starships). In 2371, when the *Enterprise* was lost opposing the El Aurians, he became captain of a new Sovereign-class starship, *Enterprise NCC 1701-E.*

Character: A career officer with no interest in marriage. He has an inquisitive mind and a deep interest in archaeology. He is also a tactician and an accomplished diplomat but is troubled by deep personal issues that he has a difficult time controlling. Although he defends Starfleet's Prime Directive (which prohibits its interference in alien cultures), he will break it if it means accomplishing a mission.

BEVERLY CRUSHER

Position: Chief medical officer aboard the starship *Enterprise NCC 1701-D.*

Year and Place of Birth: October 13, 2324, in Copernicus City, Luna.

Parents: Paul and Isabel Howard.

Marital Status: Widow (she married Jack Crusher in 2348; he died in 2355, and she is the mother of Wesley Robert, born on July 29, 2349).

Education: Starfleet Academy (2346–2350). She did her medical internship on the planet Delos IV and in 2363 passed the Starfleet Bridge Officers Examination (which permitted her to work on a starship).

Assignments: In 2364, Beverly was the chief medical officer under Jean-Luc Picard, then captain of *Enterprise NCC 1701-D.* She was reassigned in 2365 to head Starfleet Medical School for one year. Following the loss of the D-class *Enterprise* ship in battle, Beverly became a senior staff member when Picard was assigned the E-class *Enterprise* ship.

Character: Beverly has a keen interest in the theater (she formed her own theater group on the *Enterprise* and performed in such plays as *Cyrano de Bergerac* and *The Pirates of Penzance*). She is an expert at poker, is obsessed by fine woven metallic fabrics, and is an excellent dancer (she was called "The Dancing Doctor" in medical school).

DEANNA TROI

Year and Place of Birth: March 29, 2336, near Lake El-Nar on the planet Betazed.

Parents: Ian Troi (a human Starfleet lieutenant) and a Betazoid mother, Ambassador Lwaxana.

Husband: William Riker (see below).

Position: Counselor under Jean-Luc Picard.

Ability: Has telepathic powers, can emotionally bond with other species, and is also knowledgeable in languages and linguistics.

Education: Starfleet Academy (2355–2359); the University of Betazed (for advanced studies in psychology).

Assignments: In 2364, she achieved the rank of lieutenant commander and was assigned to *Enterprise NCC 1701-D*. Six years later, she became a commander; in 2372, she was transferred to the Sovereign-class *Enterprise NCC 1701-E* under Picard.

Childhood: Deanna's father died when she was seven years old. She later learned that she had a six-year-old sister, Kestra, who drowned when Deanna was an infant. She loves Earth-based stories and songs, resulting from her father telling her them at bedtime. Her love of chocolate ("I never met a chocolate I didn't like") has followed through to her adult life (she is particularly fond of chocolate desserts).

GEORDI LA FORGE

Year and Place of Birth: February 16, 2335, on the African Confederation on Earth.

Parents: Commander Edward M. La Forge and Captain Silva La Forge.

Position: Officer, then lieutenant junior grade, on *Enterprise NCC 1701-E*. He is unique among Starfleet personnel in that he is blind (from birth) but can "see" by a device called a Visor (attached to the temple through implants that are connected directly to his brain). By concentrating, Geordi can see images. As cybernetic technology improved, Geordi was given ocular implants that use complex sensors and filters that simulate a real eye. He was first assigned duty as an ensign on the USS *Victory* in 2363.

Education: Starfleet Academy (2353–2357).

Character: Totally dedicated to performing his job but insecure in his private life, especially about dating and female relationships. He enjoys playing poker, swimming, chess, and skin diving. Building scale models of old sailing ships is his hobby, and he is able to speak several languages. He most enjoys iced coffee and pasta meals.

WILLIAM RIKER

Year and Place of Birth: August 19, 2335, in Valdez, Alaska.

Parents: Kyle and Betty Riker.

Wife: Deanna Troi (see above).

Position: Commander under Picard.

Education: Starfleet Academy (2353–2357).

Assignments: Ensign aboard the USS *Pegasus* (2358); lieutenant (2362) on the USS *Potemkin*. Later, when he saved the ship's away team on the planet

Nervalla IV, he was promoted to lieutenant commander and transferred to the USS *Hood*; in 2364, he was assigned to Picard on *Enterprise NCC 1701-E*.

NATASHA "TASHA" YAR
Year and Place of Birth: 2337 on the planet Turkana IV.
Position: Security chief.
History: Natasha and her younger sister, Ishara, had a difficult and violent up-bringing. When a civil war broke out, Natasha and Ishara's parents were killed, and they were sent to a foster home. They were soon abandoned and took to the streets for survival. In 2352, when the United Federation of Planets intervened and stopped the civil war, Natasha and Ishara parted company. Natasha joined the Federation, but Ishara chose to remain behind. They never saw each other again. Sometime later, after Tasha risked her life to save a colonist in a minefield, Captain Picard's request to have her transferred to his command was granted. In 2364, during a rescue mission on the planet Vagrall, Tasha was struck with an invisible energy blast and died of severe head trauma. She was athletic and trained in the martial arts.

DATA
Position: Science officer.
History: Data, an android, was found by the crew of the USS *Tripoli* after a crystalline entity drained the life force from his 411-member colony. Data was brought to the Omicon Theta Science Colony and reactivated on February 2, 2338, by Dr. Noonien Soong and his fiancée, Dr. Juliana O'Donnell. Data was then sent to Starfleet Academy in 2341 to learn how to become human. He graduated with honors and is an expert on probable mechanics and exobiology.
Assignment: Ensign, then lieutenant, aboard the USS *Trieste*; operations officer under Picard on *Enterprise NCC 1701-D*, then again with Picard on the E-class *Enterprise*.

T.J. Hooker

(ABC, 1982–1985; CBS, 1985–1987)

Cast: William Shatner (T.J. Hooker), Heather Locklear (Stacey Sheridan), Adrian Zmed (Vince Romano), James Darren (Jim Corrigan).

Basis: A dedicated police officer (T.J. Hooker) and his efforts to fight crime in a manner that satisfies him but at the same time remain within the boundaries of the law.

T.J. HOOKER

Background: Born in California and a third-generation police officer (following in the footsteps of his father, John Hooker [John McLiam], and grandfather). Press releases indicate that T.J.'s initials stand for Thomas Jefferson.

Occupation: Sergeant with the Academy Precinct of the LCPD (initials never revealed). He originally worked in the Narcotics Division, then as a plainclothes detective, but turned down a gold shield to remain in a blue uniform and a squad car; he is also seen as a teacher at the precinct (which is also a training academy). In his time as a rookie, he was called "The Flaming Liberal" for his view of life. In his youth, Hooker was a "hill racer" (racing cars with specially tuned engines for high terrain or flatlands).

Car Code: 4-Adam-30. On days when his personal car breaks down, Hooker takes the Number "B" bus to work.

Gun: Double-action .357 Magnum.

Badge Number: Camera shots make it appear as 716, 115, 116, or 141.

Special Equipment: A Magnum Body Armor bulletproof vest (although he has a tendency to get shot in his unprotected right shoulder).

Address: A rather untidy room at the Safari Inn.

Phone Number: 555-3012.

Patrol Car License Plate: 845 126 (also seen as 93124)

Military Service: Vietnam War.

Ex-Wife: Fran Hooker (Leigh Christian, then Lee Bryant). They divorced due to Hooker's overdedication to the job.

Children: Chrissy (Nicole Eggert, then Jenny Beck), Cathy (Susan McClung), and Tommy (Andre Gower). They reside with Fran, a nurse at Memorial Hospital (also seen as Community Hospital); Cathy and Tommy attend Lakeside Grammar School; Chrissy is a student at Valley High School and works as a candy striper at Valley Memorial Hospital. Fran, like everyone else, calls T.J. "Hooker." Fran and the children reside in his former home at 1310 Forest Drive; Chrissy takes the Associated Yellow bus to school.

Awards: The Medal of Valor; numerous commendations. He has the best time (34 seconds) for accuracy on the Shooting Exhibition course and the record for the most damaged or destroyed police cars.

Favorite Hangouts: Mid-City Bar and Irene's Coffee Shop (ABC episodes; Joan Crosby plays Irene); Sherry's Bar (CBS).

Addiction: Occasionally betting on the horses and always choosing horse number 4 ("It's not scientific, but it works").

OTHER CHARACTERS

Officer Vincenzo "Vince" Romano is Hooker's patrol car partner. Prior to their teaming, Hooker rode with Officer Johnny Durrell, and their car code was 5-William-21. Romano's private car license plate reads FCC 6412. He was born in South Philadelphia and as a child had a dog named Bear. He lives at the Marina Club and is not as aggressive as Hooker. He is drawn to southern girls (as he says, "southern hospitality") and left the series when it switched to CBS. His favorite after-hours hangout was Adrienne's Bar. Romano is also an assistant training instructor at the Academy. Vince is mentioned as serving in Vietnam, but in actuality, he would have been a boy at the time. He banks at Ascott Savings and is called "Junior" by Hooker. In high school, he was called "The South Philly Flash" for his drag-racing abilities.

Officer Stacey Sheridan, the daughter of Dennis Sheridan (Richard Herd), the precinct captain (ABC episodes), is first assigned to desk duty before being promoted to patrol car duty (her car code is 4-Adam-16). She is blonde, measures 37-27-36, wears a size 7 shoe and size 5 designer jeans, and stands 5 feet, 5 inches tall. She lives in an apartment at the Marina Club and wears badge number 280. Her private car license plate reads 1LIP 826. Stacey appears to have an unlucky streak: each time she goes undercover, she is kidnapped, with the culprit eyeing to sexually abuse her. Yellow roses are her favorite flower, and she is later teamed with Jim Corrigan.

Officer James "Jim" Corrigan, a cop for 20 years (turning down a promotion to remain a street cop), is Stacey's partner. He was born in San Francisco (a member of its police department) and moonlighted as a race car driver; his and Stacey's car code is 4-Adam-16. He lives at 62 Foster Lane.

Too Close for Comfort
(ABC, 1980–1983; Syndicated, 1984–1986)

Cast: Ted Knight (Henry Rush), Nancy Dussault (Muriel Rush), Deborah Van Valkenburgh (Jackie Rush), Lydia Cornell (Sarah Rush), Jim J. Bullock (Monroe Ficus).

Basis: The incidents that affect the daily lives of a cartoonist (Henry Rush), his wife (Muriel), and their daughters (Jackie and Sarah).

HENRY RUSH

Father: Huey Rush (Ray Middleton).

Brother: William "Bill" Rush (Robert Mandan).

Year of Birth: 1930 in San Francisco.

Address: A red Victorian, two-story home (a former brothel) on Buena Vista Street in San Francisco.

Occupation: Creator and artist of the comic strip "Cosmic Cow" (a space crime fighter).

Biggest Challenge: "To draw an udder so it is not offensive."

Education: Union Bay High School; San Francisco State College (majoring in art).

Cosmic Cow Creation: Henry began his career as an artist painting turtles. While working with animals, he hit on the idea for an animal crime fighter, thus creating "Cosmic Cow." Merchandise created from the comic supplements Henry's income.

Publisher: Random Comics, a division of Wainwright Publishing.

Work Space: A minioffice in his bedroom. He uses a "Cosmic Cow" hand puppet for inspiration; he also wears a "Cosmic Cow" sweatshirt when working.

Trait: An overprotective father, easily upset, and a constant worrier (cannot accept the fact that his daughters are young women and now living on their own).

Signature Clothing: Actual college sweatshirts (varies by episodes) sent in by fans. The University of Michigan is the first one he wore. In the final season, his sweatshirts represent cities (Boston being the first one he wore).

Relatives: Niece, April Rush (Deena Freeman), a free-spirited musician who came to live with Henry and Muriel.

MURIEL RUSH
Mother: Iris Martin (Audrey Meadows).
Date of Birth: 1936 in Florida.
Maiden Name: Muriel Martin.
Occupation: Housewife. She was a singer with Al Crowler and His Orchestra. It was at this time that Henry, dining at a nightclub where Muriel was performing, first met her. They found an instant attraction to each other, dated, and married shortly after (they honeymooned at the Golden Pines Hotel and Resort).
Hobby: Photography (she becomes a freelance photographer when Jackie and Sarah move into their own apartment).
Household Expenses: Henry gives Muriel $150 a week to run the house.
Trait: More relaxed than Henry, especially when it comes to disciplining their daughters.

JACQUELINE "JACKIE" RUSH
Relationship: The eldest daughter.
Birthday: July 3, 1958 (22 when the series begins).
Place of Birth: San Francisco.
Address: The same home as her parents but in the first-floor apartment (Henry and Muriel live on the second floor); rent is $300 a month.
Ambition: To become a fashion designer.
Education: Union Bay High School; State College (majoring in business).
Occupation: Teller at the Bay City Bank; salesgirl at Balaban's Department Store; creator of her own fashion line (Designs by Jackie).
Bra Size: 32A (she is very jealous of girls with larger breasts, as she feels that a small bustline prevents her from advancing her position in life).
Character: Very pretty, neat, and tidy. She dislikes people who are sloppy and disorganized. Everything in her life must be in order for her to perform properly.

SARAH RUSH
Relationship: Jackie's younger sister.
Birthday: June 9, 1960 (20 when the series begins).
Place of Birth: San Francisco.
Address: Shares the first-floor apartment of the Rush home with Jackie.
Education: Union Bay High School; State College.

Occupation: Student. She worked as a "Wench Waitress" at the Fox and Hound Bar (she acquired the job because her figure fit the available costume; she quit when Henry complained about her skimpy apparel); a teller with Jackie at the Bay City Bank; weather girl for KTSF-TV's *Dawn in San Francisco* program.

Bra Size: 36C. Although she considers herself a perfect 10, she feels that her gorgeous looks sometimes attract undesirable men.

Height: 5 feet, 9 inches tall.

Character: A bit naive, not easily motivated, and a rather sloppy housekeeper (presenting her and Jackie as an "Odd Couple"). She has more dates in one week than most girls have in one month.

MONROE FICUS

Relationship: Sarah's friend (rented Henry's attic apartment at $300 a month).

Father: Benjamin Ficus (Pat Paulsen).

Education: State College (majoring in communications with a minor in journalism).

Occupation: Guard at the Riverwood Shopping Mall (where he was named "Security Guard of the Month" as "Officer April" for catching a lady stealing panty hose).

Salary: $200 a week.

Pet Hamster: Spunky.

Ambition: To become a stand-up comedian.

Character: A bit naive and clumsy; tries to help but often complicates Henry's life.

Note: Based on the British series *Keep It in the Family*. Here, Dudley Rush (Robert Gillespie), a strip cartoonist (of "Barney the Bionic Bulldog"), and his wife, Muriel (Pauline Yates), struggle to keep tabs on their daughters, Jacqui (Jenny Quayle) and Susan (Stacy Dorning), when they move into the basement apartment of the Rush home.

REBOOT (SYNDICATED VERSION)

Originally titled *The Ted Knight Show*. Jackie and Sarah have moved away, and Henry and Muriel are now living in Marin County, California, with their five-year-old son, Andrew (Joshua Goodwin), an infant on the ABC version. Henry and Hope Stinson (Pat Carroll) co-own the *Marin Bugler*, a paper founded by Hope's late husband Norris J. Stinson; Brutus the Bulldog is the paper's mascot. Monroe assists Henry and hopes to work as the stand-up comic Buddy Ficus at the Comedy Shack. Lisa (Lisa Antille) is Henry and Muriel's maid; Leah Ayres played Hope's niece, Jennifer.

21 Jump Street
(Fox, 1987–1990; Syndicated, 1990–1991)

Cast: Johnny Depp (Tom Hanson), Holly Robinson (Judy Hoffs), Dustin Nguyen (H.T. Ioki), Peter DeLuise (Doug Penhall).

Basis: Cops with a youthful appearance solve crimes through infiltration as members of Jump Street Chapel (the original series title), a secret undercover unit of the Metropolitan Police Department (located in an abandoned chapel at 21 Jump Street and Sixth Avenue). Only silver shields (and higher) know of Jump Street (also called a chameleon unit; Jump Street is slang for "The Start," and its officers are sometimes called "The Kiddie Cops").

THOMAS "TOM" HANSON

Mother: Margaret Hanson (Marcia Rodd). His father (Thomas Hanson Sr.), a police officer, was shot in the line of duty; Tom was a teenager at the time and never talks about what happened.

Occupation: Police officer. Tom attended rookie school and graduated at age 21 with top honors. He rode in patrol car 25 (code 1-Zebra-6) before being recruited for Jump Street (he wanted to patrol the streets but was considered

Dustin Nguyen, Holly Robinson, Peter DeLuise, Johnny Depp, and Steven Williams. *Fox/Photofest. ©Fox*

too young to be taken seriously as a cop; it was either Jump Street or desk duty at the Parker Street Station).

Mustang Car License Plate: LCH 937 (it originally belonged to his father).

First Assignment: Infiltrating Amhurst High School to uncover drug operations (he paid $200 for a pair of socks he thought was filled with drugs).

Address: An apartment at 609 West Lindsey Avenue.

Favorite Sport: Bowling (on a team called the King Pins).

Tattoo: Tom carries a tattoo of an Indian that is actually Johnny Depp's (depicting his Cherokee heritage).

Musical Ability: Plays the saxophone.

Trait: Has a sense of humor but keeps it hidden.

50 Years into the Future: Tom, now retired, married and raised a family.

Most Embarrassing Assignment: Parading as a woman.

Flashbacks: Tom, as a boy (Luke Edwards).

Note: Jeff Yagher played Tom Hanson in the original unaired pilot.

JUDITH "JUDY" HOFFS

Parents: Dolores (Lillian Lehman) and Robert Hoffs (Robert Hooks).

Place of Birth: Chicago. She was a three time all-city guard on her unnamed high school basketball team. Her middle name is given as both Marie and Anne.

First Assignment: Undercover operative (posing as a prostitute) with the Metropolitan Police Department; she was later transferred to Jump Street and was promoted from officer to detective.

Volunteer Work: Counselor (on Wednesday nights) at the West Side Rape Crisis Clinic (she herself having once been a victim of rape).

Measurements: 35-23-33; she stands 5 feet, 4 inches tall.

Most Embarrassing Assignment: Dressing as Officer Milk Carton to teach children to avoid strangers.

Bank: First City State and Loan.

Car License Plate: DVI 737.

Address: An apartment at 703 East Verona Drive.

Telephone Number: 555-3436.

Badge Number: 714 (same as Sergeant Joe Friday on *Dragnet*)

Favorite Beverage: Ocean Spray Cranberry Juice.

First Assignment: Teaching newcomer Tom Hanson the ropes.

50 Years into the Future: After leaving the force, Judy became a U.S. senator, now retired.

H.T. (HARRY TRUMAN) IOKI

Parents: Not named, played by Keone Young and Haunani Minn.

Background: His real name is Vinh Von Tran. He was born in Saigon and lived on Kanot Street. In April 1975, when he was 14 years old, the Vietcong invaded his city. He fled Saigon and made his way to St. Louis (becoming the first Vietnamese refugee in the city), where he was raised by a woman named Bessy Mason. He learned to speak English by watching *Sesame Street* and became fascinated by TV crime dramas (*S.W.A.T.* was his favorite); they instilled in him a desire to become a police officer. After high school graduation, he went to San Francisco and posed as a reporter for a college newspaper to gain access to death records. He took the name H.T. Ioki, enrolled in the police academy, finished fifth in his class, and was assigned to Jump Street.

50 Years into the Future: After leaving the force, Harry established a self-defense school; he was also married four times.

Most Embarrassing Assignment: Dressing in drag ("I was an ugly woman").

Belief: The chapel was originally a Chinese temple.

DOUGLAS "DOUG" PENHALL
Birthday: March 1, 1964.
Weight: 165 pounds. He stands 5 feet, 10 inches tall.
Address: 8137 Juniper Street.
Car License Plate: 71 6583.
Character: Often plunges into dangerous situations without thinking first. He is also claustrophobic.
50 Years into the Future: Doug became a reverend and head of the most prominent human rights organization in the world.
Most Embarrassing Moment: Accidentally shooting Tom in the butt during a case.
Belief: The chapel was originally a synagogue.
Relatives: Uncle, Nick Penhall (Dom DeLuise).
Flashbacks: Doug, as a boy (R.J. Williams); Doug, as a teenager (Michael DeLuise).

OTHER CHARACTERS
Officer Joseph "Joey" Penhall (Michael DeLuise), Doug's brother, joined Jump Street in later episodes. Infiltrating the religious cult Heaven's Gate was his first assignment. He left home when he was 15 due to his father's alcohol addiction; Doug, on the other hand, remained with their father until acute alcoholism killed him.

Dennis Booker (Richard Grieco), the rogue cop who could not do things his way, leaves the unit to become the head investigator for the Los Angeles–based Teshima Corporation (located in the Teshima Tower Building). The spin-off series *Booker* (Fox, 1989–1990) emerges with stories following Booker's case investigations. Alicia Rudd (Marcia Strassman) is his superior; Suzanne Dunne (Lori Petty) is his assistant.

Sal Banducci (Sal Jenco), called "Blowfish," is the chapel's jovial maintenance man. Mindy Cohn appeared as Sal's wife. After leaving the force, he founded Star Maintenance ("We maintain the stars") and became rich.

Richard Jenko (Frederic Forrest) is the chapel captain. He calls Tom "Sport" and plays lead guitar (on Saturday nights) with a band called the Bunco Dudes. His idol is Jimi Hendrix, and he drives a car with the license plate 9486 EO.

Captain Adam Fuller (Steven Williams) replaced Jenko when he was killed in a hit-and-run car accident. Fuller attended the University of Toronto and often poses as a schoolteacher for undercover assignments. Larenz Tate played Adam as a boy in flashbacks; David Raynt was Adam's son, Kipling "Kip" Fuller (Adam's wife left him when she discovered he had an affair with his female partner while on duty and named Kip after her love of poets). Judy claimed Adam had style, especially in the shirts he wore.

Note: The soda machine at Jump Street Chapel resembles a gas station pump with the slogan "Roar with Gilmore Gasoline"; in the opening theme, when "21 Jump Street" is spray painted, the paint runs on the letters "J" and "S."

In the season 6 Halloween episode, "Old Haunts in a New Age," the characters dressed as follows: Tom Hanson (the stalker Travis Bickle from the film *Taxi Driver*), Judy Hoffs (a devil), Ioki (Elvis Presley), Doug Penhall (Dracula), Captain Fuller (a matador), and Sal (the Phantom of the Opera).

Webster
(ABC, 1983–1987; Syndicated, 1987–1988)

Cast: Susan Clark (Katherine Papadopolis), Alex Karras (George Papadopolis), Emmanuel Lewis (Webster Long).

Basis: A young orphaned African American boy (Webster) and his experiences living with Katherine and George, a white couple who take on the responsibility of caring for him after his parents' deaths in a car accident.

WEBSTER LONG

Place of Birth: Chicago in 1976 (said to be 5, then 8, then 7 years old).

Parents: Travis and Gert Long. Travis, a pro football player, called Webster "Little Quarterback." George is Webster's godfather and promised Travis he would care for Webster if anything happened to him.

Education: Clemens Elementary School (plays triangle in the school band).

Nicknames: Calls George "George" and Katherine "Mam" (sounds like "Mom" to him).

Pets: Fred and Peggy (frogs) and Dr. Plotsman (snake).

Homemade Robot: Mr. Spielberg (after Steven Spielberg).

Favorite Breakfast Cereal: Sweeties and Farina Pops.

Favorite Number: 3.

Quirk: Keeps his "memstoes" (mementos) in an old cigar box.

Member: The Braves Boy Scout troop (he earned a merit badge for helping the Great Walnutto [Harold Gould], a 1940s magician who performed tricks on the radio, make a comeback).

Regret: Accidentally killed a mother bird with his BB gun. He cared for the eggs in the nest by placing them in the school incubator; when they hatched, he named the birds George, Mam, and Webster.

Favorite Park Pigeon: Charlie.

Teddy Bear: Teddy.
Favorite TV Series: Don't Jump (a mythical game show).

GEORGE PAPADOPOLIS JR.

Father: George "Papa" Papadopolis Sr. (Jack Kruschen); he owns a store called Papa Papadopolis You Break It, I Fix-It Shop.

Age: 41; born in Chicago.

Occupation: Sportscaster for WBJX-TV, Channel 6 (host of *Papadopolis on Sports*). He was a former pro basketball player (wore jersey 71) and failed to make a comeback with the Warriors when he discovered he was too old.

Education: Middlefield High School; Chicago University.

Address: Apartment 4B at 534 Steiner Boulevard; later in a private home (second floor; address not given) of their friends Cassandra "Cassie" Parker (Cathryn Damon) and her husband, William "Bill" Parker (Eugene Roche). They are married for 25 years in 1986, honeymooned at the Venus Arms Motel in Chicago, and spent their first Valentine's Day together seeing the movie *The Attack of the 50 Foot Woman.* They are the parents of Maggie (Jennifer Holmes).

First Meeting: George met Katherine on an ocean cruise to Greece. It was love at first sight, and they were married aboard ship.

Childhood Memory: The Tumbleweed Ranch in Arizona (stayed in Bunkhouse 7).

Favorite Eateries: Sloppy Eddie's (buys chili cheese dogs) and Angelo's Pizzeria.

Nickname for Webster: "Web."

Nickname for Katherine: "Jelly Bean."

Quirks: Sings songs from *Carmen* when upset; wears white socks with black shoes.

KATHERINE PAPADOPOLIS

Mother: Emily Calder-Young (Neva Patterson).

Age: 37 (born in Chicago).

Maiden Name: Katherine Calder-Young (the daughter of wealthy parents).

Education: W. T. Grant High School (where, as the valedictorian of her graduating class, she became so nervous that she forgot her speech and related the terms of her Bloomingdale's department store charge card); Radcliffe College.

Occupation: Consumer advocate for the mayor's office; she later quit to attend Chicago University to purse her dream of becoming a child psychologist.

Childhood Memories: Katherine had her own butler named Chives; a horse named Binky ("His real name was Mortimer but we called him Binky") and dogs named Derek and Farnsworth. She attended Camp Kitchecuwowa (at age 12), loved ballet, and hoped to become a ballerina.

Hope: On Valentine's Day, Katherine wishes George would give her "a large, heart-shaped box of chocolates—the 50,000-calorie kind. But what do I get? Sensible gifts like a Water Pik."
Nickname for George: "Cuddle Bunny."
Relatives: Aunt, Charlotte (Gwen Verdon); uncle, Charles (John Astin).

OTHER CHARACTERS
Jerry Silver (Henry Polic II) was originally Katherine's assistant at the mayor's office. When Katherine quit, he became the owner of Jerry Silver's Health Club; he also does volunteer work for the Oak Shore Hospital.

Phillip Long (Ben Vereen) is Webster's uncle (Travis was his brother). Although Phillip is a blood relative, Travis and Gert believed that if anything happened to them, Webster would be better with George. Phillip, a professional entertainer (dancer), had an unstable life. Although Phillip petitioned the court to raise Webster, he withdrew the petition when he realized his brother was right. Phillip calls Webster "Baby."

Who's the Boss?
(ABC, 1984–1992)

Cast: Judith Light (Angela Bower), Tony Danza (Tony Micelli), Alyssa Milano (Samantha Micelli), Katherine Helmond (Mona Robinson), Danny Pintauro (Jonathan Bower).
Basis: A widower (Tony Micelli) and the father of a young daughter (Samantha), becomes the live-in housekeeper to Angela Bower, a divorcée with a young son (Jonathan). Also living with Angela is her mother, Mona Robinson.

ANGELA BOWER
Parents: Robert and Mona Robinson.
Place of Birth: Connecticut on October 16, 1950.
Measurements: 34-25-32; she stands 5 feet, 7 inches tall and has blonde hair.
Ex-Husband: Michael Bower (James Naughton). They divorced when Michael, a documentary filmmaker for the Geographic Institute, insisted that Angela accompany him on global assignments and not pursue her own career goals.
Address: 3444 Oak Hills Drive in Fairfield, Connecticut.
Telephone Number: KL5-6218.
Education: The Montague Academy for Girls; Harvard Business School.
Occupation: President of the Wallace and McQuade Advertising Agency in Manhattan; later, owner of the Angela Bower Agency at 323 East 57th Street in Manhattan (she is in the 39 percent tax bracket).

Character: As a teenager, Angela was lonely and shy and felt that her small breasts were the cause of all her problems. She tried stuffing her bra with tissues "to become one of the cool girls" but was rejected. She used food to suppress her sorrow but became overweight. It was at this time that she learned to respect herself and lost weight. In her spare time, she manages a softball team called John's Giants and mentioned her first job was rowboat manager at the Fairfield County Boat Club. In college, Angela was a member of the Curletts and attempted to play the cello (she was so bad that her mother hid it in the attic to prevent her from playing it). At age 13, Angela attended the Cataba Summer Camp and pretended to be a girl named Ingrid. It is here that she met and shared her first kiss with a boy named Tony (11 years old; he would later become her housekeeper).

Favorite Color: Emerald.

Favorite Beatles Song: "Hey Jude."

Car: A Jaguar with the license plate MX8 266.

Flashbacks: Angela as a girl (Lani Golay).

TONY MICELLI

Place of Birth: Brooklyn, New York, on April 23, 1952.

Full Name: Arthur Morton Micelli (Anthony is also mentioned as his first name).

Marital Status: Widower.

Education: In Brooklyn: P.S. 86 grade school; Pikerin High School (where he was a member of the Dream Tones band). In Connecticut: Tony, scoring a 545 on his entrance exam, enrolls in Ridgemont College (majoring in business, later education; he became a legend "when he liberated the monkeys from the bio lab"). He first teaches history and coaches baseball at Wells College in Bradford, Iowa, then English, science, and history at the Nelson Academy for Boys in Connecticut.

Religion: Roman Catholic (he was an altar boy at the Blessed Sacrament Church).

Military Service: Navy.

Occupation: Angela's live-in housekeeper. Prior to leaving Brooklyn to find a better environment for Samantha, Tony was second baseman for the St. Louis Cardinals. His baseball career ended when he injured his arm two years later; it was at this time that he married his high school sweetheart (who died shortly after Samantha's birth) and acquired a job as a fish market truck driver. In Connecticut, Tony was also the sportscaster on the Ridgemont College Sports Channel.

Attributes: Excellent cook and housekeeper; he buys groceries at Food Town.

Sports: Enjoys golf (at the Ridgemont Golf Club) and bowling (a member of Dr. Whittier's Drill Team league). He also manages Tony's Tigers, a kids' softball team.

Model: Posed as "Mr. November" for a calendar.

Cars: A 1967 blue Chevy van (license plate 780 AGN); a 1989 black Jeep Cherokee (plate PH 3925); a sedan (plate 518 68Q).

Proposal: Love eventually developed between Tony and Angela, and Tony proposed to her in the episode of November 16, 1991 (but a marriage never occurred).

Relatives: Father-in-law, Nick Milano (James Coco); grandfather, Anthony Micelli (Tony Danza); cousins, Anna (Ana Obregon), Mario Micelli (Richard Grieco), and Dominic Micelli (Louis Gus); uncle, Aldo (Vito Scotti); aunt, Rosa Micelli (Antonia Ray).

Flashbacks: Tony, as a boy (Danny Geuis); Tony, as a teenager (Kenny Morrison).

SAMANTHA "SAM" MICELLI

Birthday: May 16, 1973 (11 years old when the series begins).

Place of Birth: Brooklyn, New York.

Allowance: $15 a week. She worked as Angela's girl Friday at her ad agency and as a waitress at the Yellow Submarine (fast food).

Education: P.S. 86 grade school (Brooklyn). In Connecticut, she attended Fairfield Junior High School, Fairfield High School, and Ridgemont College. Sam most wanted to attend Tate College in California but didn't meet the requirements; she later moves into the Ridgemont college dorm and shares a room with Melinda (Andrea Elson).

Car: A yellow 1968 Oldsmobile with the license plate SAM'S CAR. It had red reflectors on the sides, a tire on the rear bumper, and five rear brake lights; Sam called it "my yellow nightmare."

Best Friend: Bonnie Munson (Shana Lane-Block). They met in sixth grade while waiting in the milk line. Bonnie cut in, and Sam pushed her to the ground and called her a "chowderhead"; they became best friends. Bonnie calls herself and Sam "The Three Musketeers" (Sam doesn't understand it either); their hangout is the Burger Palace.

Marriage: In 1992, Sam married Hank Tomopopolus (Cunal Aulisio), a struggling puppeteer. Candice Azzara and Vic Poliza appeared as Hank's parents, Fran and Joe.

Favorite Dinner: Pasta (which she calls "Mr. Linguini").

Favorite Breakfast: French toast (which she calls "Mr. Frenchie").

Teddy Bear: Freddy Fuzzy Face.

Character: A very pretty tomboy and in love with sports, especially hockey (she wears a size 5½ hockey skate). Her tomboyish ways came to an end when she turned 12 and wanted her first bra ("the one with the little pink bow"). Tony thought pink was too "girlie" and bought her the no-bow model 304 "My Training Bra" (seeing that Tony just didn't understand Sam's feelings, Angela took charge and changed the tomboy into an elegant young lady).

MONA ROBINSON

Relationship: Angela's sexy, young-at-heart mother.
Birthday: July 5, 1928 (a fact she tries to keep secret).
Mother: "Nana" Reynolds (Marian Seldes).
Maiden Name: Mona Rockwell.
Brothers: Archie Rockwell (Gordon Jump) and Cornelius Rockwell (James B. Sikking).
Marital Status: Widow. Her late husband, Robert Robinson, was played in ghost sequences by Efrem Zimbalist Jr.
Occupation: Angela's ad agency assistant.
Pet Dog: Grover.
Character: Very proud of her large breasts (called "all boobs and no brains" by her mother); enjoys reminding Angela that she has small breasts and lacks cleavage. Mona has had many affairs and appeared on the cover of *Mature Woman* magazine.
Flashbacks: Mona, as a girl (Candace Cameron).
Proposed Spin-Off: Mona. Here, Mona and her brother, Cornelius Rockwell pool their resources to operate the Nottingham Hotel.

JONATHAN BOWER

Parents: Angela and Michael Bower.
Education: Oak Valley Grammar School; Fairfield High School.
Pet Snake: Wilbur.
Favorite Musician: Lawrence Welk (he has a Welk record collection).
Musical Ability: Attempting to play the accordion.
Character: A bit shy and not as outgoing as Samantha. He enjoys sports (but rarely plays any) and helping Tony around the house.

SPIN-OFF

Living Dolls (1989) finds Samantha's friend Charlene "Charlie" Briscoe (Leah Remini) attempting to become a fashion model under the direction of Trish Carlin (Michael Learned), the owner of the Carlin Modeling Agency at 68th Street and Madison Avenue in Manhattan. Emily Franklin (played by Halle

Berry), Martha Lambert (Andrea Ellison), and Caroline Weldon (Deborah Tucker) are the other "Living Dolls" (models).

The Wonder Years
(ABC, 1988–1993)

Cast: Dan Lauria (Jack Arnold), Alley Mills (Norma Arnold), Fred Savage (Kevin Arnold), Danica McKellar (Winnie Cooper), Olivia d'Abo (Karen Arnold), Jason Hervey (Wayne Arnold), Daniel Stern (narrator as adult Kevin). In the pilot episode, Arye Gross was the narrator.

Basis: A look at life in a small, unnamed town as narrated by the adult Kevin Arnold but seen from 1968 to 1973 in flashbacks from his point of view as a youngster living with his parents (Jack and Norma) and siblings (Karen and Wayne). Buster is the family dog.

KEVIN ARNOLD

Birthday: March 18, 1956 (12 years old when the series begins).

Education: Hillcrest Grammar School; Robert F. Kennedy Junior High School (a member of the Glee Club); William McKinley High School (where he has pictures of actress Raquel Welch in his locker). He scored 1,240 on his SAT test but is undecided about his future (aspirations to become an astronaut, a member of the first manned flight to Mars, a writer, or a center fielder for the San Francisco Giants baseball team).

Wardrobe Feature: Wears a New York Jets football jacket.

Band: The Electric Shoes.

Favorite Hangout: The Pizza Barn; the Moonlight Roller Rink.

Allowance: 50 cents a week (1969), $2.50 a week (1970), $3.00 a week (1971).

Occupation: Student. He worked as a caddy ($20 a game), a stock clerk at Harris and Sons Hardware, a busboy at the Cascades Resort and Tennis Court, a delivery boy (later waiter) at Chong's Chinese Restaurant, and a clerk at the family-owned furniture store.

Sports: Wore jersey 24 on his school football team and number 6 for the soccer team. In the pilot episode, a wildcat is seen as the logo for the football team, the Kennedy Wildcats (the logo becomes an Indian for the series).

Girlfriend: Winnie Cooper, his neighbor, with whom he had an on-and-off romance. His actual first crush was on his seventh-grade English teacher, Miss White (Wendel Meldrum). Kevin mentions that since he turned 12, he has always been confused by girls. When breakups do happen, he has what he calls "The *Star Trek* Dream," where he is Captain Kirk and Winnie, "the

Fred Savage and Danica McKellar. *ABC/Photofest. ©ABC*

beautiful alien with long hair and a short skirt," is his interest ("Hey, it's my fantasy, I figured I might as well do it right"). Even as Kirk, it didn't help.

Backup Girlfriend: Becky Slater (Crystal McKellar, Danica's real-life sister), whom Kevin often turned to when he and Winnie broke up.

Other Girlfriends: In 1969, while vacationing with his family in Ocean City, Kevin befriended a 15-year-old girl named Teri (Holly Sampson). She called him "Brown Eyes," and it appeared they had a crush on each other. When it came time to leave, Teri returned to New Mexico and said she would write. She did so but only once. As Kevin said, "I keep that letter in an old shoe box." On Labor Day in 1970, during the Norcom Annual Picnic, Kevin developed a crush on Mimi Serweiler (Soleil Moon Frye), a former childhood friend who was nicknamed "The Stick" but had since developed. During the summer of 1971, Kevin fell in love with a girl named Cara (Lisa Gerber); the infatuation lasted until it was time to return home. Julie Aidem (Wendy Cox) is the stunning girl who attached herself to Kevin when he and Winnie broke up in 1972. Julie had a dog named Poo Poo and smothered Kevin so much that it caused a breakup.

Pet Dog: Buster (given to him by his grandfather).

Car: Blue four-door Oldsmobile (plate QGF 846).

Best Friend: Paul Joshua Pfeiffer (Josh Saviano). Attended the same schools (until the fall of 1971 [1991 episodes], when his parents sent him to the Allenwood Academy Prep School; he returns a year later and joins Kevin at McKinley High). He suffers from a number of allergies, and he and his family are members of the Fairlawn Country Club. He later attended Harvard and became a lawyer. John C. Moskoff and Stephanie Satie are Paul's parents, Alvin and Ida Pfeiffer; Torrey Ann Cook is Paul's sister, Debbie Pfeiffer.

Flashbacks: Young Kevin (Benjamin Daskin).

JACK ARNOLD

Birthday: November 6, 1927. He passed away in 1975 after a heart attack.

Military Service: The army during the Korean War.

Occupation: Manager of distribution for Norcom, a government contracting company. Jack gets up a 5 a.m., hates his job, and quits to open a furniture store. As a kid, he dreamed of becoming a baseball player, then a ship's captain.

Cars: Chevrolet Impala (plate GPW 385; later BEQ 326); Dodge Polaris (plate XDH 975).

Address: A home (street number 516) in an unnamed suburban town depicting "Anywhere, U.S.A." In some episodes when car license plates are visible, they indicate California. In another instance, when Wayne receives his license plates from the Division of Motor Vehicles, the envelope address is seen as Culver City, California 90230.

Character: Jack often feels the whole world is against him. He is rather strict in disciplining the children and rarely takes any nonsense from them.

Relatives: Father, Albert Arnold (David Huddleston); cousins, Lloyd Arnold (Arlen Dean Snyder), Opal Arnold (Helen Page Camp), and Philip Arnold (John Brandon).

NORMA ARNOLD

Birth Year: 1928.

Occupation: Housewife. She worked as a secretary and salesgirl prior to her marriage. She returned to work as the attendance room secretary at Kennedy Junior High School and later enrolled at Fremont Community College (although the narrator calls it "State College") to improve her secretarial skills. She later acquires a job as comptroller at Micro Electronics, a computer software company, at $225 a week.

Marriage Year: 1949 (she and Jack honeymooned in Ocean City). It is first mentioned that Norma met Jack when she worked as a salesgirl at Macy's and he approached her to return a necktie; it is later stated that they met at a dance (where Jack engaged in a fight with another boy to win her over).

Childhood Dream: To become a singer. As a high school student, Norma was caught smoking on campus and suspended for two weeks.

Character: A gentle, trusting person who tries to be subtle when dealing with family issues; her wisdom and understanding are actually the glue that holds the family together.

GWENDOLYN "WINNIE" COOPER

Birthday: July 16, 1956.

Education: Hillcrest Grammar School; Robert F. Kennedy Junior High School (where she was a cheerleader for the Wildcats football team and starred in a production of *Our Town*; Kevin worked the spotlight). She left Kennedy Junior High in the spring of 1970, when her family moved to a new home (house number 525) four miles away. She attended Lincoln Junior High and completed her education at McKinley High School; she scored 1,482 on her SAT exams.

Hobbies: Tennis, reading, and dancing.

Boyfriend: Kevin Arnold. Although their relationship became rocky over the years, they remained close; as Kevin says, "I'm a part of Winnie, and Winnie is a part of me; for as long as I live, I will never let her go." She and Kevin shared their first kiss at the large rock in Harper's Woods. It appeared that Kevin and Winnie were meant to be with each other forever. In the final episode, Kevin and Winnie make a promise to never let their friendship end. Kevin's words during the final seconds of the episode tell us what happened after they graduated from high school: "Winnie left the next summer [1974] to study art history in Paris. Still, we never forgot our promise. We wrote to each other once a week for eight years. I was there [the airport] to meet her when she came home—with my wife and my first son. Things never turn out exactly as you planned. Growing up happens in a heartbeat. . . . The memories of childhood stay with you for the long haul . . . and the thing is, after all these years, I still look back in wonder."

Character: Very pretty, sweet, and trusting, the typical 1960s girl next door. Kevin always found Winnie to be a friend, a person he could share his deepest thoughts with. She listened, and she cared.

Occupation: Student. She worked as a lifeguard at the Cascades Resort and Tennis Club during the summer of 1973.

Relatives: Brother, Brian (Bentley Mitchell), killed in Vietnam; parents (unnamed), Lynn Milgrim and H. Richard Greene.

KAREN ARNOLD

Age: 16 (when the series begins).

Education: Hillcrest Grammar School; Robert F. Kennedy Junior High School; William McKinley High School. In 1971 (1991 episodes), Karen enrolled in "McKinley College up North." She returned in 1972, married Michael (David Schwimmer), and moved to Alaska to begin a new life. A son is later born to them. Michael drives a Ford Econoline van.

Character: A typical flower child of the 1960s with her own thoughts on what she wants to do and what she hopes to become.

Flashbacks: Young Karen (Jodie Rae).

WAYNE ARNOLD

Birthday: April 6. In the actual Vietnam War lottery held in 1969, Wayne's birthday was drawn as number 312, indicating that he would not serve in the military (as drafting would never reach that high).

Education: Same schools as Kevin. Kevin mentions Wayne scored 317 on his SAT exams (this is impossible, as 400 is the lowest possible score a student can get).

Nickname for Kevin: "Butthead."

Character: Obnoxious and delights in annoying Kevin. The only thing they apparently ever had in common was agreeing that, in 1969, they wanted a color TV for Christmas (it didn't happen until 1971).

Occupation: Student. After graduating from high school, Wayne went to work in the family furniture store and eventually took over the business when Jack passed away.

Index

Aames, Willie, 25, 26
Ackroyd, David, 24
Adams, Joey Lauren, 138
Akerling, Maya, 91
Alden, Norman, 91
Alexander, Erika, 44
Allen, Chad, 205
Alley, Kirstie, 29
Ameche, Don, 85
Amos, John, 105
Andersen, Bridgette, 86
Anderson, Dana, 71
Anderson, Harry, 169
Anderson, John, 124, 175
Anderson, Pamela, 14
Anderson, Richard Dean, 122
Applegate, Christina, 135
Aprea, John, 145
Archer, Beverly, 130
Argenziano, Carmen, 115
Argoud, Karin, 130
Arquette, Lewis, 26
Arthur, Bea, 82, 89
Arthur, Rebeca, 174
Astin, John, 26, 170, 225
Atkinson, Bruce, 129
Atwater, Edith, 71
Austin, Karen, 173
Ayler, Ethel, 44

Babcock, Barbara, 103
Baca, Sean, 160
Baio, Scott, 25

Bakula, Scott, 53, 177
Ball, Sue, 110, 175
Banes, Lisa, 119
Bardolph, Alice, 24
Bardolph, Paige, 24
Barilla, Courtney, 105
Barnes, C.D., 61
Barr, Douglas, 62
Barrie, Barbara, 71
Barron, Jenn, 82
Basehart, Richard, 113
Bateman, Justine, 68
Battimo, Max, 194
Baxter, Meredith, 68
Bearse, Amanda, 135
Beasley, Allyce, 33, 147
Beaubian, Susan, 191
Beck, Jenny, 215
Beckham, Brice, 150
Begley, Ed, Jr., 203
Belford, Christina, 86
Bell, George, 29
Benedict, Dirk, 1
Berber, Andrea, 75, 79
Bergan, Judith Marie, 57
Bergen, Candice, 156
Berger, Claire, 119
Berkley, Elizabeth, 189
Bernard, Crystal, 107
Berry, Halle, 228
Berry, Ken, 130
Beytner, Andrea, 115
Bialik, Mayim, 158

Billingsley, Barbara, 59
Birkett, Bernadette, 34
Birney, David, 203
Blacque, Taurean, 97
Blair, Linda, 138
Blake, Ellen, 103
Bledsoe, Tempestt, 43
Bleeth, Yasmine, 14
Bloch, Scotty, 112
Bond, Raleigh, 74
Bonerz, Peter, 155
Bonet, Lisa, 43
Bonsall, Brian, 68
Borgnine, Ernest, 6
Bosley, Tom, 153
Bosson, Barbara, 97
Bouvier, Charles 53
Boxleitner, Bruce 194
Bradford, Richard 24
Brandon, John, 232
Bridges, Lloyd, 144
Brighton, Barbara, 190
Brill, Charlie, 137
Britt, Kelly, 110
Britt, Melendy, 35
Brosnan, Pierce, 180
Brown, Eric, 130
Brown, Henry, 191
Brown, Pat Crawford, 49
Bruce, Scott, 160
Bruening, Justin, 116
Bry, Ellen, 208
Bryant, Clara, 186
Bryant, Lee, 215
Bryde, Eyde, 109
Buckland, Robyn Faye, 84
Bullock, Jim J., 216
Bundy, King Kong, 138
Burke, Chris, 117
Burke, Delta, 49
Burnett, Carol, 134
Burnette, Olivia, 27, 177
Burns, Jere, 47
Burrell, Maryedith, 71, 182
Burton, LeVar, 210
Buzzi, Ruth, 192

Cadogan, Alice, 129
Call, Brandon, 14, 128
Callan, K, 108
Callahan, James, 25
Cameron, Candace, 74, 79, 228
Cameron, Kirk, 76, 92
Camp, Helen Page, 48, 232
Campbell, Heather, 14
Campbell, Jennifer, 14
Campion, Michael 79
Carey, Clare, 40
Carl, Adam, 71
Carlson, Hunter, 140
Carr, Jane, 47
Carroll, Janet, 161
Carter, Dixie, 49
Carter, Ginna, 51
Carter, Mary Dixie, 51
Carter, Nell, 80
Cartwright, Nancy, 197
Caruso, David, 103
Caspary, Tina, 140
Cast, Tricia, 107
Castellaneta, Dan, 197
Castillo, Gerald, 193
Cavanaugh, Michael, 105
Chainey, Eva, 161
Chalke, Sarah, 183
Chapman, Judith, 63
Charvet, David, 21
Chokachi, David, 21
Christian, Leigh, 215
Clark, Bryan, 159
Clark, Oliver, 194
Clark, Susan, 223
Cobb, Julie, 25, 128
Coca, Imogene, 131
Coco, James, 227
Coffey, T. Scott, 124
Cohan, Billy, 48
Cohen, Jeff B., 71
Cohn, Mindy, 26
Colasanto, Nicholas, 29
Coleman, Marilyn, 53
Collins, Gary, 160
Connelly, Christopher, 7

Conrad, Michael, 97
Conway, Tim 137
Cook, Torrey Ann, 231
Cooper, Jackie, 155, 205
Cord, Alex, 6
Corley, Jerry, 162
Corley, Pat, 156
Cornell, Lydia, 216
Cornthwaite, Robert, 112
Cosby, Bill, 43
Coulier, Dave, 74, 79
Cox, Courteney, 74, 155
Cox, Wendy, 231
Crosby, Denise, 201
Cross, Marcia, 34
Culea, Melinda, 1
Culp, Robert, 89
Currie, Sondra, 82
Curtin, Jane, 111

d'Abo, Olivia, 229
Daggett, Jensen, 11
Daly, Tyne, 23
Dana, Bill, 88
Daniels, William, 113, 203
Danson, Ted, 29
Danza, Tony, 225
Darlow, Linda, 124
Darren, James, 214
Dash, Stacey, 209
Daskin, Benjamin, 231
Davies, Geraint Wyn, 8
Davis, Clifton, 11
Davis, Duane, 115
Davis, Josie, 25
Davison, Bruce, 105, 115
Delany, Dana, 36
DeLuise, Dom, 221
DeLuise, Michael, 221
DeLuise, Peter, 219
DeMay, Janet, 183
Depp, Johnny, 219
DePrina, Marietta, 49
D'Errico, Donna, 14
DeVito, Danny, 198
Dewhurst, Colleen, 158

Diamond, Dustin, 189
Diamond, Selma, 173
Dick, Jamie, 24
Diol, Susan, 171, 179
Dooley, Paul, 42, 61
Doyle, Richard, 35
Dryer, Fred, 103
DuBois, Marta, 126
Duff, Howard, 125
Duffy, Julia, 49, 163
Duggan, Debra, 131
Durrell, Michael, 182
Dussault, Nancy, 216

Eads, George, 125
Easton, Sheena, 146
Eaton, Meredith, 125
Ebsen, Buddy, 145
Edelman, Herb, 206
Edwards, Paddi, 171
Eggert, Nicole, 14, 25, 27, 215
Elcar, Dana, 122
Elder, Judyann, 64
Electra, Carmen, 14
Eleniak, Elena, 14
Ellerbee, Bobby, 103
Elliott, Bob, 163
Elliott, Stephen, 48
Ellison, Andrea, 229
Elson, Andrea, 8
Evans, Troy, 40

Fabares, Shelley, 40
Fagerbakke, Bill, 40
Fairchild, Morgan, 158
Faustino, David, 135
Fenmore, Tanya, 74, 120, 134
Ferrer, Miguel, 105
Fielding, Dorothy, 206
Fishman, Michael, 183
Fitzgerald, Geraldine, 206
Flanders, Ed, 203
Flores, Erika, 60
Fluegel, Darlanne, 105
Foch, Nina, 48
Foley, Ellen, 173

Ford, Faith, 156
Foster, Meg, 23
Fox, Michael J., 68
Foxworth, Jaimee, 64
Frakes, Jonathan, 210
France, Jo Marie Payton, 64
Francis, Genie, 155
Frann, Mary, 162
Franz, Charles, 97
Freeman, Dena, 217
Freeman, Sarah, 186
Friedman, Andrea, 121
Friedman, David, 132
Frye, Soleil Moon, 231
Fuller, Penny, 37
Furst, Stephen, 209
Fusco, Paul, 8

Gaffin, Melanie, 205
Gagnier, Holly, 21
Galecki, Johnny, 186
Gallagher, Megan, 36, 102
Garland, Beverly, 182, 196
Garlington, Lee, 86
Garrison, David, 135
Gatti, Jennifer, 78
Gemignani, Rhoda, 77
Gentry, Mimmie, 43
Getty, Estelle, 82. 89
Ghostley, Alice, 54, 87
Gibson, Henry, 167
Gilbert, Sarah, 183
Gilford, Jack, 88
Gilyard, Clarence, Jr., 141
Ging, Jack, 1
Goez, Mike, 106
Golay, Lani, 226
Gold, Tracey, 92
Goldthwait, Bobcat, 138
Goodman, John, 183
Goranson, Alicia, 183
Gorrell, Ashley, 14
Gosselaar, Mark-Paul, 158, 189
Gould, Harold, 55, 86
Gower, Andre, 215

Graff, Ilene, 150
Grammer, Kelsey, 29
Grant, Lee, 56
Graves, Christopher, 36
Graves, Kevin, 36
Greene, H. Richard, 232
Greene, Lynnie, 87
Greer, Dabbs, 27
Gregory, Benji, 8
Gregory, Debbie, 78
Grieco, Richard, 221, 227
Griffeth, Simone, 89
Griffith, Andy, 141, 143
Grizzard, George, 84
Grizzard, Lewis, 50
Groener, Harry, 47
Gross, Michael, 68
Grovernor, Linda, 155
Guest, Lance, 119
Guilbert, Ann, 60, 166
Gus, Louis, 227
Guy, Jasmine, 46

Haake, Effie James, 138
Haid, Charles, 97
Hairston, Jester, 13
Hale, Barbara, 89
Hall, Christopher Kent, 78
Hallahan, Charles, 105
Halop, Florence, 173, 210
Hamel, Veronica, 97
Hamilton, Murray, 82, 132
Haney, Anne, 142
Hanks, Tom, 71
Hansen, Judith, 103
Hardison, Kadeem, 46
Harger, Elias, 79
Harmon, Angie, 21
Harmon, Deborah, 95, 173
Harmon, Mark, 207
Harrelson, Woody, 29
Harris, Cassandra, 182
Harris, Joshua, 205
Haskins, Dennis, 189
Hasselhoff, David, 14, 113

Hatcher, Teri, 177
Hauser, Fay, 129
Haydn, Lili, 108
Haynie, Jim, 59
Heard, John, 111
Heasley, Marla, 1
Hecht, Gina, 21, 118
Hecht, Paul, 112
Hedaya, Dan, 32, 36, 73
Heffner, Kyle, 89
Helgenberger, Marg 36
Helmond, Katherine, 225
Hemmings, David, 1
Hemsley, Sherman, 11
Hendler, Lauri, 80
Hensley, Pamela, 144
Herd, Richard, 215
Herrmann, Edward, 205
Hervey, Jason, 229
Hewitt, Christopher, 150
Hill, Dana, 63
Hillerman, John, 125, 129
Hirsch, Judd, 47
Hirschfeld, Robert, 102
Hirson, Alice, 49, 75, 159
Hoffman, Isabella, 47
Hoffman, Joshua, 190
Holbrook, Hal, 50
Holliday, Kene, 141
Holliday, Polly, 85
Holm, Celeste, 35
Holt, Sandrine, 125
Hood, Don, 78
Hooks, Jan, 49
Hooks, Robert, 220
Hopkins, Telma, 64
Hopper, Heather, 194
Horsford, Anna Maria, 11
Horsley, Lee, 144
Houser, Christine, 76
Howard, Barbara, 7
Huddleston, David, 126, 232
Hunt, Helen, 207
Hunter, Robert, 24
Hyman, Earle, 43

Ingber, Mandy, 32
Ivey, Judith, 49

Jackson, Jeremy, 14
Jackson, Kate, 194
Jacoby, Billy, 84
Jaeckel, Richard, 20
Jagger, Dean, 205
Jenco, Sal, 221
Jillian, Ann, 107
Johns, Glynis, 31
Johnson, Ashley, 92
Johnson, Don, 145
Johnson, Georganne, 108
Jones, Clayton Barclay, 146
Jones, Dean, 190
Jordan, Jan, 124
Jovovich, Milla, 137
Jump, Gordon, 92, 228
Jurasik, Peter, 97

Karen, John 32
Karlen, John, 24
Karnes, Brixton, 115
Karras, Alex, 223
Kasem, Jean, 36
Katt, William, 89
Kauders, Sylvia, 150
Kava, Caroline, 177
Kavner, Julie, 197
Kayser, Allan, 130
Keene, Virginia, 108
Keller, Mary Page, 117
Kerns, Joanna, 92
Kerns, Sandra, 25
Kerr, Heather, 134
Kilmer, Val, 115
Kimbrough, Charles, 156
Kirchenbauer, Bill, 95
Kirkconnell, Claire, 4
Kissir, John, 115
Kline, Richard, 108
Knight, Ted, 216
Knotts, Don 141
Knox, Terrence, 208

Kober, Jeff, 37
Koehler, Frederick, 111
Korman, Harvey, 134
Kramer, Stepfanie, 103
Kreppel, Paul, 107
Krige, Alice, 155
Kruschen, Jack 78
Kumagai, Denice, 173
Kuter, Kay E., 142
Kuzyk, Mimi, 102

Lampkin, Charles, 173
Landry, Karen, 71, 208
Lane, Lauren, 105
Laneuville, Eric, 209
Langenkamp, Heather, 95
Lanier, Monique, 117
Lansbury, Angela, 153, 155
Larroquette, John, 169
Lasser, Louise, 107, 207
Latham, Louise, 50
LaTorre, Tony, 24
Laughlin, John 37
Lauren, Tammy, 71
Lauria, Dan, 229
Lawrence, Joey, 60
Lawrence, Vicki, 130, 131, 132
Learned, Michael, 228
LeBeauf, Sabrina, 43
Lee, Ruta, 26, 184
LeGault, Lance, 1
Leisure, David, 55
LeNoir, Rosetta, 13, 65
Lenz, Kay, 27, 63
Lerman, April, 25
Lewis, Dawnn, 46
Lewis, Emmanuel, 223
Lewis, Sagan, 209
Light, Judith, 207, 225
Lind, Heather, 120
Linn-Baker, Mark, 174
Littman, Lisa, 32
Lizer, Kari, 141
Lloyd, Norman, 203
Lockhart, June, 91

Locklear, Heather, 214
Lockwood, Vera, 78
Logan, Adam, 178
Long, Shelley, 29
Lopez, Mario, 189
Loughlin, Lori, 75, 79
Lowe, Chad, 120
Lucchesi, Vincent, 104
Lucking, William, 1
Luke, Keye, 173
Luner, Jamie, 95
LuPone, Patti, 117, 118
Lyman, Dorothy, 130

MacWilliams, Caroline, 208
Madsen, Virginia, 149
Mahan, Kerrigan, 115
Majors, Lee, 62
Malick, Wendie, 112, 194
Mandel, Howie, 208
Manetti, Larry, 125
Manning, Ruth, 167
Manoff, Dinah, 55
Marcus, Dee, 78
Marie, Rose, 160
Marin, Jason, 166
Markham, Monte, 21
Markham, Monty, 82
Marsden, Jason, 162
Martin, Barney, 160
Martin, Keil, 97
Martin, Kellie, 117
Marx, Margaret, 71
Masak, Ron, 153
Matarazzo, Heather, 187
Matheson, Michelle, 120, 150
McCay, Peggy, 165
McClain, Cady, 33
McClanahan, Rue, 27, 82, 84
McClung, Susan, 215
McClure, Bryton, 68
McCrary, Darius, 64
McCullough, Linda, 115
McDaniel, George, 190
McFadden, Gates, 210

McGavin, Darren, 158
McGinley, Ted, 135, 175
McGrath, Derek, 166
McGuire, Betty, 92
McIntire, John, 171
McKellar, Crystal, 231
McKellar, Danica, 229
McKenzie, Richard, 108
McLiam, John, 214
McNichol, Kristy, 55, 155
Meadows, Audrey, 217
Meadows, Jayne, 207
Melton, Sid, 89
Mercer, Marian, 60, 87, 107
Metclaf, Laurie, 183
Michaelsen, Kari, 80
Middleton, Ray, 216
Milano, Alyssa, 225
Milgrim, Lynn, 232
Miller, Denise, 26
Miller, Jeremy, 92
Miller, Lara Jill, 80
Miller, Linda G., 110
Mills, Alley, 229
Mills, Hayley, 194
Mills, Samantha, 194
Milner, Martin, 124
Mitchell, Bentley, 232
Mitchell, Keith 107
Miyori, Kim, 209
Mobley, Mary Ann, 160
Moffatt, Donald, 37
Moll, Richard, 1969
Montgomery, Belinda J., 146, 155
Mooney, Laura, 158, 189
Moore, Sheila, 124
Moreno, Rita, 61
Morrill, Priscilla, 71
Morris, Garrett, 104
Morse, David, 203
Morton, David, 58
Morton, Greg, 195
Moskoff, John C., 231
Mosley, Roger E., 125, 173
Mr. T, 1

Mulgrew, Kate, 159
Mulhare, David, 113
Mulligan, Richard, 55, 56
Mumy, Billy, 142
Murphy, Rosemary, 112
Myers, Ari, 111

Naughton, James, 225
Neal, Mark, 189
Needham, Tracey, 117
Nelson, Craig T., 40
Nettleton, Lois, 78
Neuwirth, Bebe, 29
Newhart, Bob, 163
Newsom, David, 177
Nguyen, Dustin, 219
Nielsen, Leslie, 84
Nincz, Melanie, 76
Noble, Chelsea, 95
Nolan, Jeanette, 171
Nolin, Gena Lee, 14, 19
Norman, Susan, 115
North, Sheree, 82

Obregon, Ana, 227
O'Connell, Annie, 131
O'Keefe, Michael, 187
O'Leary, William, 11
Olin, Ken, 102
Olsen, Ashley, 75
Olsen, Mary Kate, 75
O'Neal, Tricia, 63
O'Neill, Amy, 134
O'Neill, Dick 23, 27, 33, 94
O'Neill, Ed, 135
Orsi, Leigh Ann, 121
Overall, Park, 55
Owens, Geoffrey, 43

Packard, Kelly, 14
Pankin, Stuart, 71
Parker, Norman, 71
Parsons, Estelle, 183
Pastorelli, Robert, 156
Patterson, Lee, 104

Patterson, Neva, 224
Paul, Alexandra, 14
Paulin, Scott, 205
Paulsen, Pat, 218
Pearlman, Michael, 25
Peppard, George, 1
Perlman, Rea, 29
Petty, Lori, 221
Pickles, Christina, 142, 203
Pinchot, Bronson, 174
Pine, Robert, 128
Pintauro, Danny, 225
Pleshette, Suzanne, 168
Polinsky, Alexander, 25
Pollin, Tracy, 74
Pontig, Sally, 129
Post, Markie, 169
Poston, Tom, 163
Potts, Annie, 49
Pratt, Deborah, 7
Preston, J.A., 102
Price, Marc, 74
Prosky, Robert, 34
Pulliam, Keshia Knight, 43
Purl, Linda, 141

Quinn, Glenn, 186

Ralph, Sheryl Lee, 107
Randall, Lexi, 50
Randolph, John, 69
Rappaport, David, 151
Rashad, Phylicia, 43
Ratzenberger, John, 29
Ray, Antonia, 227
Raz, Kavi, 208
Read, James, 183
Redgrave, Lynn, 155
Reese, Della, 4, 173
Regalbuto, Joe, 156
Remini, Leah, 32, 192, 228
Remsen, Bert, 119
Reynolds, Debbie, 185
Richter, Deborah, 100
Rieffel, Lisa, 55

Roberts, Doris, 60, 75, 183
Robinson, Charles, 169
Robinson, Holly, 219
Rocket, Charles, 149
Rodd, Marcia, 219
Roebuck, Daniel, 144
Rogers, Melody, 191
Roseanne, 183
Rosenberg, Arthur, 105
Rosenthal, Rick, 119
Ross, Shavar, 129
Runyon, Jennifer, 26
Ruscio, Al, 117
Rush, Barbara, 128
Russell, Howard, 37
Russo, Deanne, 116

Sabella, Ernie, 33, 191
Sagal, Katey, 135
Sagat, Bob, 74, 79
Saint, Eva Marie, 147
Saint James, Susan, 111
Sampson, Holly, 231
Sander, Casey, 86
Sanderford, John, 191
Sanders, Beverly, 78
Sanderson, William, 138, 163
Santiago, Saundra, 146
Santon, Penny, 117, 145
Satie, Stephanie, 231
Savage, Ben, 48
Savage, Fred, 229
Saviano, Josh, 231
Savidge, Jennifer, 209
Scarabelli, Michelle, 8
Schaal, Wendy, 48, 107
Schallert, William, 158
Schedeen, Anne, 8
Schultz, Dwight, 1
Scolari, Peter, 163
Scott, Jean Bruce, 6
Scott, Karen Lynn, 137
Scotti, Vito, 227
Seagrave, Jocelyn, 50
Seeley, Eileen, 53

Seldes, Marian, 111
Sellecca, Connie, 89
Selleck, Tom, 125
Seymour, Anne, 69
Shankman, Matt, 95, 194
Sharrett, Michael, 205
Shatner, William, 214
Shaud, Grant, 156
Sheen, Martin, 11
Shepherd, Cybill, 147
Short, Dana, 205
Sikes, Cynthia, 208
Sikking, James. B., 97, 228
Silva, Trinidad, 103
Simmons, Jaason, 21
Singleton, Penny, 155
Sirtis, Marina, 210
Slaten, Troy, 24, 158
Smart, Jean, 49
Smith, Allison, 111
Smith, Martha, 196
Smith, Peter, 48
Smith, Yeardley, 197
Smitovich, Bill, 117
Snyder, Arlen Dean, 78, 194, 232
Soden, Maura, 108
Sommars, Julie, 141
Sorvino, Paul, 149
Spano, Joe, 97
Spiner, Brent, 210
Stafford, Nancy, 141
Stahl, Richard, 60, 110
Stamos, John, 74, 79
Steele, Christine, 115
Stephens, Garn, 74
Stephens, James, 205
Stern, Daniel, 229
Sternhagen, Frances, 33
Stevenson, Cynthia, 56
Stevenson, McLean, 87
Stevenson, Parker, 21
Stewart, Mel, 196
Stewart, Patrick, 210
Stockwell, Dean, 177
Stone, Rob, 150

Stout, Paul, 195
Strassman, Marcia, 221
Strickland, Gail, 173
Stuart, Mary Ellen, 91
Sullivan, Susan, 107
Summer, Donna, 68
Swanson, Jackie 35
Swanson, Jandi, 87
Sweet, Dolph, 80
Sweetin, Jodie, 74, 79
Swenson, Inga, 85
Swit, Loretta, 24

Tablak, Juliet, 141
Tambor, Jeffrey, 103
Tanner, Richard, 87
Taylor, Clarice, 43
Taylor, Meshach, 49
Tenney, Jon, 162
Thayer, Brynn, 143
Theiss, Brooke, 95
Thicke, Alan, 92
Thiegen, Trevor, 151
Thiessen, Tiffani-Amber, 189
Thomas, Betty, 97
Thomas, Heather, 62
Thomas, Jay, 32
Thomas, Michelle, 68
Thomas, Philip Michael, 145
Thomas, Robin, 159
Thompson, Sada, 32
Till, Lucas, 125
Todd, Hallie, 84
Tomei, Concetta, 37
Tomei, Marissa, 46
Tomlin, Lily, 162
Toussant, Beth, 105
Tragester, Kathy, 115
Travanti, Daniel J., 97
Travolta, Ellen, 26
Tucker, Deborah, 229
Turman, Glynn, 46

Uecker, Bob, 150
Urich, Robert 160

Van, Dorothy, 131
Van Dyke, Barry, 8
Van Dyke, Jerry, 40
Van Valkenburgh, Deborah, 216
Vaughn, Robert, 1
Velez, Eddie, 1
VelJohnson, Reginald, 64
Venuta, Beany, 52
Verdon, Gwen, 126, 225
Vereen, Ben, 225
Vincent, Jan-Michael, 6
Viola, Herbert, 147
Vogel, Darlene, 75
Volstad, John, 163
Voorhies, Lark, 189

Walker, Nancy, 88
Walsh, Leigh, 7
Walters, Susan, 47
Ward, Jonathan, 25
Warfield, Marsha, 55, 169
Warlock, Billy, 20
Warner, Malcolm-Jamal, 43
Warren, Michael, 97
Watanabe, Gedde, 168
Wayne, David, 82, 144
Webb, Chloe, 36
Webber, Robert, 147
Wechsler, Nick, 115
Wedgeworth, Ann, 185
Weitz, Bruce, 97
Welles, Orson, 129
Wells, Tracy, 150
Wendt, George, 29
West, Natalie, 185
Wettig, Patricia, 207
Whalen, Justin, 26
Wheeler, Ellen, 105
Wheeler, Susan, 158
White, Betty, 82, 134

White, Deborah, 207
White, Jaleel, 64, 68, 194
Widdoes, James, 25
Wiener, Sabrina, 32
Wilder, Yvonne, 77
Willette, Jo Ann, 95
Williams, Brandon, 89
Williams, Frances E., 53
Williams, Joe, 44
Williams, Kellie Shanygne, 64
Williams, R.J., 128, 221
Williams, Steven, 222
Williams, Timothy, 32
Willis, Bruce, 147
Wilson, Melanie, 174
Wimmer, Brian, 37
Windom, William, 153
Windust, Penelope, 124
Winfield, Paul 68
Winnery, Barbara 208
Winters, Shelley, 185
Witting, Steve, 143
Wohland, Sean, 124
Woodard, Alfre, 209
Woods, Nan, 36
Wright, Max, 8
Wyatt, Jane, 206
Wyner, George, 103
Wyss, Amanda, 24

Yagher, Jeff, 220
Yothers, Tina, 68
Youngfellow, Barrie, 107

Zabriski, Grace, 59
Zeigler, Heidi, 95
Zimbalist, Efrem, Jr., 181
Zimbalist, Stephanie, 180
Zmed, Adrian, 214

About the Author

Vincent Terrace has worked as a researcher for ABC and is currently the TV historian for BPOLIN Productions, LLC (for which he created and wrote the pilot episode for a projected TV series called *April's Dream*). The author of 37 books on television and radio history, Terrace has teamed with James Robert Parish for the *Actors' Television Credits* series of books for Scarecrow Press. Other books include *The Encyclopedia of Television Pilots, 1937–2012* (2013), *Television Specials, 1936–2012* (2013), *The Encyclopedia of Television Subjects, Themes, and Settings* (2011), and *The Encyclopedia of Television Programs, 1925–2010, Second Edition* (2011). Terrace is also the author of *Television Introductions: Narrated TV Program Openings since 1949* (Scarecrow Press, 2013) as well as *Television Series of the 1950s: Essential Facts and Quirky Details* (Rowman & Littlefield, 2016), *Television Series of the 1960s: Essential Facts and Quirky Details* (Rowman & Littlefield, 2016), and *Television Series of the 1970s: Essential Facts and Quirky Details* (Rowman & Littlefield, 2017).